WORST JOURNEYS

Volume 2

Keath Fraser

ISIS

LARGE PRINT

Oxford, England

Copyright © Keath Fraser 1991, 1992, 1993

First published in Great Britain 1992
by Picador

Published in Large Print 1994 by Isis Publishing Ltd,
7 Centremead, Osney Mead, Oxford OX2 0ES,
by arrangement with Picador

British Library Cataloguing in Publication Data
Worst Journeys. — Vol. 2
I. Fraser, Keath
910.4

ISBN 1-85695-225-8

Printed and bound by Hartnolls Ltd, Bodmin, Cornwall

CONTENTS

Introduction

PART ONE

LUCKING OUT WITH A BAD PATCH OF ROAD

NORMAN LEWIS *from* Golden Earth 3

PATRICK MARNHAM *from* Road to Katmandu . . 13

STEPHEN BROOK *from* Honkytonk Gelato . . . 20

MARK ABLEY *from* Beyond Forget 30

COLIN THUBRON *from* Where Nights Are Longest 36

PAUL THEROUX *from* The Old Patagonian Express 43

MARY MORRIS *from* Nothing to Declare 50

RONALD WRIGHT *from* Cut Stones and Crossroads 59

CHARLES NICHOLL *from* The Fruit Palace . . . 73

JONATHAN RABAN *from* Old Glory 87

TED CONOVER *from* Rolling Nowhere 101

PART TWO

WRITERS AND THE EFFECTS OF WAR

IRVING LAYTON Postcard 111

DIRK BOGARDE *from* Backcloth 113

JAMES FENTON *from* All the Wrong Places . . . 122

P. J. O'ROURKE *from* Holidays in Hell 132

GAVIN YOUNG The Murder of Hué 151

BRUCE CHATWIN A Coup 166

JOHN RYLE *from* The Road to Abyei 192

CAROLYN FORCHÉ Return 206

PEREGRINE HODSON *from* Under a Sickle Moon . 211

PART THREE

CLASSIC QUESTERS IN EXTREMIS

AL PURDY When I Sat Down to Play the Piano . 229

RUSSELL BANKS *from* Continental Drift . . . 233

J. M. COETZEE *from* Waiting for the Barbarians . 243

GRAHAM GREENE *from* The Lawless Roads . . 253

ERIC HANSEN *from* Stranger in the Forest . . 265

REDMOND O'HANLON *from* In Trouble Again . . 275

WILFRED THESIGER *from* Arabian Sands . . . 286

MICHAEL ASHER *from* A Desert Dies . . . 292

ERIC NEWBY *from* A Short Walk in the Hindu
  Kush 301

PETER MATTHIESSEN *from* The Snow Leopard . . 309

JOHN MILLS The Night of Lucia 316

ANNE MICHAELS Pillar of Fire 332

INTRODUCTION

Here is one way to have a bad trip.

You are lying in your underwear on a bed in a Havana hotel room in the late sixties when travel to Cuba is still widely restricted, and a young man in the next bed refuses to discuss anything about money until you follow him into the bathroom. Only here will he let you continue counting aloud the Cuban pesos in your wallet. We're being watched he says.

You walk back into the bedroom and discover it's true. Tapestry palms hanging on either side of the large mirror aren't embroidered on a cloth so much as planted in a kind of webbing common to old-fashioned radio speakers set into the wall. You prod the coconuts, nestling in behind a design of iron filigree, and discover the adjoining mirror is also lodged into the wall. It doesn't take much imagination to figure it goes both ways.

Suppose you have been trading in black market currency with a Pakistani diplomat the evening before in his colonial suburban home. And now your conversation has been careless. It's a hot day in December, say. The ceiling fan cranks slowly.

Your journey is already a debacle, with an Ilyushin that had mechanical trouble reaching Cuba, forcing it to re-land in Mexico City and then take off again — bringing you into San Martí airport long after dark, on a Cubana flight that oddly enough felt hijacked (the sixties' new mode of arrival in Havana). But worse, in the days that follow, officials are loath to let you leave Cuba, where, while no visa was required to enter the country, an exit visa is now harder to come by than a peace medallion on a leather thong. They're toying with you. Perhaps you've been eating too well in the dining room, spending too freely on boxes of Havana cigars.

You are an odd couple, you see now, you and this neurotic French Canadian, meeting by chance at the airport in Mexico City, flying in as celebration of the Revolution's tenth anniversary happens to be getting under way, a pair of gringo good-timers in an otherwise discreet pool of earnest Russian advisors. It's important for Cuban agents to harass you. It's their duty.

Even then, while trotting from pillar to post, you know that some day you will use your journey. You feel fortunate to be suffering. Perhaps a Catholic childhood prepared you for worse. On this, your first trip abroad, travel has become after reading and eating out the third great pleasure in life. It has also become, like repetition and indigestion, a curse. A demon to be exorcised in a little black diary. It's important to record this. It's your duty.

You are coming to learn that destination achieved is seldom what it promised when you first set off. "Ay," as Touchstone says, "now am I in Arden, the more fool I. When I was at home, I was in a better place, but travelers must be content." Not content, but rather, as the writers in this volume will show, interested in exploring the folly in forsaking more familiar surroundings.

Home in an absolute sense is where we come from.

The thoughtful traveler willy-nilly is instructive about the moral differences between the relative and absolute meanings of that place. In the relative sense home is as likely to be a ledge with two sleeping bags on the side of a mountain in the Hindu Kush as it is a bugged hotel room in weather-beaten Havana. The relative meaning, we suspect, is but a convenience on some exotic way to the other meaning, however idealized real home may become in the struggle to survive the perils of the road.

Whoever claimed that travel is merely home in motion was traveling in an armchair — or else engaged in travel (as Samuel Butler once put it) too easy to deserve the name. Travel still suggests "travail" to those who know that by leaving home they risk wire-walking without a net.

Among living writers, Redmond O'Hanlon goes further than many in mining the gap between home and wherever it is he finds himself — usually up a jungle river full of tropical dread and having the worst journey of his life. His book *In Trouble Again* has the ideal title, coming as it does from a writer determined to be funny about trouble. So has *Arabian Sands*, from another writer determined to traverse the waterless desert of Arabia's Empty Quarter. Assuming "the worst" to be over, after crossing what he has taken to be the grueling dunes of the Uraq al Shaiba, Wilfred Thesiger is told it isn't and they weren't. "For a moment, I thought he was joking, and then I realized that he was serious, that the worst of the journey which I had thought was behind us was still ahead."

In recalling Apsley Cherry-Garrard's account of Scott's Antarctic expedition in *The Worst Journey in the World*, George Woodcock may be right when he observes that a worst journey, in an absolute sense, is one that ends in death. Anything this side must presumably be governed by what Martha Gellhorn considers the subjective nature of all the other "horror journeys." Thus in Saigon, we learn that when James Fenton narrates a grotesque encounter with an apparently dying baby, "There was not the slightest element of drama. Indeed, I began to see that I was now the only person who was panicking." Indeed, not even the ghastliest cities nor vilest bureaucracies have managed to dissuade the peripatetic Jan Morris that she has *had* a bad journey. She won't stop smiling. *"What a lovely journey this is!"* Invited to tell of her worst journey she is thus forced to make one up — we presume with the same zest used to cook up her favorite and apocryphal city of Hav, also situated in the Levant.

No entire journey, nor even the greatest portion of it, is likely to be bad. Edward Hoagland considers himself a rhapsodist and essentially a Good Trip man who discerns no value in making an "ado" about bad journeys. But he concedes, "In Mexico and the southern Sudan I've seen whimpering hunger. In Casablanca and Chicago I've seen people viciously clubbed. I know that life is an abyss, among other things, and like other travel writers, I enjoy wire-walking a bit, courting, in a sense, a catastrophe." Why?

"The only aspect of our travels that is guaranteed to hold an audience is disaster," Martha Gellhorn tells us in her preface to *Travels with Myself and Another*. "That's what [people] like. They can hardly wait for us to finish before they launch into stories of their own suffering in foreign lands. . . ." The skeptic is likely to point out that such cherishing really begins with the retrospective arrangement of these disasters (the shaping of what once seemed shapeless) in reclaiming control of a temporarily disarranged self. In ascribing significance to what looked like hopeless boredom at the time, a good writer will discern humor where it never before revealed itself. She will no doubt tinker till a bad journey is, at least for her, a resolution of anxiety, indifference, fear. Gellhorn would agree: "As a student of disaster, I note that we react alike to our tribulations: frayed and bitter at the time, proud afterwards. Nothing is better for self-esteem than survival."

It is no wonder survival is central to the journeys writers record. It makes them feel good. "Look, we have come through!" wrote Lawrence of his and Frieda's rocky journey of elopement. "They may have come through," replied Bertrand Russell, "but I see no reason to look." Armchair travelers have no such scruples. We are voyeurs, carefully set up by the writer.

Martin Amis sets us up, with his confessed fear of flying and the emergency landing that follows, before he undresses even more: "Now, all writers secretly maintain a vampiric attitude to disaster; and, having survived it, I was unreservedly grateful for the experience." To no one's surprise Paul Theroux has gone so far as to conclude, in confessing his own bent as a professional travel writer, that "the worst trips make the best reading." Bad journeys, it seems, lead straight to the confession box. And as readers we take as much pleasure in listening to the blunders as writers do in confessing them. Invited to contribute to this collection, Anita Desai writes from Delhi: "Then, then at last I knew I had been had," aboard a small steamer in the dead of an Arctic winter night, having responded to a UN invitation to visit Norway to help celebrate the Decade of Women. Another contributor, William Trevor, responds by forgoing any account of a conventional trip in favor of a simple bus journey back to boarding school at the age of twelve. "What possessed me was dread," he confesses, "and the misery of anticipating the unavoidable." Such were the joys, all these travelers would agree, of recollections in misfortune.

* * *

Travel writing is a genre, but the literature of travel isn't, with antecedents as much in imaginary literature as in explorers' logbooks. Before Eric Newby's *A Short Walk in the Hindu Kush*, Norman Lewis's *Golden Earth*, Graham Greene's *Journey Without Maps*, all classics of twentieth-century travel — and earlier, before Robert Louis Stevenson's *The Amateur Emigrant*, Melville's *Typee*, and Alexander Kinglake's *Eothen* — easily lay the fictions of *Gulliver's Travels, Robinson Crusoe,* and *The Unfortunate Traveller*. If writing impelled by travel is circumscribed by an ever unruly exotic (the case in all these books, and in *The Odyssey,* come to think of it), then it will probably follow that survival flirts with us from the center of such travel, because the storyteller has understood as much if not more about human nature than the sociologist and historian. Lévi-Strauss has suggested, "The first thing we see as we travel round the world is our own garbage, flung into the face of mankind." Escape this, presumably, and we escape ennui, though the journey to that point may be difficult. To escape the self, to remake Caliban's face in the mirror, the writer as traveler uses his journey to see home even while distancing himself from it.

In John Updike's "Venezuela for Visitors" we are offered a mock anthropological report on a third-person journey into discomfort by contrast, which distances the traveler from poor Indians on one side — their lives "not paradise but full of anxiety" — and the rich who exploit them. We are not so far from home as we imagine, for introduced slyly is flirting, a cultural habit indigenous to the locally insignificant middle-class. Elsewhere, Updike has admitted that the helicopter crash on a mountaintop in Venezuela nearly killed him. He is strangely casual about it here, and possibly for a reason. This original piece of travel writing first appeared in pages of *The New Yorker* normally reserved for fiction; something stranger than fiction might have ruined its welcome.

Our itinerant wanders unbounded, much taken by what travel can tell us of the self and of the world it would escape to and be transformed by. A bad journey mirrors its exotic circumference, throwing back an image of the writer in extremis, who is willing to be tested, mocked, and remain remarkably undaunted when it begins to rain on his parade . . . when the rim of the troddened world degenerates into a *via dolorosa*.

Incidentally, it is doubtful whether my favorite title from nineteenth-century travel literature, *On Sledge and Horseback to Outcast Siberian Lepers*, by one intrepid lady traveler, misled many novel readers. But neither, for that matter, would Eric Hansen's recent title *Stranger in the Forest: On Foot Across Borneo*, though its dual declaration reminds us, with a novel's hint of mystery to the left of the centering colon, how far the travel book has come back (if that is the term) to mirroring the survival interests of fiction. "It was clear to me that at any moment I might be ambushed and killed." Hansen sounds a little like Crusoe, minus Defoe's cultural blinders.

The Australian novelist Murray Bail, whose novel *Homesickness* uncovers the kind of tourist ethnocentrism the real traveler reviles, raises the moral question of voyeurism and intervention on safari in Central Park, when a group of Australians visiting New York City finds itself in a tree house watching human predators attracted by darkness and a human prey. Obsessed with the way we see the world, the novel subverts travel in brilliant ways, not the least of them on this terrible journey into a metropolitan wilderness.

Tension and resolution, but also character and insight: these characteristics of the novel have been absorbed by many contemporary travel writers who may or may not be novelists. Graham Greene, Norman Lewis, Colin Thubron, Edward Hoagland, Paul Theroux, Peter Matthiessen, Jonathan Raban, Mary Morris, Bruce Chatwin — novelists know how central drama is to the stories they tell us in their travel books. We read these writers for the plots of their frequently self-inflicted predicaments. ("What do people *do* in Morgan City?" asks Jonathan Raban, finding himself in the "worst" motel room he has ever seen, having just motored two thousand miles down the Mississippi in a sixteen-foot boat. He finds out. "Fight. Get drunk. Pick up women.")

The novelist Timothy Findley, flying to Moscow in 1955 as a young actor in Peter Brook's production of *Hamlet*, describes how "increasingly, as the flight wore on, it became apparent that we really were in trouble. It became very cold in the plane. Everyone put on an overcoat. Blankets were offered. The pilot was attempting to climb above the storm, but he was failing to achieve his goal. The snow, apparently, went all the way to heaven." On an earlier leg of this flight, Findley has looked around the cabin to discover with some solace a furtive Graham Greene on the same journey to Moscow. "His knuckles, just like mine, were bone white and rigid." Findley's fear of flying scrambles for any metaphysical comfort he can find in his hope that perhaps God takes "special care of special people." So the fear of flight creates its own drama in a story.

So do the fears of fellow tourists, dark and squalid conditions of the road, mutterings of war, and possible death by rain forest Indians, thirst, or hypothermia. Survival is all. In the finest travel writing the storyteller resolves his fears through the catharsis of narrative. Without fear, travel has no meaning; the writer is without a secret. He goes on to create epiphanies where the scholar would be tempted merely to recycle the past.

If the scholar is right, that we learn from history, even more may we learn from what fictional narrative teaches us about journeying in time.

Think of Sartre's autodidact. He is looking for "adventures" only because he thinks travel, which he has never done, is the best "school." (". . . Getting on the wrong train. Stopping in an unknown town. Losing your wallet, being arrested by mistake, spending the night in prison. Monsieur, it seems to me that you could define adventure as an event which is out of the ordinary without being necessarily extraordinary.") Yet even while longing for adventure, the autodidact fears the upheaval of travel, and moreover is unable to look at photographs and see journeys abroad as anything except confirmation of what he already knows. He knows history, but cannot tell a story. He lacks the imagination for metaphor.

(Not novelist Umberto Eco, who is able to use history in a bold and indivisible way. Listen to his mock horror on a culture crawl down the California coast in *Travels in Hyperreality*: "The poor words with which natural speech is provided cannot suffice to describe the Madonna Inn. . . . Let's say that Albert Speer, while leafing through a book on Gaudi, swallowed an overgenerous dose of LSD and began to build a nuptial catacomb for Liza Minnelli. But that doesn't give you an idea. Let's say Arcimboldi builds the Sagrada Familia for Dolly Parton. Or . . ." etc. He can barely contain his imagination, set free by its recollected arrival amidst the *horror vacui* of pop vulgarity.)

In one obvious sense, then, a writer's worst journey is

also his best. It contains the seed of a vivid story in which he is the welcome survivor. The worse the journey the more fortunate the writer. Long before Defoe, Thomas Nashe saw that a bad journey could be very useful in his imaginary story of Jack Wilton. *The Unfortunate Traveller* is suitably mistitled — as is James Fenton's recent *All the Wrong Places*, which of course points to all the *right* places for a writer to be in when trouble breaks out. Jack Wilton fortunately survives, as if the advice he is given on the requisite anatomy of a traveler — from a banished English earl who, in despising life abroad, believes that what the wandering Israelites consider to be an enslaving curse, masochistic Englishmen count as their chief boon — has somehow made the difference: "He that is a traveller must have the back of an ass to bear all, a tongue like the tail of a dog to flatter all, the mouth of a hog to eat what is set before him, the ear of a merchant to hear all and say nothing." Scoundrels, murderers, liars — why, wonders the earl, is Jack interested in trucking with foreigners abroad? Better learn of their treachery from books at home.

Well, we hasten to agree, home is a place of fortune that allows writers sufficient funds to leave it at their leisure. Writers who tell of bad trips through peaceful or even plentiful lands, not to mention war-torn and impoverished lands, recognize instinctively how fortunate they are to have their particular homes (those gauges of fortune) to return to. Compared with the struggling and even starving strangers they will certainly meet along the road, these travelers will indeed feel fortunate and perhaps morally sensitized.

Over the traveler's head hang evils Joseph Brodsky offers advice about avoiding, instructing us winningly on how to *prevent* a worst journey, in his imagined Asian landscape ("Advice to a Traveller"). Yet a traveler will find some way to thwart the evils of the road by turning misery to his advantage. Reflecting upon a lifetime of travel, little of it easy, the splendid English traveler Norman Lewis once observed that "insurgents and bandits, malaria, curtains of various kinds, whether lowered by politicians or by the priest-kings of their day . . . I am reminded that those parts of the world where I have travelled most happily . . . always seemed to suffer from these disadvantages. . . ." Lewis has always felt happiest traveling when the going was manifestly not good. As Edward Hoagland correctly grasps, T. E. Lawrence was not necessarily happier than V. S. Naipaul for having had trips that sounded more agreeable.

Happiness for the writer who travels certainly seems earned in proportion to exhaustion brooked. Note Graham Greene on his arduous journey to Palenque in the thirties: "I lay wet through with sweat for four hours — it was very nearly like happiness. In the street outside nobody passed: it was too hot for life to go on." Paul Theroux is also happiest when unhappy. The success of his own travel books owes something to the persona he creates for himself in the tradition of Evelyn Waugh and Greene himself. He's the antidote to Jan Morris. One might even wonder if, like her, he is here making *up* his worst journey, at home in his study once the hard traveling is past, and Limón has become a minor inconvenience with confessional potential. However contrived his drama, in his engaging little story of survival (no more or less contrived than other writers' stories), his unflattering portrait is recognizable to anyone who has visited the Caribbean coast of Costa Rica.

The fifty living writers collected here have engaged me in different ways and with varying degrees of drama. All these writers — whether as tourists, professional travel writers, war correspondents, poets, rugged explorers, memoirists, or imaginary travelers in the personae of novelists like Russell Banks or J. M. Coetzee with journeys of grim irony and moral dilemma — all transport me in directions I like my armchair to go. Writers remaking themselves remake us. By their surviving so do we, in mini catharses, in armchair journeys of descent and resurrection, feel life renewed.

The fruit of bad journeys should be redemptive. The writer escapes, feels wiser perhaps, survives to bring back tales of ennui and strangely focused mirrors. (Kicked out of Cuba, with a visa at last, you are refused a visa back into Mexico.) Peter Matthiessen in *The Snow Leopard* notes: "Tibetans say that obstacles in a hard journey, such as hailstones, wind, and unrelenting rains, are the work of demons, anxious to test the sincerity of the pilgrims and eliminate the fainthearted among them." In a beguiling sense the pilgrims today have become Matthiessen's readers. We as readers can be grateful to such fortunate travelers for bringing back reports of the demonic. Of the amusingly corrupt. Of bugs and hot hikes: "No," writes Wilfred Thesiger in *Arabian Sands*, "it is not the goal but the way there that matters, and the harder the way the more worthwhile the journey." These survivors, fortunate all, save us from faintheartedness.

* * *

Not every writer, of course, who travels is a traveler — no more than is every traveler who writes a writer. Writers from a number of countries were invited to tell of their (mis)fortunes on the road. I would especially like to thank those who took time to contribute essays on their worst journeys, along with the rest and their publishers who were asked for excerpts from previously published works.

I suppose many landscapes described here in passing aren't really different in degree from the harsh ones of India — to which this collection of journeys happens to be devoted, and its people assisted by the generosity of these writers, who have agreed to donate all their royalties to Canada India Village Aid. CIVA is a registered, non-salaried charity dedicated to building medical and agricultural facilities in some of the poorest areas of rural India.

In addition, I would like to extend my gratitude to Ed Carson, Louise Dennys, Cynthia Good, Ellen Levine, Michael Ondaatje, John O'Brien, and George Woodcock for their support and interest in this project in variously crucial ways; and to Trevor Carolan.

No thanks, of course, is ever really adequate to express the deep appreciation I feel for the continuous support of my wife, Lorraine.

Keath Fraser
Vancouver, 1990

PART ONE

LUCKING OUT WITH A BAD PATCH OF ROAD

It was as if I had burst through the bottom of my plans and was falling through darkness. I would continue to fall: there was absolutely nothing to do until dawn. My feet hurt; I was tired, dirty, sweating; I had not eaten all day. This was not the time or the place to reflect on the futility of the trip, and yet Costa Rica had seemed to promise better than this dark end.

—*Paul Theroux*

NORMAN LEWIS

Born in London in 1903, Norman Lewis served in North Africa and Italy during World War II, and his Naples '44 *is considered by some to be one of the best books about the war. His travels in the early 1950s to Southeast Asia and Burma are narrated in* A Dragon Apparent *and* Golden Earth. *In later years he continued to travel all over the world, to Arabia, Africa, India, and especially to the Spanish-speaking countries of Central and South America.* A Goddess in the Stones, *his account of a journey in north-east India, was published in 1992. His many novels often include exotic settings abroad. A selection of his best journalism was recently collected in* A View of the World, *which includes what he considers his most influential work, the account of a 1968 journey to Brazil, when he reported at length on Indian genocide. His earlier travels to Asia were more disinterested. In the following excerpt, from his journey to Burma, he is traveling by lorry to Lashio.*

from GOLDEN EARTH

Through the brazen hours that followed high noon, we crept onward through a tunnel of glittering verdure.

Then in the early afternoon came the official stop for breakfast. We were in a tiny hamlet, a few branch-and-leaf huts around a well. A single half-blind pariah dog slunk up to inspect us and was immediately chased away by a pair of lean, hairy swine that came rushing out of one of the huts. A cavern had been hollowed out of the wall of rock that formed the background to the village, and wisps of smoke trailed up through a sort of bamboo veranda that had been built over the mouth of it. This infernal place was the restaurant.

The moment had now come when all European prejudices about food had to be abandoned; all fears of typhoid or dysentery had to be banished resolutely from the mind. Even if I held back now and refused to enter this murky grotto, there was a long succession of others awaiting me, and ultimately sheer hunger would settle the matter. Remote journeyings had their advantages, the occasional sense of adventure, the novelties of experience. They also had their drawbacks, and this was one of them. And as there was no turning back from them, it was just as well to be bold.

In the dim interior — a model of most remote oriental eating houses — we were awaited by a cook who was naked to the waist. Tattooed dragons writhed among the cabalistic figures on his chest and arms. A snippet of intestine was clinging to a finger, which, shaken off, was caught in mid-air by an attendant cat. Tin Maung gave an order and in due course the headwaiter arrived, a rollicking Shan with shining bald head and Manchu moustaches, carrying a dish heaped with scrawny chickens' limbs, jaundiced with curry, a bowl of rice, and a couple of aluminum plates. When uncertain how to behave, watch what the others do. A few minutes later I was neatly stripping the tendons from those saffron bones; kneading the rice into a form in which it could be carried in the fingers to the mouth. But the *spécialité de la maison* was undoubtedly pickled cabbage, with garlic and chili pepper. This Shan delicacy was gravely recommended by Tin Maung as "full of vitamins." It had a sharp, sour flavour, for which a taste was easily acquired; I should certainly have missed this and many other similar experiences had I been able to follow the advice given in the *Burma Handbook*: ". . . there are no hotels, and the traveller, when he quits the line of railway or Irawadi steamer, must get leave from the deputy commissioner of the district to put up at government bungalows, and must take bedding, a cook, and a few cooking utensils."

* * *

Although Tin Maung had said that it was most unlikely that we should reach Lashio in one day, we found ourselves by the late afternoon within a few miles of the town. We had just crossed the Nam Mi river, where I had admired the spectacle of landslides of the brightest red earth plunging down the hillside into deep, green water, when we were stopped by a posse of soldiers. They told us that Chinese Nationalist bandits had temporarily cut the road, only four kilometres from Lashio, and had shot up and looted the truck in front of ours. As this had happened several hours before, it was not exactly a narrow escape. But there was a delay until an officer of the Shan police arrived to tell us we could carry on. As we came into the outskirts of Lashio, the sun set. Flocks of mynas and parakeets had appeared in the treetops, where they went through the noisy, twilight manoeuvres of starlings in a London square.

In accordance with the recommendations already quoted from the *Burma Handbook*, I asked the driver of the lorry to put me down at the Dak Bungalow, but there appeared to be some difficulty, and Tin Maung told me that it had been taken over by the army. He invited me to come to his house, where I could leave my luggage while making further inquiries. Lashio had been partly destroyed by bombing but, it seemed, rebuilt along the lines of the English hill-station it had once been, with detached bungalows, each with its own garden. We stopped at one of these. It was now nearly dark, and a young man clad only in shorts came running down the path, and opened the gate. Approaching us, he crossed his arms and bowed in a rather Japanese fashion, only partially straightening himself when he turned away. Tin Maung nodded toward the baggage, and uttered a word, and the still stooping figure snatched up both suitcases and hurried away to the house with them. He was not, as I imagined at the time, a servant, but a younger brother.

I was then invited to go and sit on the balcony of the house, where I was met by Tin Maung's father. U Thein Zan looked like a lean Burmese version of one of those rollicking Chinese gods of good fortune. Even when his mouth was relaxed his eyes were creased up as if in a spasm of mirth. He had learned, in fact, as I soon discovered, to express his emotions in terms of smiles: a gay smile (the most frequent), a tolerant smile (for the shortcomings of others), a roguish smile (when his own weaknesses were under discussion), a rueful smile (for his sharp losses, the state of Burma, and humanity in general).

In the background hovered the mother. In her case no formal presentation was made. The three of us, father, son, and myself, sat there on the balcony making occasional disjointed remarks about the political situation. From time to time the younger brother came out of the house, bowed, and went in. The mother appeared, curled herself up in a chair well removed from the important conclave of males, and lit up a cheroot. There was no sign of stir or excitement. Later I learned that this was the return of the eldest son after an absence of two years, during which time the brother next in age to him had been killed by insurgents. I could have imagined Chinese etiquette imposing these rigid standards of self-control, but it came as a great surprise that old-fashioned Burmese families should follow such a rule of conduct.

The matter of finding somewhere to sleep now came up, and the younger son was sent off to make inquiries about a bungalow belonging to the public works department. He was soon back to say that it was full of soldiers, although there might be a room free the next night. Upon this Tin Maung said that I would have to sleep in his father's house, and signalled for my baggage to be taken inside. I apologized to the old man for the trouble I was putting him to, whereupon he handsomely said, "Anyone my son brings home becomes my son," accompanying this speech with such a truly genial smile that it was impossible to feel any longer ill at ease.

But before there could be any question of retiring for the night, U Thein Zan said, there were formalities to be attended to. He thought that owing to the unsettled local conditions I ought to be on the safe side by reporting, without delay, to the deputy superintendent of police, and after dressing himself carefully, he took up a lantern and accompanied me to the functionary's house. The D.S.P. soon mastered his surprise at the visit, seemed relieved that I was under the control of such a pillar of local society as U Thein Zan, and found me several forms to fill in. In the morning, he said, I must report to the office of the special commissioner for the region, and to the commanding officer of the garrison. The latter obligation was one of which nothing had been said in Rangoon, and I decided to avoid it if possible. With Chinese bandits in the vicinity I could imagine this officer considering himself justified in putting me under some kind of restrictive military protection, or even sending me under escort back to Mandalay. When I brought up the matter of the attack on the truck, the D.S.P. firmly announced that it had been the work of local Shans.

We went back home and sat for a while chatting desultorily and listening to the radio. Two stations were coming in faintly well: La Voix d'Islam broadcast on a beam from Radio Toulouse, and a station which might have been Peking, because the announcements were in Chinese, and the music Western and evangelical in flavour, with the exception of one playing of a marching song of the Red Army. U Thein Zan was a fervent Buddhist and liked to talk about his religion whenever he could. He was delighted because the next day a famous abbot would be preaching several sermons at the local monastery and he was to play a prominent part in the welcoming ceremony.

Soon after this the family retired to bed. The house was a rather flimsy construction raised on piles about three feet from the ground. It consisted of two main rooms and a kitchen, had a palm-thatched roof and a floor of split bamboo. I was left to myself in one of the rooms, while the five members of the family — another brother had just turned up — were to sleep in the other. Clearly the old mother did not approve of this arrangement, which I gathered, from her gestures, probably went against her ideas on true hospitality. Perhaps she felt that I was not being treated as a member of the family. At all events she protested and was with difficulty overruled by Tin Maung, who probably told her that communal sleeping was not a European custom; and with a shrug of bewildered resignation she let the thing go as it was. Bars were put over the door and a shutter fitted to the window. The younger brother appeared carrying a camp bed, which he erected in a corner. By the side of this Tin Maung set a stool with a lamp, a glass of water, a saucer of nuts, and several giant cheroots. Before going into the other room he told me not to put the lamp out. I wondered why.

Taking off my clothes, I put on a cotton longyi which I had bought in Mandalay. It had been recommended as the coolest thing to sleep in. Turning the lamp low,

9

I lay down on the camp bed, and was just dozing off when I heard a slight creaking, and through half-opened eyes saw Tin Maung, going slowly round the room, flashing an electric torch on the walls and ceiling. I asked him what he was looking for, and he said, "Sometimes there are moths." He then tip-toed quickly from the room. My eyelids came together and then opened, reluctantly, at a faint scuffling sound. The bungalow consisted of a framework of timber upon which sheets of some white-washed material had been nailed. It was like a very ramshackle example of a small black-and-white Essex cottage. On one wall, just above my feet, was a Buddha shrine, containing a rather unusual reclining Buddha and offerings of dried flowers in vases. From behind this there now appeared several rats, not large, but lively, which began to move in a series of hesitant rushes along the beam running round the room. There were soon seven of them in sight.

I watched this movement with dazed curiosity for a time, and then began to doze again. Then, suddenly, an extraordinary protective faculty came into use. Once during the recent war, I had noticed that whilst my sleep was not disturbed by our own howitzers firing in the same field, I was inevitably awakened when the dawn stillness was troubled by the thin whistle of enemy shells, passing high overhead. Now, on the verge of unconsciousness, I felt in the skull, rather than heard, a faint scratching of tiny scrambling limbs. Something, I half-dreamed and half-thought, was climbing up the leg of the camp bed. Turning my head I caught a brief, out-of-focus glimpse of a small black body on the pillow by my cheek. Then in a scamper it was gone. It was a scorpion, I thought, or a hairy spider of the tarantula kind. I linked its appearance with Tin Maung's mysterious inspection of the room with his torch. What was to be done? I got up, thinking that whatever this animal was, it would come back to achieve its purpose as soon as I fell asleep. I thought of sitting up in the chair and staying awake for the rest of the night, but when I picked up the lamp to turn up the wick, it felt light, and shaking it produced only a faint splashing of oil in the bottom of the container. In a short time then, the lamp would go out, and my scorpion or whatever it was, with others of its kind, would come boldly up through the interstices in the bamboo floor. The next impulse was to spend the night walking round Lashio, and I went to unfasten the door bar. Immediately the pariah dog that lived under the house, where it lay all night snuffling and whining, burst into snarling life, furiously echoed by all the dogs in the district. I thought of the trigger-happy police of Lashio, who would have Chinese bandits on their mind.

The best thing, I decided, was to use my mosquito net and hope that I could sleep without any part of my body coming into contact with the sides. Fixing it up as best I could, I crawled in and tucked the net well under me. For a while I watched the movement, blurred through the net, of the rats; then consciousness faded again. I was awakened by a not very sharp pain in the lip and putting up my hand found myself clutching a cockroach which had fastened there. This was the last disturbance; when I next woke it was to the mighty whirring of hornbills flying overhead, and the daylight was spreading through the shutters.

PATRICK MARNHAM

Patrick Marnham was born in Jerusalem in 1943 and educated at Oxford University in jurisprudence. His first book, Road to Katmandu, *describes his trip overland from Turkey to Nepal in 1968. His second book,* Fantastic Invasion: Dispatches from Africa, *is a report for the Minority Rights Group on the nomads of Sahel. He has published a book on Lourdes, another,* So Far from God: A Journey to Central America, *about a journey to Central America in the mid 1980s, which won the Thomas Cook Travel Book Award, and in 1992 a biography of Simenon,* The Man Who Wasn't Maigret.

from ROAD TO KATMANDU

The Indian trains were filthy, unreliable, stifling, and hopelessly over-crowded. And the third class had one other distinction. It was virtually free. Because of the great numbers traveling, it was quite impossible for any ticket collection to take place during the journey, and at the stations most of the mob just rushed the barrier.

Euphoric at the thought of a free ride as far as the Nepalese border, we took the wrong train and did not discover our mistake until we reached Patna on the south side of the Ganges. Not only was this too far

13

south. It was too far east as well. The great trek to the southeast had to be completed by a final northwestern leg. At Patna we climbed wearily off the train and made inquiries for the Ganges ferry. In Delhi it had been reliably reported that the monsoon had reached Patna some weeks ago. The men in Delhi should not believe everything they read in the weather reports. Patna lay under an identical yellow pall, and the people waited sullenly for the rain.

We found the river with the aid of a bicycle rickshaw boy. There were no buses in town, and so we succumbed to his blandishments and loaded our packs and ourselves onto his carriage. He carved a path through the packed streets and the solid air, ringing his bell furiously — the sinews on his legs standing out like cords. Even on this short journey we both managed to sleep; free train rides are not restful. At the quay a great crowd was gathered waiting patiently for the boat. By the booking office window an old lady was sitting in a pool of her own water, a few feet away her grandchildren slept on the floor. Other children played by the river edge, jumping in and out of the brown flood and occasionally retrieving charred wooden trays that floated downstream. These they raced against one another: They were the cremated remains of the funeral rafts from Benares.

Eventually a tubby paddle steamer with a thin smokestack slipped its moorings and drew into the quay. There was a great rush to board the single gangplank. Somehow the press forced itself up, and after another pointless delay we set off. Out into the holy Ganges we paddled, while the glutinous tide rushed past the ship, its surface speckled with ashes and garlands. For the first time since the ferry over the Bosporus we had to cross more than a stream; it was an unnatural experience for islanders. Nobody could say when we would reach the far shore, or whether there would be a train there. Nothing was visible out on the water except the haze and the rushing ashes. Shortly after sailing we went aground.

The voyage dragged on during the afternoon, Perkins slept heavily sitting on a bench, and a curious crowd gathered silently around him to puzzle over the contrast between his ragged shoes and his expensive cameras. Smuts from the smokestack soon covered every passenger. They were less visible on us than on the white-clad Indians. Toward evening the mist cleared a little, and we could make out a mud bank on the horizon. Slowly, silently, we approached it — beyond, a rise in the ground revealed a railhead. As the boat drew in fifty men in black shorts and faded red vests, oblivious of the churning blades, leaped on with a wild shout. They were not dacoits but free-lance porters, and gangs of them fought for the privilege of carrying the richer-looking bags. We stumbled ashore and began the ascent to the train. Someone had said that it went to the border.

Even by Indian standards (we had heard of a train in Delhi which started twenty-four hours late), this train was remarkable. For a start it was the most crowded train we had yet seen. It was physically impossible to board it. People were already standing along its outer side, clinging to the window frames and climbing onto its roof. There was no question of us *and* our packs getting a ride. One or the other had to go. Nor were we the only disappointed travelers. Struggling up the hill behind us came a litter borne by two porters. A girl lay inside it, thin and pouring sweat. At every lurch she cried out in pain; she was followed by her family, her mother murmuring to her, the rest silent. There was apparently no room for her either.

The train was already an hour late, and there seemed every possibility that it would be lingering here for most of the night. In the event, and following the litter to the front, we found a better solution. There was a first-class truck which was virtually empty. The girl in the litter was lifted into one-half of this. We explored the other. Within were four major generals. And two empty seats. We climbed up. "One moment. This is a first-class compartment."

We knew. Did we have tickets? Of course. Could they see them? No, they were not ticket inspectors. So sorry; without our tickets being seen we would not be allowed to enter. The generals would see to that. And so reluctantly we departed to buy two first-class tickets from Manendru Ghat to Raxaul. And reluctantly the major generals allowed us to rejoin them. At least we had found out where we were and where we were going.

The generals next devoted themselves to interrogation. A toothy one began it. "Where are you going?" "Where have you come from?" "How?" "Are you from the Peace Corps?" "Are you students?" They could understand none of the answers. Why were we moving around India in this unkempt condition at this time of year? "What is the *aim* and *object* of all this movement?" Wearily we tried to explain, but the result was a failure. "Are you on a government grant?"

For the rest of the journey they stared at us, solemnly marking down each detail for some future identification. The train jolted slowly through the night from one crowded halt to the next. The electric fans did not work. The iron bars on the windows proved useful hand holds for the people outside. By the light of two dim bulbs I could make out the enormous cockroaches on the floor. It became a point of honor with me to kill any that moved. The generals were bemused by this — "Those creatures are *to*tally harmless."

Slowly the heat and the wagon melted us down; we began to resemble two half-consumed lollipops that had been dropped on a cinema floor. To boost morale, we applied a liberal sprinkling of baby powder. Then we curled up on the benches and slept. Powdered lollipops sleeping like babies in a nest of generals. Nobody who smelled like us could be really dirty. The generals sat erect in their starched British uniforms, cross-legged on their bench, brown-brogued and sockless, looking inscrutably on.

Once again the journey passed into a dream phase, only remembered through waves of tiredness and confusion. The train crawled along without the least sense of urgency. It paused on the half-hour for half an hour. At each halt, one could just make out the dim forms of a packed crowd lying on the platform. Nobody stirred. The engine, whenever one went forward to inspect it, was deserted. The signal room equally so. Suddenly without warning or reason we might jolt forward again through the night. It became possible to understand Indian Railways' enormous casualty figures. On the signal-box door, there was a prettily embroidered motto: "THERE IS NO ONE SO DESERVING OF PRAISE AS THE CAREFUL MAN . . ."

In the deserted stationmaster's offices there would be a wood fire and a bank of gleaming brass levers. There were mugs of cocoa stamped with the company's monogram, and a jumble of Victorian telegraphic machinery. The whole place snugged and glowed like a northern Christmas. It was as though one had been transported to a small Welsh mountain branch line of fifty years ago. The machinery lay to hand, the domestic details were authentic, the stove had been cast in Derby. Only the will to operate the system was absent. But the relics of this impeccable plan remained — to render grotesque the chaos which had succeeded it. In the dark corner behind the broom cupboard one expected to see the ghost of Isambard Kingdom Brunel wringing his hands over these cunning and now misused devices. He would have felt at one with the legionnaires haunting Hadrian's Wall.

Somehow during the night, stumbling across stations with unreadable names, we managed two changes. At one of these we were told that we would have to wait a few hours for the train to Raxaul. The platform was too crowded to lie on. We dragged out two kitchen chairs from the stifling heat of the stationmaster's office and slept on these. We woke at dawn. It was freezing, it was misty, slowly the recollection returned that we had spent the night on a station platform. Farther down, groups were lighting fires and huddling close to them. Something was wrong with the day, something was different. Rain. The first since Teheran. Stiffly we made our way down to the waiting train. We were hopeful that the last day had begun.

STEPHEN BROOK

Stephen Brook was born in 1947 and grew up in London. He was educated at Trinity College, Cambridge, and then worked for seven years for a variety of publishers in America. He returned to England, and was an academic editor before becoming a full-time writer: he edited The Oxford Book of Dreams *in 1983. He is best known as a travel writer, and his books include* New York Days, New York Nights, Maple Leaf Rag, The Double Eagle, Winner Takes All, Los Angeles Love *and* Claws of the Crab. The Club: The Jews of Modern Britain, *published in 1991, was a bestseller.*

from HONKYTONK GELATO

A HITCH

To be exact: all my clothes, my typewriter, my passport and driving licence, my diaries, notebooks, address book, house keys, a few hundred photographs and negatives, and a large amount of cash. Even my razor and toothbrush had gone, and the book I'd left lying open on the bed when I'd gone out. All that remained were the few items I kept in the car, and my credit cards which I was carrying with me. Since I hadn't unpacked much, it must have been a joy to rob me, and I could picture the thieves scarcely able to believe their luck as they simply picked up my bulging cases and carried them away. It couldn't have taken them more than a minute to wipe me out.

I strode towards the motel office. Again I passed the loitering girls but this time I didn't so much as glance at them. They were silent, motionless. It seemed obvious to me that they knew what had happened. The office was locked — it was after midnight — but my hammering roused the night clerk. I indulged in some therapeutic yelling and ordered him to call the police. Then I marched back to my empty room, where I tried to calm myself. Two feelings were paramount: the sense of outrage, violation, that anyone who has been robbed experiences, and a sickening desolation at the thought that almost a month's notes had been stashed in one of the stolen cases. It seemed distinctly possible that with no notes, no money, no photographs, and no clothes, I would have to abandon the journey.

Checking the room once more, I spotted two items that the thieves had missed. Indeed, they were of no value, except to me. One was the notebook from which I'd typed up the stolen notes. That meant that I could in theory reconstruct much of what had been lost. Secondly, a blue folder in which I'd thrown the addresses and phone numbers of every single contact I'd made or would be making in Texas. It dawned on me that if I could rewrite my notes, get my hands on some more money, and replace some clothes, I could continue after all.

There was a flashing light outside my door, then a knock. Not the police, but a security man employed by the hotel. I told him what had occurred; he was sympathetic, until I pointed out that his visit and his concern came rather late in the day. The motel, I opined, had some cheek sending round their security man, since my room, situated on the ground floor and facing the main forecourt, had not been broken into but had been entered with a key. It was therefore painfully evident that the motel had no security to speak of. He went away.

Another fifteen minutes went by. Just to sit in that room depressed me, so I went out and paced up and down the forecourt. Even at such a late hour the place was humming, and it didn't take long to realize that the motel fulfilled a very different function at night from that of resthouse for the road-weary. Large battered sedans swooped in and out. Pairs of men sat quietly in darkened cars, talking, watching. The tall woman in the singlet spoke to some of them on her way to visit her dour friend again. One of those cars, bumping on spongy springs towards the Main Street exit, could well have my property stowed in its boot. The thought was intolerable, so the next time I saw a car making for the exit, I stepped out and flagged it down.

"Excuse me," I said politely as the driver, bemused, lowered his window, "but I've just been robbed at this motel and am anxious to recover my possessions. Now I've no right to ask this, but I'd like to inspect your car. It's not that I suspect you, it's just that I suspect everybody. You're perfectly at liberty to refuse, but I should tell you that I've noted your licence number and if you refuse to let me look inside your car, I shall pass it on to the police."

To which pretty speech the driver replied: "Hey man, you're crazy. You think I got your stuff? That's crazy, man. I don't want you givin' no number to the police. I ain't got your stuff but this car — well, I just don't want you giving out no number."

"I promise you I won't if you open the trunk."

Shaking his head in disbelief, the youth got out of his car and opened the boot. Tyres, toolbox, comic books. No suitcases. I apologized for troubling him and, muttering, he drove off.

The next motorist I stopped was less co-operative. He refused absolutely to let me search his car. I didn't argue. He was with a girl, and it was unlikely he'd back down in front of her. Off he went, and I jotted down the number. It began to occur to me I wasn't getting anywhere.

As an alternative way of passing the time, I approached the dour whore. Had she seen anything suspicious going on near my room?

"Ain't seen nothin'."

After half an hour the police arrived. I explained what had happened. They nodded, made notes; they'd heard similar stories too often before.

"It's real tough, something like this happening your first night in the city, but can I ask you something?"

"Of course. "

"What are you doing staying in a whorehouse?"

"How was I to know this is a whorehouse? It's

obvious now, but when I checked in this afternoon in broad daylight it looked like any other cheap motel. How could I tell?"

"Because every motel on Main Street is a whore-house."

"I didn't know that. They don't tell you that in the brochures your tourist offices hand out."

The Astro had, on its signboard, not only advertised its proximity to the Medical Center but offered a shuttle bus service to its hospitals. Like most of the other establishments on the street, it looked minimally respectable. How wrong I'd been. Whores who make regular use of a room almost certainly have a duplicate key. How easy it must have been for a whore, observing my departure at dinnertime, to let someone know that the sucker in Room 102 had just driven off.

"Think I'll get my stuff back?" I plaintively asked the police.

"You'll never see it again. Maybe they'll throw your papers and those notes you're so anxious about into a dump truck or a pile of trash near the road. You could check 'em in the morning. But my guess is you won't see your clothes again unless you check out every flea market in Houston."

"I did try searching some cars that were leaving the motel."

"You what?"

I explained how I'd flagged down vehicles and attempted to search them.

"That was not smart," said the horrified cop. "If you'd

stopped the guy who had your stuff, he'd probably have shot your face off. They shoot first round here."

"Mmm, that hadn't occurred to me. Look, I can't search this place, but can't you?"

"No sir. It's possible that your luggage is sitting in some other room in this motel — either that or it's on the other side of Houston by now. But we can't just go into people's rooms and search them."

"Of course not. All you can do is pat my shoulder and tell me I'll never see my things again."

"Just count yourself lucky you were out when it happened. Listen. We're gonna take a statement from you, and then after we've gone my advice to you is to have a word with those whores out there. If it's just those papers you're worried about, they just may be able to get through to some guy who had something to do with it and he may agree to dump your stuff somewhere. You could give it a try."

I did. The dour whore was sullen, said she knew nothing about it, but I made sure she understood my message. I woke the night clerk again and screamed at him till he gave me the room number of the tall tart. I gave her a call.

"Yeh?" It was a man's voice.

I explained who I was and why I was phoning, but he interrupted me. "Hey man, will you quit botherin' me and my ole lady?"

"Look, this is terribly important. I know you have nothing to do with what happened, but —"

"It's two in the morning. Will you leave us alone? She don't want to talk to you. It's too bad some guy ripped you off but it ain't nothin' to do with me or my ole lady."

"It's my papers, you see — I don't care about the clothes. They can keep all that — all I want . . ." I was hopeless. I was talking to a pimp in the middle of the night, and could I really expect him to work up much interest in some sheets of paper? If the police had no intention of investigating the robbery, why should a pimp put himself out? In the ice bucket sat what was left of a bottle of 1980 Chateau St Jean Gewurtztraminer (Frank Johnson Vineyard), a stunning wine I'd picked up quarter-price in Lubbock. At least some pleasures were left to me. I carried it to bed and drank myself to sleep in style.

I woke two hours later, got up early to begin an exciting day that consisted mostly of searching rubbish dumps and checking pawn shops. I bought myself a razor so I could at least shave, and moved to another motel. I returned to the Astro later in the afternoon, when I'd been told the manager would be there. To my astonishment Mr Khan had not yet been informed that one of his guests had been relieved of his worldly goods during the night. In my presence he called in a clerk and reprimanded him, but I wasn't fooled for a second. I informed Mr Khan that I had no intention of paying my bill.

"I must remind you, Mr Brook," said the glacial Mr Khan, "that this motel is not liable for your losses."

"I dare say, but if you think I'm going to pay you thirty dollars for the privilege of having been robbed here, you're mistaken."

After a further exchange of courtesies, he agreed to tear up the bill. I probably could have sued him, especially in litigation-crazed Texas, but from across the Atlantic there would have been little point. Instead, I had the grim satisfaction of warning some travellers about to check into the motel that they would be better advised to go elsewhere.

It was a miserable weekend. On Sunday evening an acquaintance came by with her boyfried to take me out for the evening. "I'm so shocked that something like this should have happened to you in Houston," said Regina, and to show she meant it she tried to thrust a hundred dollars into my hand, thinking I might be short of cash. I successfully resisted, as I had enough to get by until fresh supplies arrived from London. But her thoughtfulness to a near stranger struck me as remarkably generous. After dinner we went to a protest meeting about the treatment of Soviet Jewry, and there I met Republican Congressman Bill Archer. We talked about grapefruit.

The weekend was punctuated by frequent phone calls to the Astro and to the police just in case any of my belongings had been handed in. No, nothing. As my hopes gradually sank, my determination to recoup rose. I borrowed a typewriter from the sculptress Gertrude Barnstone and began to rewrite the notes that had perished.

On Monday I went to the British Consulate to apply for a new passport. The staff there were efficient and impersonal and postponed payment of the fee until the passport would be ready for collection a fortnight later. They also gave not the slightest indication of regret or concern. Oh, I know, British subjects are murdered, raped, mugged, and robbed all the time in Houston — why should I expect special treatment? Yet it was disheartening to this innocent abroad that my consulate didn't so much as inquire whether I might need anything, while strangers were pressing money into my hands.

Despite the kindness of strangers, I didn't want to lean too heavily on their goodwill. I recognized that my morale needed a major overhaul. My labours at Gertrude's typewriter in the air-conditioned gloom of my motel room were dogged but dispiriting. I needed rest, even pampering. I had another reason for wanting to leave Houston. I was, to my shame, developing mild paranoia around black people. The whores and pimps at the Astro were all black, and I assumed that whoever robbed me probably was black too, though I had no proof. When a pair of black men would walk towards me on the street, I would tense with fear and anger. It might have been them, was the unreasonable thought that invaded my mind. If a black laughed anywhere near me, I immediately suspected he was laughing at me. This, I recognized, was preposterous. Not that a small measure of paranoia comes amiss in Houston, where there was public rejoicing because there hadn't been a murder for two whole days. If the trend continued, the murder rate for the city would drop that year from over 700 to a mere 550. "Houston," someone later explained to me, "lulls people into a false sense of security. They come down from New York or Chicago, and find a city that's open and tolerant. The weather's hot and balmy. So they walk the street late at night under the palm trees. Next thing they know five kids from Baytown are leaping out of a pickup that's arrived from nowhere and you're being beaten to a pulp. To pass the time. This is a dangerous city."

I decided to take refuge with Christopher and Ann in Austin, and phoned to warn them of my imminent reappearance in downcast condition. Four hours later I was there.

"You're in luck," said Christopher. "Ann's been trying out some recipes for her book. And we've chilled a bottle of something good in the hope of cheering you up."

So we sat down to a dinner of redfish with scallions and ginger, stuffed pompano, salmon with raspberries, and trout bourguignon, and drank a bottle of 1973 champagne. For that hour at least I felt I was happily back in a corner of sweet, intense, cosy, much missed Europe.

"That was wonderful," I murmured, replete and even content. "I must get robbed more often."

MARK ABLEY

Mark Abley was born in England in 1955, grew up on the Canadian prairies, and graduated from the University of Saskatchewan. He then attended Oxford as a Rhodes scholar. He now lives and works as a critic and free-lance journalist in Montreal. In 1985, he returned to the prairies in an attempt to rediscover his place in their vastness. He drove south from Saskatoon, to the town of Forget (pronounced For-jay), and thence through Saskatchewan, Manitoba, and Alberta.

from BEYOND FORGET

Two days before my thirtieth birthday, I almost killed myself. I had warning: on the train ride from Churchill back to Thompson, I dozed into a dream that carried me along Clarence Avenue in the middle of Saskatoon. While my car moved from the riverbank toward 8th Street, gathering pace, I couldn't find its brake. In the dream I approached the clotted traffic of 8th Street expecting disaster, and the car threaded the free spaces like an engine-powered needle. I relaxed — but the car continued to speed down the tranquil suburban avenue. When it was out of control and racing across a sidewalk, I woke up sweating, the unpaved wilderness serenely all around.

In Thompson I had a long night's sleep and a fatty breakfast. It was the eve of Mother's Day, and I wanted to make good headway on the drive to Saskatoon. Unfortunately I had to wait for a bank to open. Churchill had emptied my wallet.

"Are you up here for business or pleasure?" the bank clerk inquired.

"It's sort of business."

She nodded sympathetically. "Nobody comes here for pleasure in May."

I drove then for three hours without stopping. The paucity of traffic and the day's cool brightness combined to make wildlife abundant: a swimming muskrat in a soaking ditch; a pair of mergansers; a spruce grouse immobile by the roadside, its black breast and barred belly vivid even at a glance. By the highway's side, the railway line to Soab Lake was unused. It stands on a high embankment from which, in three or four places, the gravel has crumbled away, leaving yards of track exposed crazily in midair. I thought of a long bone that had lost its flesh.

At Ponton I continued west, rather than following the main highway south toward Grand Rapids. More than a hundred miles of trees, boulders, and water awaited me, unbroken by a town or village: an asphalt tunnel through the green world. By the time I met another vehicle — a red station wagon heading my way, twenty-five miles out of Ponton — it seemed a hallucination, a trick of the coniferous light. The forest bowed and produced, for its next act, a sandhill crane above the road, turning as though lost, flapping slowly south to the Mitishto River.

31

I pondered its direction, and the highway turned pink. From sandstone, not embarrassment, I assume.

When the road was grey again, I switched on the radio. The only signal that could penetrate the tunnel came from the mining town of Flin Flon far to the northwest. Out of the mouths of zinc and copper came the program "Meet the Legion." I listened to a song called "Mr. Sandman, Bring Me a Dream." Then I paused for a rest.

That lakeshore picnic site in the Grass River Provincial Park has lodged in my mind with absolute clarity: the clearing in the woods, the feeble pier, the white-throated sparrows with their treble yearnings, the stained brown table where I munched my raisins and sipped my northern water. The car sat quietly on its gravel sofa, ready for a few more thousand miles in the weeks to come. I had great plans for it in the newborn summer of the prairies and the western foothills. The farther I drove that day, the more I was recapturing spring: already the domain of needles and leafless branches had given way to a forest studded with green poplars. I looked up once from the leaves and the lake to find a flock of thirteen snow geese turning lazily against a high cloud. When the sun caught them, their feathers flashed a brilliant white. They turned again, and a serration of black wings appeared to cut the sky. I got back into the car and regained the straight, empty road.

It was early afternoon. The Flin Flon station was broadcasting a country-and-western lament. The male voice whined, the forest gleamed in the sun, and I looked down at the highway map to see how much longer this road would go on before I had to turn south to The Pas. I felt glazed by all the green. Or could I take a different route? I revolved the map, glanced up, and found that the car had left the asphalt and was hurtling over the gravel shoulder at more than sixty miles an hour.

I veered left to escape the ditch, slammed my foot on the brake, and lost control. The car swung onto the wrong side of the highway, lurched back toward the right shoulder, and pulled left again. The singer whined as the Dodge fought the road. Everything was happening so fast that I had no time to panic; my only emotion was a numb amazement that such chaos could emerge from nowhere. My sporadic fears of big-city pile-ups, slippery blacktop, treacherous backroads, misplaced wildlife, and drunken drivers had left no space in the imagination for me to abandon an excellent highway without another vehicle in sight. My body refused to believe the danger. I recovered concentration too late to scream or pray.

The only thing that flashed before my eyes was a green line of trees turning upside down as the car deserted the road. It flipped in midair and landed on its rear. An instant later, the front of the car joined the back in a grassy ditch, and the world fell silent. Maybe, for a second or two, I lost consciousness.

I found myself sitting in an upright wreck, stunned. If the first feeling was relief — *alive, can move, not in pain, not burning* — the second was shame. *What happened, why did it, how could I?*

My mind battled for order. After I had removed the keys from the ignition, I switched off the silent radio and pushed the gear lever from "drive" to "park". Then I unstrapped the seat belt, which had possibly saved my life, and tried to open the door. It was jammed. But the glass had shattered out from the side windows, allowing me to clamber across the passenger seat and jump to earth. I could hear nothing other than a small breeze playing through the forest.

The car was ruined. Its windshield lay in fragments, its roof was bent, and its hindquarters had the crumpled appearance of a shed skin. It looked like the surprised victim of some monstrous rite of spring. Or was it a rite of passage? The impact had forced open the trunk, and my belongings — everything from a hefty blue suitcase to a couple of fifty-dollar bills — lay scattered like old fillings in the jaw of the ditch. My first impulse was to gather up the money and the small objects that had rested, along with my wallet, on the passenger seat: an address book, a journal, a little camera, the map. I was still doing this when I noticed the distant throb of an engine.

It was approaching, I thought, from the west. I stepped into the highway and started to wave when the throbs became visible. A blue half-ton truck, empty except for the driver, a middle-aged man with short brown hair and a face of dismay, slowed and stopped.

"I've had an accident," I said through the window. "That was my car."

"Is there anyone inside?"

"No, I didn't have any passengers. I just drove off the road."

He looked relieved.

34

"How long ago did it happen?"

"Don't know. A couple of minutes?"

The man climbed out of his truck. "I'll take you into The Pas," he said. "Let's load up the back."

"But that's where you're coming from," I said.

He gazed at me and silently, gently, shook his head.

I had my directions completely askew. Only at that moment did I understand: after flipping over, the car had landed off the wrong side of the road, facing east. The half-ton had been following my path.

We lifted my possessions into the truck and sped away. I sat in the passenger seat of the cabin, my hair stuffed with shards of gravel, pressing a Kleenex against my only wound: a tiny cut on the left ear. Behind me, a sleeve of my plaid dressing gown protruded from the ripped suitcase and flapped for fifty miles until The Pas. In retrospect, I was beginning to feel afraid.

Apart from some loose change, there was only one item we had failed to discover, either in the car's shell or in the ditch: the golden pen I had been using to write my daily journal. I had passed the pen through Al Hochbaum's inukshuk to bring good luck. Perhaps it had accomplished its task.

COLIN THUBRON

A descendant of John Dryden, Colin Thubron was born in London in 1939. The account of his journey alone by car through western Russia was published in 1984 as Where Nights Are Longest *in the United States and as* Among the Russians *in Great Britain. His difficult but uncomplaining trip through China in the mid-eighties is recounted in* Behind the Wall, *which won the Thomas Cook Award. The author of several books on the Middle East, including* Journey into Cyprus *and* The Hills of Adonis, *he also makes documentary films about travel. Among his five novels are* A Cruel Madness, Falling, *and* Turning Back the Sun. *He is a Fellow of the Royal Society of Literature.*

from WHERE NIGHTS ARE LONGEST

For . . . four days I was followed everywhere. I came to recognize the techniques of the white Volgas (they were always white), sheltered by lorries a hundred yards behind me. Highly trained, they behaved in ways which were eventually so recognizable that by the fifth day I would pick them out at a glance. But by now I was riddled with nerves. I was afraid above all that my travel notes, compressed into the form of an illegible diary, would be discovered and taken away. Isolated, I began to partake in the condemnation of my silent spectators. I began to feel deeply, inherently guilty. A single friend might have saved me from this, but I didn't have one. I understood now the precious intensity of personal relationships among the dissidents. Because around me, as around them, the total, all-eclipsing Soviet world, which renders any other world powerless and far away, had become profoundly, morally hostile.

In the long, carpetless halls of the hotel, the walled-up faces of waiting men and the sunny voices of the Intourist girls became the scenario of nightmare. I began to behave guiltily. For a whole day I incarcerated myself in my room, illegibly writing up and disguising notes. I searched for a bugging device in vain; I did not dare even curse to myself. Then I wondered if I had implicated anybody else, and decided to destroy my list of Russian addresses and telephone numbers. The irony was that there was no person on it, dissident or other, who did not feel passionately for his country's good. But I could not decide how to destroy this paper. The problem became tortuous. If I shredded the list into my wastepaper basket, it might be reconstructed. If I went into the passage, the eyes of the concierges followed me; and all the public rooms were heavy with scrutiny. If I went out, I would be followed. So, like a cunning schoolboy, I burnt the list in my lavatory.

"Fire!" A fat laundry-maid burst in. "Fire! Where's all this smoke from? Fire!" She had a blotched, porcine face which sloped neckless into her body. I stared at her with pure hate.

A young concierge appeared behind. Her gaze hardened and flew round the room. "What's this?"

"I've been smoking."

"Only smoking?"

"Yes."

I felt angry, shaken by my own lie. The concierge marched back past her desk and descended the elevator. I imagined myself under inquisition, trying to clear myself. I never smoke. But in one corner of the stairway landing stood an ash bin where I found three cigarette stubs. As if participating in some third-rate thriller, I took them back to my room, lit them to foil forensic tests, and left them in the lavatory. Then I walked downstairs and out into the sun, refusing to look behind me. I was shaking.

It seems foolish, in retrospect, that Kiev should be so contaminated for me. I thought it a handsome city, but it remains discoloured in my mind. I remember staring into foodshops whose stock was wretchedly little and expensive: in one only a heap of decapitated chickens, in another some crates of aubergines. And this was the capital of the Ukraine, of the Black Earth! I began to feel terribly tired, as if some unnoticed strain from the past months were finally spilling over. In the hotel that afternoon I found a Soviet Greek, an engineer from Kazakhstan with a delicate, mobile face. I befriended him with neurotic relief. His parents had come from Istanbul to Sukhumi after Ataturk's victories in 1922 and had died in old age without ever talking a word of Russian. But he himself never spoke Greek, although he understood it; and his children could barely even understand it. I prompted him anxiously about his people's history. The Greeks, founders of freedom! Had he read Sappho, Cavafy, Herodotus? Those books were hard to get, he said. But did he still feel Greek, I demanded? Absolutely, he said. Yet I could not tell in what the feeling lay. He knew the date of Lenin's birthday, but he could not remember who had built the Parthenon. In my present state this struck me as a parable of total corruption.

I had been given other addresses in the city: those of a priest, a journalist, and the wife of a poet who had recently been arrested. But all would have been compromised if I had met them. Although I did not know it at the time, the poet, a Ukrainian nationalist, was sentenced to ten years' hard labour on the day I arrived. I confined my trips to conventional tourist sites. I did not even see Babi Yar, where the Germans massacred over a hundred thousand Kievan Jews and others. ("It's discouraged to go there," an Armenian had told me. "I suppose they're afraid of it becoming a Jewish shrine.")

The only people I had warned of my coming were a Georgian agronomist and his Russian fiancée, who appeared by taxi one evening to take me to their home for supper. They greeted me like old friends — he a man of mercurial darkness, she motherly, blond, and Slavic-calm. I warmed to them at once. In the taxi we talked at ease of mutual friends in England. But through its back window I glimpsed the number-plate of the white Volga following us. I felt sick. But I didn't tell them. The contrast between their blithe chatter and this

39

paranoid shadow was somehow horrific. And I, in my knowledge, was condemned to the shadow. My guilty diary bulged in my coat pocket.

The Volga drifted to a halt beyond us when we stopped, and as we ascended in the flat-block elevator, I glimpsed a man in a leather jacket enter below. His face was enclosed, leaden, and I could hear the noise of his feet keeping pace with the rickety elevator as we rose, until he knew which apartment we entered.

But the moment the door closed, we were at peace. Mehrab and Vera had both left behind broken marriages, and were palpably in love. Theirs was a timeless attraction of opposites. Mehrab had the trim, agile physique of his people. In his swarthy face, with its high forehead and prominent but rather delicate bones, the eyes glittered with a febrile restlessness. He spoke to me about his work, but was distracted by the closeness of Vera, seated heavy-breasted beside him. His gestures incorporated a tender searching of her body with the elucidation of drainage around the Black Sea. Irrigation ditches somehow found their way across her thighs; harvest failures were offset by a consoling crop of squeezes; a bumper year collected her breasts.

And all the time, framed in page-boy hair, her blue eyes and broad lips gave out a happy and uncomplicated strength. The word "definitely" kept recurring in her talk. She was outspoken and often (said Mehrab) wrong. She had a puritan love of Siberia, where she had been born, and all of northern Russia. She preferred Leningrad to Kiev. "The people are more open-hearted there. Definitely. Here in

Kiev they're enclosed, they live in their own circles."

When she went into the kitchen to prepare supper, Mehrab laughed affectionately: "She's biased. She was a child in Siberia, you see, and a student in Leningrad, living among students — but an adult only here. She looks back on those student days with nostalgia and on her childhood with love. So of course she sees the places in that order. But really, I think, the old gradations of north to south apply here too. Kiev, you know, is more casual and dirty than northern Russia, and the Ukrainians a bit more open. But Georgia is better still!"

Love, in many permutations and disguises, pervaded our evening. The flat was full of it: thumbed books, taped music, Black Sea driftwood which they had collected on holiday and lacquered in curious shapes. "A man should love his work," Mehrab said, "that's the secret, but I'm not sure if the young do that any longer." He spoke of "the young" as if they were another race; I supposed he was about thirty-five. "They're somehow more diffuse, perhaps more imaginative than we were at that age."

I said I hoped so. I was thinking of peace, the trust which needs imagination.

"If real peace comes, it'll come because people are selfish," Vera said. "Definitely. They'll have too much to lose."

"Yes," I said. That sounded like life.

A storm rumbled outside. I went to the window. The rain was lashing down on the road, the darkened trees, and the white car sheltered under them.

"The young have ten times as much as we had," Vera went on. "When I was five, I remember, I ached for a doll. I used to make wooden ones myself, but I longed for one with proper hair and a body made of something smooth, like skin, which I could dress and undress and wash." She laughed boisterously. "I got one when I was twenty! And I loved it just as much as if I was five! And now I see children with bicycles, radios, everything, and it hasn't improved them." She looked puzzled and fed up. "And you in the West, you have so much, but are you happier?"

I didn't know, I said (whatever we meant by happiness). *But we couldn't go back.*

*   *   *

When I returned to my hotel, I knew that something was wrong. The comfortable old concierge who had taken over duty on my floor, and who had previously shown a maternal benignity, now gaped at me with horror.

My room, in my absence, had been searched. It had been done near perfectly, everything repositioned almost precisely as it was. Only by the pinpoint siting of several objects before I left, and by the insertion in notebooks of tiny threads now dislodged, did I realize that everything I possessed — letters, clothes, wallet, books, documents — had been removed, scrutinized, and fastidiously replaced.

But my diary was in my pocket, and my address list ashes down the lavatory.

PAUL THEROUX

Paul Theroux's books of train travel include The Great Railway Bazaar, The Old Patagonian Express, The Kingdom by the Sea, *and* Riding the Iron Rooster, *an account of a year's travel in China. He has also published a book describing his travels in the Pacific,* The Happy Isles of Oceania, *and in 1992 his collection* Travelling the World. *Among his numerous novels is the recent* My Secret History, *about a travel writer and based on some of its author's own experiences. Theroux believes you must travel alone. Of Costa Rica he writes: "I craved a little risk, some danger, an untoward event, a vivid discomfort, an experience of my own company, and in a modest way the romance of solitude. This I thought would be mine on that train to Limón." Unfortunately, scant experience of his own company has arisen, for he has been beset aboard by a garrulous Mr. Thornberry, from whom he now hopes to flee.*

from THE OLD PATAGONIAN EXPRESS

Limón looked like a dreadful place. It had just rained, and the town stank. The station was on a muddy road near the harbor, and puddles reflected the decayed buildings and over-bright lights. The smell of dead barnacles and damp sand, flooded sewers, brine, oil, cockroaches, and tropical vegetation which, when soaked, gives off the hot moldy vapor you associate with compost heaps in summer, the stench of mulch and mildew. It was a noisy town as well: clanging music, shouts, car horns. That last sight of the palmy coast and the breakers had been misleading. And even Mr. Thornberry, who had been hopeful, was appalled. I could see his face; he was grimacing in disbelief. "God," he groaned. "It's a piss hole in the snow." We walked through the puddles, the other passengers splashing us as they hurried past. Mr. Thornberry said, "It blows my mind."

That does it, I thought. I said, "I'd better go look for a hotel."

"Why not stay at mine?"

Oh, look, it's raining. It blows my mind. Kind of a pipeline.

I said, "I'll just sniff around town. I'm like a rat in a maze when I get to a new place."

"We could have dinner. That might be fun. You never know — maybe the food's good here." He squinted up the street. "This place was recommended to me."

"It wasn't recommended to me," I said. "It looks pretty strange."

"Maybe I'll find that tour I was supposed to be on," he said. He no longer sounded hopeful.

"Where are you staying?"

He told me. It was the most expensive hotel in Limón. I used that as my reason for looking elsewhere. A small, feeble-minded man approached and asked sweetly if he could carry my suitcase. It dragged on the street when he held it in his hand. He put it on his head and marched bandy-legged, like a worker elf, to the market square. Here, Mr. Thornberry and I parted.

"I hope you find your tour," I said. He said he was glad we had met on the train: it had been kind of fun after all. And he walked away. I felt a boundless sense of relief as if I had just been sprung from a long confinement. This was liberation. I tipped the elf and walked quickly in the opposite direction from Mr. Thornberry.

I walked to savor my freedom and stretch my legs. After three blocks, the town didn't look any better; and wasn't that a rat nibbling near the tipped-over barrel of scraps? *It's a white country,* a man had told me in San José. But this was a black town, a beachhead of steaming trees and sea stinks. I tried several hotels. They were wormy staircases with sweating people minding tables on the second-floor landings. No, they said, they had no rooms. And I was glad, because they looked so disgustingly dirty and the people were so rude; so I walked a few more blocks. I'd find a better hotel. But they were smaller and smellier, and they too were full. At one, as I stood panting — the staircase had left me breathless — a pair of cockroaches scuttled down the wall and hurried unimpeded across the floor. *Cockroaches,* I said. The man said, *What do you want here?* He too was full. I had been stopping at every second hotel. Now I stopped at each one. They were not hotels. They were nests of foul bedclothes, a few rooms, and a portion of verandah. I should have known they were full: I met harassed families making their way down the stairs, the women and children carrying suitcases, the fathers sucking their teeth in dismay and muttering, *We'll have to look somewhere else.* It was necessary for me to back down the narrow stairs to let these families pass.

In one place (I recognized it as a hotel by its tottering stairs, its unshaded bulbs, its moth-eaten furniture, its fusty smell), a woman in an apron said, "Them — they're doublin' up." She indicated a passageway of people — grandmother, young women, sighing men, glassy-eyed children, black, fatigued, pushing old valises into a cubicle and several changing their clothes as they stood there in the passageway.

I had no idea of the time. It seemed late; the people in Limón who were not room hunting were strolling the wet streets. They had that settled look of smugness that the stranger interprets as mockery or at least indifference. Saturday nights in strange cities can alienate the calmest of travelers.

Further on, a man said to me, "Don't waste your time looking. There are no hotel rooms in Limón. Try tomorrow."

"What do I do tonight?"

"There is only one thing you can do," he said. "See that bar over there?" It was a peeling storefront with a string of lights over the door; inside, shapes — human heads — and smoke; and broken-crockery syncopations. "Go in and pick up a girl. Spend the night with her. That is your only hope."

I considered this. But I did not see any girls. At the door were a gang of boys, jeering at men who were entering. I tried another hotel. The black owner saw that his reply to my question distressed me. He said, "If you really get stuck and got no other place, come back here. You can set out here on that chair." It was a straight-backed chair on his verandah. There was a bar across the street: music, another mob of gawking boys. I slapped at the mosquitoes. Motorbikes went by; they sounded like outboard motors. This sound and the boys and the music made a scream. But I left my suitcase with this man and searched more streets. There were no hotels, no bars, no rooming houses; even the music was muffled. I decided to turn back, but I had gone too far: now I was lost.

I came to a precinct of Limón known as Jamaicatown — in this white Spanish-speaking country, a black English-speaking area; a slum. These were the worst streets I had seen in Costa Rica, and each street corner held a dozen people, talking, laughing; their speech had a cackle in it. I was watched, but not threatened; and yet I had never felt so lost. It was as if I had burst through the bottom of my plans and was falling through darkness. I would continue to fall: there was absolutely nothing to do until dawn. My feet hurt; I was tired, dirty, sweating; I had not eaten all day. This was not the time or the place to reflect on the futility of the trip, and yet Costa Rica had seemed to promise better than this dark dead end.

At one corner I asked some loitering men the way to the market. I asked in Spanish; they replied in English:

they knew I was a stranger. Their directions were clear: they said I couldn't miss it.

I saw the row of hotels and rooming houses I had entered earlier in the evening. I had been disgusted by them then, but now they didn't seem so bad to me. I kept walking, and near the market square, skipping feebly across the street, one shoulder lower than the other because of the bag he carried, funny blue cap, bright green shirt, sailor pants, shuffling deck shoes: Thornberry.

"I've been looking all over for you."

I needed his company: I was glad — someone to talk to. I said, "I can't find a room anywhere. There aren't any in Limón. I'm screwed."

He took my arm and winced. "There are three beds in my room," he said. "You stay with me."

"You mean it?"

"Sure — come on."

My relief was inexpressible.

I got my suitcase from the hotel where the man had said that I could spend the night on his verandah chair. Mr. Thornberry called the place a piss hole (and over the next few days, whenever we passed it, he said, "There's your verandah!"). I went to his room and washed my face, then we had a beer and grumbled about Limón. In gratitude I took him out to eat; we had broiled fish and hearts of palm and a bottle of wine, and Mr. Thornberry told me sad stories about his life in New Hampshire, about his loneliness. Maybe he'd rent a house in Puntarenas for the winter. He couldn't take another cold winter. He had made a mess of his life, he said. It was the money — the IBM stock his sister had bequeathed to him. "The things I want, money can't buy. Money's just bullshit. If you have it. If you don't have it, it's important. I didn't always have it."

I said, "You saved my life."

"I couldn't let you walk around all night. It's dangerous. I hate this place." He shook his head. "I thought I was going to like it. It looked okay from the train — those palm trees. That travel agency was lying to me. They said there were parrots and monkeys here."

"Maybe you can get on a tour tomorrow."

"I'm sick of thinking about it." He looked at his watch. "Nine o'clock. I'm bushed. Shall we call it a day?"

I said, "I don't normally go to bed at nine o'clock."

Mr. Thornberry said, "I always do."

So we did. There was only one room key. We were like an elderly couple, fussing silently at bedtime, yawning, chastely putting on our pajamas. Mr. Thornberry pulled his covers up and sighed. I read for awhile, then switched off the light. It was still early, still noisy. Mr. Thornberry said, "Motorbike . . . Music . . . Listen to them yakking . . . Car . . . Train whistle . . . Those must be waves." Then he was asleep.

MARY MORRIS

Mary Morris has published two collections of stories, Vanishing Animals *and* The Bus of Dreams, *and two novels,* Crossroads *and* The Waiting Room. *Early on in* Nothing to Declare: Memoirs of a Woman Traveling Alone *she confides that traveling alone often isn't easy, and is never easy for a woman. "Brace yourself for tremendous emptiness and great surprise. Anything can happen. The bad things that have occurred in my travels . . . have happened because I wasn't prepared. At times I wonder that I am still alive." In the following journey to Palenque, not even a traveling companion is enough to ensure immunity from surprise and emptiness. Morris lives with a young daughter in New York City. Her most recent book is* Wall to Wall: From Beijing to Berlin by Rail.

from NOTHING TO DECLARE

Nobody goes to Palenque in mid-August, and what we were doing there then remains a mystery to me. Perhaps it was just a case of bad planning. But there we were, and we experienced it in its full force. The minute we stepped outside in the morning the heat struck us, bowled us over like a blast furnace. Our jeans, which we'd washed out the night before, were stiff as boards, dry as clay in the morning sun. But my hair never felt dry the entire time I was in Palenque; it was always soaked with sweat. As we walked to the ruins, the people swung in their hammocks, expressionless, barely moving, dead-looking, brains boiled. The jungle of Palenque was not like that of the highlands. Here there were no hills, no vistas, no gentle rolling of the land. In Palenque you were at the bottom of a pit of the lowlands, enclosed in a jungle prison. No breeze blew through this hollow. It felt ominous, treacherous, omnivorous, and indifferent, as if it would swallow you with a single gulp. If you stood still for just a moment, vines would engulf you, snakes would poison you, small crawling things would devour you, the air would be stolen from you. And you would be forgotten.

* * *

We entered the lost city of Palenque, a city of overgrown trails and crumbled ruins, a mysterious place about which little is known. Once a thriving city, Palenque was abandoned suddenly in the tenth century when all the great Mayan centers were abandoned for reasons unknown. I walked through its main causeways, among its temples and houses and courts where sports were played. I walked through these ruins with steam baths, public toilets with septic tanks, aqueducts, and drainage systems. I tried to imagine the city that had been.

Palenque, whose civilization was concurrent with that of the dawn of civilization in Greece and Egypt, is a place of questions, of things you must accept because no answers are forthcoming. Palenque isn't even its original name. After many years archaeologists have deciphered a date, which translates to 682 B.C.; they believe it is the completion date of the first pyramid. But no one can explain those pagoda-like temples reminiscent of those in China or at Angkor Wat in Cambodia. No one knows about Pakal, the prince entombed in an obsidian mask at the bottom of the great pyramid of the same name. He is believed to have been a captive, a prince of another tribe, yet the people of Palenque spent years building him the only pyramid in all of Mexico that is also a tomb.

Catherine and I climbed. We climbed each temple, every pyramid. We descended into the cool, wet depths of the tomb, then rose to see the astrological markings at the observation tower. We saw the entire valley from the observation tower, where the Mayan rulers observed the stars and charted their course and made their calendar — a calendar more accurate than ours. No one knows how they accomplished this, and no one knows why the Mayan people dispersed, leaving their cities and their religious centers centuries before the conquistadors arrived.

I left Catherine and climbed to the top of the Temple of the Sun; I saw the Temple of the Foliated Cross and imagined in the distance people struggling up the hill. Mayans going to their places of worship, dragging boulders, building their temples, stone by stone, painting beautiful pictures on the walls. I saw them fighting back the jungle, futilely pushing it away. I could see them from where I stood, a great, passionate, religious people who had disappeared but for their ruins.

Then I walked into the jungle a little ways. A horde

of soldier ants descended a tree. In my path were a red-bellied spider with skinny legs, reminding me of the black widow we thought we'd seen the night before, and butterflies of topaz, amber, turquoise, earth brown. Tigers, monarchs, delicate lace-leafed butterflies, little pearl and azul ones, big yellows and the giant blues — the cobalt-blues — all flew past me. I heard the sounds of strange animals as I made my way through the lush vegetation.

* * *

At dusk Catherine and I staggered back to the hotel with only one thought in our minds. We would strip, put on our suits, and take that swim. We walked in silence and I do not recall ever being quite so exhausted. As we approached the hotel, the pool appeared before us, turquoise. We kept walking, but the pool was not so shimmering as it had seemed the day before. As we drew nearer, I did not take my eyes from it. Catherine gaped as well. When we were only twenty feet away, I stopped. "Look," I said.

Catherine nodded. "It's not possible," she said.

We reached the edge of the completely empty swimming pool, the pool which had been full of water the afternoon before but did not have a drop in it now. We rushed to the man who sat in the office drinking a warm Coke, feet on his desk, and he told us that the pool was dirty so they had decided to drain it. We shook our heads in utter disbelief. We went to our room to shower and I felt someone was playing a cruel joke on us — there was no water. We rushed back to the man at the desk. He told us that they'd run out of water. For reasons we've never understood the hotel decided to drain the swimming pool on the same day they ran out of water. "When will you have more water?" Catherine asked.

The man shrugged. "Later," he said.

We went back to our room and lay on the bed, miserable, not speaking. Then we wiped ourselves off with half a dozen Wash 'n Dris each and went to the restaurant where we'd eaten the previous night. Petunia, who seemed to know me now, rolled over on her back to have her stomach rubbed throughout the meal, much to Catherine's annoyance. Eventually the owner came over and sat down. He asked if we liked Palenque and we said we did, but we were very hot and our hotel had no water. "Then you must go to Agua Azul," he said. "It is beautiful. Dozens of waterfalls. Yes, you must go there and swim."

* * *

We were lucky that morning. About a hundred people were waiting to push onto the local bus that would take us to Agua Azul, but the ticket taker took pity on Catherine and me. He was a young man of about seventeen with a kind and handsome dark face, warm brown eyes. And he wore pink. He wore a shiny pink shirt with some kind of animal — elephants, I think — all over it, and pink pants. One doesn't normally see a man dressed all in pink. That fact has stayed with me, and always will.

Since we were going all the way to Agua Azul, two hours up the mountain — not just to Egipto or Santa María, the mud and thatch villages along the way — and since we were the only blue-eyed gringas around, the ticket taker got us seats before the local people piled on. Then he opened a window for us and let everyone else board.

There seemed to be no limit to how many people the bus could hold. As many as showed up squeezed on. Mothers clutched screaming babies and pushed and dragged their chickens and goats. Men with machetes stood bleary-eyed in the heat. All had misery in their faces, the pain of drudgery.

The bus climbed and the breeze and the cooler air made everyone feel better. Slowly, as people got off, we felt the terrible heat letting up. The ticket taker in pink joked with us. He asked if Palenque had been hot enough for us. And he said Agua Azul was a beautiful place.

In two hours we reached Agua Azul, with its twenty or so main waterfalls and a series of lesser ones; small pools formed at the bases of some falls, and we could swim in these. Our driver said we'd stay for about two hours, then return. Catherine and I changed into our suits in a small wooden dressing room. A dead tarantula lay on the floor.

I headed for one of those little pools at the base of the falls while Catherine got a beer and started off on a walk. Our bus driver, a very gentle, elderly man with soft gray eyes, sat on the edge of a rock and pointed to a pool near him. He told me this was not a bad place to swim. I eased my way into the icy water and felt the cool go through me. I felt alive, tingly, happy to be in water. I began to swim. I swam out into the pool and back again, but about midway I could feel the current — strong, pulling at me.

Catherine came back. She said she'd seen a large wild boar, drowned, in one of the pools. "Be careful," she said. I looked at where I'd been swimming. The pool where I swam fed into a waterfall that fell about ten yards. It didn't look so treacherous and I wasn't very concerned. Catherine went to make us sandwiches with some vegetables, bread, and cheese we had brought from town. She said she'd be back with lunch.

I went into the water again. A boy had entered the pool and was swimming beside me. I swam out and back a few times, and each time I felt the current at that one place. Finally I decided it was dangerous and that I should not swim all the way across and back. But the boy, flailing about like a puppy, was not a very controlled swimmer, and he was making his way back and forth well beyond the place where I was stopping. I remember thinking to myself, I should tell him that the current is very strong. I should say something. But I did not. I didn't want to pry or bother him. He must know what he is doing, I told myself. Then Catherine called me for lunch.

I hoisted myself out of the water. As I walked toward her, my body felt cool for the first time in days and I smiled. I felt incredibly vigorous and content as Catherine held a sandwich out to me. Hungry and ready to eat, I reached for it, but our hands never connected. Her face changed from one of greeting to one of stunned horror. Her mouth opened, but all she could do was point to the place where I had been swimming.

From the corner of my eye I saw the boy who had been swimming next to me. He seemed to be riding one of those carnival watersled rides because he was practically sitting up and the current was just taking him along. I could see his face now and he looked familiar to me, like an old acquaintance you meet after many years but cannot quite place.

He was silent. That is what I remember most. The silence. He never screamed or shouted or cried for help. His face had the concentration of a good student taking an important exam. When he got to the falls, he twisted his body, trying to grab onto a branch, and then he was gone without a sound. Suddenly we were both screaming and pointing at nothing, at nothing at all except the rush of water.

The Mexicans did not believe us. They said no boy was missing. No one was missing anyone, but we were hysterical. "Someone went over that fall," we told them. At the same time I could not help thinking how I had done nothing. How that boy had been swimming near me and I had thought to say something and had said nothing. And then I thought how close it had come to being me. If I had gone out just a little farther, it would have been me.

Then our bus driver came toward us slowly, eyes glassy. He clasped in his hands the pink shirt and pink pants of the ticket taker, who had given us our seats. He said nothing. He simply held out the boy's clothes.

It took a while, but a search party was organized. About a dozen young Mexican men stripped down to their shorts and with sticks went to the base of the falls, where they formed a line. We sat on the bank over the falls, watching. Catherine seemed nervous and soon began pacing. But I sat, transfixed, never taking my eyes off the search party. I watched the bodies of young men, bodies so perfect and beautiful that I wanted to touch them as they bent over the water and put their faces in, like divers after mother-of-pearl. They walked and probed as I sat and waited, but no body was found.

A Mexican who seemed to be in charge came over to us. "He is at the bottom of the falls. It has happened here before. The body will be trapped there forever." The bus driver was in tears now. He knew the boy and his family well. The Mexican shrugged. "We'll keep looking," he said. They searched for two hours while we waited on the bank.

Finally the driver patted me on the shoulder. "Let's go," he said.

"I should have done something," I said to Catherine as we got on the bus. "When we were swimming, I should have said something."

"Be grateful it wasn't you," she said.

"I am, but I should have done something."

Catherine opened up a copy of *Tropic of Cancer* and read all the way back to Palenque. I tried to talk to her, but she would not discuss the incident with me. She just said, "It wasn't your fault. It was an accident, so forget it."

RONALD WRIGHT

Born in England in 1948, Ronald Wright read archaeology and anthropology at Cambridge, where he received his M.A. in 1973. His books include Cut Stones and Crossroads: A Journey in the Two Worlds of Peru, On Fiji Islands, *and* Time Among the Maya: Travels in Belize, Guatemala, and Mexico. *He has traveled widely in the Americas, Africa, and the South Pacific, and now lives near Toronto. His latest book is* Stolen Continents, *a history of the New World through Indian eyes.*

from CUT STONES AND CROSSROADS

My copy of the *South American Handbook* is out-of-date. I was planning to take the Santa railway to Huallanca at the north end of the Callejón de Huaylas. But I learned at breakfast that the line was another victim of the earthquake. It seems that the tracks have been taken up and the railbed is now being used as a road. Moreover, my informant (a cook with a filthy vest and a forearm so covered in scales that it looked like a large fish) suggested this "road" is dangerous. Peruvians seldom remark on the hazards of roads. . . . Still, a detour will be tedious and probably no safer.

I wait all morning at a service station on the edge

of Chimbote for a vehicle going my way. Gasoline architecture varies little around the world: this place has two greasing bays, four pumps, and an office full of oil tins and girlie pinups. Blondes, of course. Latin Americans' ideal of beauty has nothing at all to do with racial fact. Advertising, pornography, and images of Christ all share a taste for pallid Aryans. They like the girls a little heavier than the current gringo vogue: skinniness is too suggestive of poverty.

A salient concrete roof shades the pumps. The only clues to my whereabouts are the sign for PETROPERU and the fact that urine defeats diesel in the contest of smells.

The sun chases me and the shadows beneath the roof. Outside, greasy asphalt shimmers and stinks, soft as toffee, a mosaic of embedded bottle caps.

After siesta a three-ton Ford arrives. A sticker on its windshield says: VIRGINITY CAUSES CANCER — GET YOUR VACCINATION HERE. The driver is a young, intelligent man with a shock of black hair and supple movements. He offers me a place on top of the load, says the road is perfectly safe, and makes me promise one thing: "Lie absolutely flat when we come to the tunnels or you'll lose your head. There isn't clearance for a fart in most of them."

"How many are there?"

"Sixteen."

* * *

For a long time we wind through a former sugar hacienda, now a co-op; we stop often to pick up small loads and people wanting short rides. The usual yellow haze veils the sky, intensifying the heat, robbing the landscape of contrast. Wherever is water, is color — greenery and flowers: frangipani, bougainvillea — infrequent and insecure, like patches of paint left on a peeling fresco. Dust coats everything near the road; even the trees and gaudy houses seem camouflaged for desert warfare.

There is harvesting in the fields, which have been burned to remove the dense, rasping leaves from the cane. Workers wearing only briefs slash rhythmically at the charred stems with machetes. Their bodies run with sugar, soot, and sweat; the air reeks of molasses.

Have things improved for these workers since the reforms? The answer, as far as I can tell, is a much-qualified yes. At first the rhetoric of worker control alarmed the supervisors and technicians on these estates. They threatened to resign en masse, and were placated only by the gift of disproportionate power in co-op affairs. This alienated the laborers, who went out on strike after calls from their APRA union bosses. Then there came an uneasy truce presided over by "military coordinators," resented by both sides. The situation was more complex than the architects of the land reform had realized — many of the cane cutters were seasonal workers, and the co-ops' fulltime members were reluctant to share their new wealth with these outsiders as the army insisted they must. Now the army has backed off and the co-op members have become a proletarian élite; but recent drops in world sugar prices will no doubt threaten their prosperity.

* * *

At last we leave the desert plain and enter the lower Santa canyon, so rocky that one sees no life here, even beside the river. I long for the sierra. Already Chimbote is a memory of only three colors: khaki land, houses, and sky, and rock islands white with guano standing in a black sea.

The old railbed soon leaves the valley floor, which becomes too wild, and clings to the canyon wall on a ledge blasted from the rock. It is seldom more than six inches wider than the truck on either side: the former railway was narrow-gauge. Abandoned mine workings pack the cliffs like rodent burrows; long tongues of debris depend from their small black mouths. The tunnels are indeed low, unlined and jagged inside. According to the other passengers, more than one traveler has had his head "smashed like a melon."

In twilight we reach one of those tiny hanging pampas that one finds so unexpectedly in the Andes. "Pampa" in Peru has a less specific meaning than in English: it is the Runasimi adjective for "flat," and a noun for any flat space, no matter how small. There are a few huts here, some chickens, children, and dark green-orange trees. Though we are a thousand feet above the river, its water is brought from upstream by a long channel cut into the valley wall.

The driver stops and shouts up: "Flat tire. Good thing it happened here!" Yes, very. I climb down and walk to the edge of the gorge. The sky has cleared with the height we have gained and is navy blue with approaching night. All around are folded masses of rock torn by shadow. At the bottom of its dark, dry vee, the river's violence makes it conspicuously white.

The spare is flat (of course), and the puncture is on the inner dual, requiring removal of both wheels. It takes half an hour of hammering and cursing to break the bead from the rim; but it's not until the tube has been patched and replaced that the real work begins. The problem is the pump, one of those tiny plunger jobs suitable for bicycles. It needs lots of spittle inside before yielding any air. The driver, his helper, and one of the more vigorous passengers take turns at a hundred strokes each. I remember an earlier flat tire, on the Huancayo road in 1975, the driver shouting exhortations to his helper — a dull-witted and potentially rebellious teenager — exhortations satirizing government propaganda: "Pump for Peru! I'll tell Velasco how valiant you are. Work hard so the country can afford to buy him a wooden leg."

It is now quite dark. An hour's pumping has failed to inflate the tire to within a quarter of its working pressure. Lights can be seen in the distance coming down the mountain. The driver says, "That's strange. The road is one-way going up today." As with several roads in the Andes, traffic is supposed to switch directions on odd and even days. One of the pumpers hopes for a new Dodge truck with compressed air, but the wish is unfulfilled. Ten minutes later another violator of the traffic code arrives (or is it we who are wrong?) and he does have air.

I return to the *canasta*, the extension of the truck box that overhangs the cab, and get comfortable on my back among some sugar sacks. The stars seem very close, blotted from time to time when tunnels sweep overhead.

Much'aykusqayki Pacha Ruwaq	Blessed Maker of the World
Qhawarillaway	Watch us
Sumaq qoyllur ñawiyki-wan.	With your eyes, the glorious stars.

I must have slept. Around midnight, very cold, the driver shakes me awake: "This is Yuraqmarka. We can eat here, and there's lodging." He leads me through the darkness to a restaurant. An old woman is shuffling about, half asleep. It takes her ten minutes to bring a candle. I ask how much I owe for the ride. Nothing, the driver says, but he wants the miniature flashlight I lent him while the tire was being repaired. I have to refuse, and feel mean: I need it for camping and there are none available in Peru.

The woman serves an execrable cold dish that was once hot: *seco de cordero*, an old foe of mine, but I am hungry enough to eat it. Seco is usually made from sheep neckbones braised in a gravy flavored with cilantro, coriander leaves. It sounds harmless enough, but so much cilantro is used that the result is cloying and sickly, like rotten parsley. The flavor is utterly different from coriander seed, a main ingredient of curry powder.

"Lodging" turns out to be a tin shack behind the restaurant. Two of the four beds are already occupied by bulky forms, from which come snores and gusts of alcoholic breath.

* * *

My first sight of the day is the avalanche of refuse that begins at the back door of the kitchen and drops away into the ravine: plastic, tins, corncobs, offal, and rags. Three very hairy black pigs are scuffling for the edible items. Yuraqmarka means White Town; I had imagined a pleasant sierra village, but daylight reveals a collection of metal huts that is little more than a truck stop. I go inside the kitchen, looking for water, and do not immediately realize that what appears to be an old coat hanging from the ceiling is in fact a sheep's haunch, invisible beneath a regiment of flies. The insects settle on me as I wash. Their feet are cold and moist.

* * *

The old railbed joins a true road at Yuraqmarka; the truck carrying advice to virgins has left for the north. After the vision of the kitchen I am content with a cup of tea for breakfast. The only other customers are two men conversing intently through the forest of empty beer bottles on their table. One is tall, thirtyish, European-looking, but obviously, from his neat polyester shirt and slacks, a well-to-do Peruvian; the other, a sallow mestizo with Asiatic eyes and blighted four-day stubble. He wears — or, rather, appears to live in — a wrinkled suit and a shirt with no collar.

The tall one (also the soberer of the two) speaks: "Gringo! Where are you going?"

"Huallanca, and Huarás."

"So are we. Come and have a drink with us." I take my tea over to their table.

"Carlos García Cárdenas *a sus órdenes!*" the tall one

65

says, "and my fellow traveler Policarpo Ruíz Huillca." I give my name, we shake hands. Their touch is soft and clammy and reminds me of the flies. (Handshaking in Latin countries is always frequently and lightly done, with the loose grip that Anglo-Saxons believe shows lack of "moral fiber.")

"I am from Lima," García says, in the voice of the Peruvian *Herrenvolk*; "my . . . friend here lives in Carás, in the Callejón." Ruíz looks up, belches, swallows quickly, says nothing. "He's a justice of the peace."

At this Ruíz comes to life, nods at the Limeño as if he were far away, and leans toward me conspiratorially: "He's a PIP. You understan'?" The voice drops to a whisper. "Policía de Investigaciones del Perú!"

The PIP is the élite plainclothes police force. It has political functions (not always those of the government), a reputation for corruption, and a taste for power. Its members are supposed to operate undercover, but are usually too swaggering to be inconspicuous. The acronym is pronounced, appropriately, as *peep*.

"Peep," the judge continues, "you'll see. When a truck comes we'll get a ride. No problem. Nothing to pay. Peep!" He flashes his hand as if he held a badge. García looks embarrassed. Ruíz calls for more beer. I decline.

"From what country?" García asks.

"England originally — I live in Canada."

"You're my friend!" Ruíz interrupts, seizing my hand and continuing to hold it in a flabby grasp. "This gentleman is a PIP! If anything comes by . . . he'll stop it for us. . . ."

66

"So, what do you think of us two 'bad functionaries' of the government?" (García must be making ironic reference to the newspaper campaigns of Velasco's day calling on people to denounce corrupt officials.)

"That's not for me to say."

"Have a beer. I'd feel much better if you'd join us."

"No, really I'd rather not."

"Yes! Waiter, three beers!"

"No, please. I'll have a soft drink instead."

"You don't drink?"

"Never before lunch."

"'Never before lunch' — you gringos have such rules, such discipline. We Peruvians . . ."

"There are plenty of gringos who drink."

"But not you, Ronald?" The "peep" persists.

"Not when I'm traveling. I seem to lose the taste for it."

"You don't smoke marihuana, do you?"

"Of course not." I don't like this line of questioning.

Ruíz revives again and leans across: "What country you from?"

"He's from England . . . and Canada."

"Ah," Ruíz sighs, "England. England is the mother country of Canada and the United States. That so? Just as Spain is the mother country of Peru!"

I reply without thinking: "It's not really the same. Spain isn't the mother country of Peru in the same sense. In North America most of the people have originally come from Europe, but Peruvians are mostly native, descended from the Incas. . . ." The look on Ruíz's face tells me how he has taken my effort to instill national pride. He knocks over his chair and shoots to his feet with impossible speed.

"There are no Indians in Peru! *No Indians in Peru!*"

Huillca, his Runasimi matronymic, must be a terrible shame to him.

* * *

At eleven, a truck comes at last. Ruíz is now at the incapable stage. García and I hoist him up the tailgate and the passengers inside haul him over the top. He props himself in a corner, crimped at the middle like a furled rug.

A woman sitting on the floor nearby has a large basket holding about a hundred eggs; when the driver puts the motor in gear the truck lurches and the judge's foot goes in. "*Ay, señor!*" the woman wails, pushing him away. He has smashed at least a dozen — equivalent in value to a laborer's daily wage, or two bottles of the beer that has brought him to this state. But the woman does not dare ask compensation and none is offered.

Later there is poetic justice: Ruíz tries to climb out of the moving vehicle and his fedora blows away in the wind.

* * *

Judge and "peep" decide to stop at Carás, where the Callejón proper begins. It is already early afternoon; I continue to Huarás by colectivo.

There has been plenty of rain here. From Carás south the valley is a study in greens and reds: silver-green maguey and eucalyptus saplings, emerald stands of young maize, bottle-green alfalfa; the adobe walls and houses are russet, and so are the wounds of paths and erosion channels on the land.

"Callejón" (Spanish for "alley" or "corridor") is an apt name for this long valley running between the two cordilleras. The Cordillera Negra is a sad range. Its eighteen-thousand-foot heights are too low to capture eternal snows; too low, even, to receive much of the scanty moisture that remains in the winds sweeping up from the sea. For that reason it is black, and the ranchers of sheep and llamas on its slopes are forced into conflict with the farmers of the valley whenever drought sears their pastures. But the White Cordillera, which forms a great wall to the east, is magnificent. Clouds are hiding the twenty-two-thousand-foot summits of Huascarán and Huandoy, but as I watch, the vapors swirl and part to reveal a kaleidoscopic world of illusion, dazzling against the blue-black sky. I cannot tell what is cloud, what ice, what blowing snow; and when the sun catches the glaciers their refulgence stabs my eyes.

Climbers look on these mountains the way some men regard beautiful women: as objects to be wooed, conquered, and then left. Only a new ascent, like a new sexual practice with an old lover, will tempt the mountaineer to a longer dalliance.

In the case of mountains I am the "pedestal" type, content to worship them from afar. The Runa call the mountains *Apu*, "Lord," the same title that was applied to the Lord Inca and the four Apus who ruled over each quarter of the Tawantinsuyu. To Runa the mountain is an ancestor, a protective deity, as well as a kind of underworld in which life and flesh are held in reserve.

All life is cycled through the mountains that preside over an ayllu, just as water is recycled by the process of condensing on the peaks and running down through the streams and irrigation channels of the ayllu lands. Apus are "fed" with offerings of coca, alcohol, and food. Only if an Apu is given the proper respect will he provide for his community's needs. When José María Arguedas was doing anthropological research in Puquio, he was given this description of the Apu concept by the head of a Runa ayllu (in that region, the Apu as a spiritual entity is more often called *Wamani*):

> The Wamani is really our second God. The Wamani exists in all the mountains; all high places have the Wamani. He provides the pasture for our animals, and to us he gives his veins, the watercourses.

The mountains can also be dangerous, not only to foolhardy climbers, but to anyone living in the shadow of their influence. The 1970 earthquake dislodged a great mass of partly frozen mud and rock from the upper slopes of Huascarán. The *aluvión* hurtled down the mountainside, reaching a speed of more than sixty miles per hour. At one place in its path a sudden rise in the topography was sufficient to launch the whole slide into the air. It is said that it flew over a small Runa settlement, inflicting no physical harm, though several people were deranged by the sight and sound of it passing overhead.

A large town near the valley bottom was not so lucky: the mass dropped on Yungay like an Old Testament judgment. All the buildings and twenty thousand people were buried. When the first relief helicopters arrived they saw an unbelievable sight: sticking up from the middle of the waste of boulders, ice, and clay were the tops of four palm trees, still in place, marking the corners of the central plaza.

Until now, the road has been straight, but at Yungay it must snake its way between colossal boulders. The driver and other passengers cross themselves repeatedly. I see only a raw landscape like the bed of a dry river, in which some hardy shrubs are starting to grow.

The valley rises gently from Carás at seventy-five hundred feet to Huarás at ten thousand. The slope is barely perceptible, except perhaps by the drowsiness brought on by gradual rarification of the air. People are more numerous as we draw near the city. Everywhere Runa are returning home, the men dressed dowdily in shabby Western clothes, the women bright and traditional in flowing skirts of crimson, blue, or black. Both sexes wear battered felt hats that look like Humphrey Bogart hand-me-downs. The rest of the female costume has changed little in its essentials since the Indian writer and illustrator Felipe Waman Puma captured it in his great work, *El Primer Nueva Corónica y Buen Gobierno*, which he wrote between 1585 and 1615. Now, as then, the women wear the handwoven *lliqlla*, a shawl and carrying cloth, fastened in front with a large pin or brooch still called *tupu*. Beneath the *lliqlla* and skirt are frilly blouses and petticoats elaborately stitched in a style that must have been introduced during the eighteenth century. Those with fields to guard carry the slings that were once an Inca war weapon but are nowadays used for killing birds; those with livestock wear homespun lariats around their waists.

Munankichu willanayta	Do you want me to tell you
Maymantachus kanichayta?	Where I'm from?
Haqay urqu qhepanmanta,	I'm from behind that hill,
Clavelinas chawpinmanta,	Amid the carnations,
Azucenas chawpinmanta.	Among the lilies.
Castillamantam warak'ay,	My sling is of Castilian fabric,
Merinomantam seqolloy:	And my lasso of merino wool:
Enteramente durable,	Very long-lasting,
Enteramente aguante.	Very strong.

Night has fallen when we reach Huarás. Unshaded lightbulbs shine dimly from the doors of one-room shops and bars. Some people are dancing to *waynos* played on scratchy phonographs. No matter how gay the tune, Andean music always wrenches me: there is a desperation to the gaiety that evokes the tragedy of Peru.

CHARLES NICHOLL

Charles Nicholl was born in London in 1950 and now lives in Herefordshire. His journalism has appeared in Granta, Rolling Stone, the Sunday Times, *and* the New Statesman. *He has published a book on Elizabethan alchemy and a biography of the pamphleteer Tom Nashe, and an investigation into the death of Christopher Marlowe,* The Reckoning. *Nicholl's interest in the storytelling techniques of fiction are evident in both his travel books, the recent* Borderlines: A Journey in Thailand and Burma *and* The Fruit Palace, *an adventurous investigation into the cocaine underworld of Colombia.*

from THE FRUIT PALACE

The San Felipe slaughterhouse lay behind a supermarket in the nebulous northern outskirts of Bogotá, where the city laps around the old outlying villages of Suba and Nissa, depositing its flotsam of shopping malls and housing projects on the high green savannah. I presented myself at the gates and said I wished to see Señor Santander Gomez Cuartas, Junior Vice-Superintendent of the slaughterhouse.

Getting this far had indeed been easy enough. A visit to the offices of the Colombian Meat Producers'

Federation had secured, along with reams of information and statistics about the meat trade, the name of Señor Gomez. As Jefe de Relaciones Públicas at the slaughterhouse, he was the official unfortunate delegated to deal with occasional visiting nuisances like myself. I flourished my business card at the security man. This describes me as a "consultant researcher," with a Mickey-Mouse-company address and telex number underneath, a useful tool in the nose-poking trade. Judging from the security man's blank gaze it might just as well have described me as an Egyptian rope-dancer, but the general effect was enough. He telephoned through to Gomez and told him he had a visitor at the front gate.

Presently Gomez appeared, a small, worried man with a goatee beard. He wore a white coat with splashes of blood on it, and carried another over his arm. Oozing plausibility, I explained my mission. I was compiling a "business opportunities" report on Colombia, was very interested in the meat business, had your name from Señor So-and-so at the Federación, and would be most grateful — esteemed *señor* — to be shown around this major meat-processing plant of yours. He said he would show me round with pleasure. He gave me the white coat to put on, and I was in. If Rikki was right, this was where the Snow White pipeline disgorged 100 kilos of cocaine a week. I didn't quite know what I was looking for, but surely something must show. I noted the trucks parked at one end of the abattoir, dusty flat-bed trucks and larger covered lorries that brought the cattle up from the lowland grazing plains of the east. There must have been thirty or forty trucks there. How to spot a few sacks of coke?

The job in hand, however, was my guided tour of the slaughterhouse. I wasn't looking forward to this. We watched the cattle being herded into the corrals behind the abattoir. Most of them were *cebú* oxen — big, placid, humped, white beasts, South American versions of the Brahmin ox, though unfortunately for them not sharing their Hindu cousins' immunity from slaughter. Gomez rubbed his hands and said that a stout, well-covered *cebú* bullock was worth upward of 30,000 pesos. Each of these big fellows would weigh about 500 kilos and yield over half that weight in meat and assorted offals. Meat is measured in the traditional unit of *arrobas* — 12.5 kilos — and a good animal is always said to yield *una arroba mas*, one *arroba* more than half its body weight.

As we walked round the block of the corrals, Gomez stopped. Gesturing me to follow him, he walked over to a group of three men standing round a station wagon. A fourth was sitting in the opened back, pulling on a pair of rubber boots. Gomez introduced me to a tall, lugubrious man, the *matadero*'s senior vice-superintendent, and to the young, bearded manager of the Cafam supermarket next to the abattoir. Small talk was exchanged. Sixty million kilos of beef left the slaughterhouse every year, I learned.

The small, elderly man in the back of the station wagon was discussing something with a white-coated official — instructing him, it seemed, for now the official said, "Yes, señor, right away," and hurried off, checking his watch like the White Rabbit. Gomez promptly launched into obsequious greetings. "What a pleasure it is to see you, Don Rafael," he cried, ducking and bobbing like a courtier. He plucked fussily at my sleeve. "May I present to you Señor Rafael Vallejo Aragon? He is one of our most distinguished and successful figures in the meat business."

The small man took this heralding as no more than his due. He wore a smart tweedy suit, check shirt, heathery woollen tie. His rubber boots were brand new: blue with bright yellow soles. The whole gave a careful effect of well-breeched country gent. He stood to shake hands. The palm was hard and calloused, the figure beneath the squire's tweeds stocky and powerful. He hadn't been born distinguished, I guessed.

I fired in a couple of polite questions about his meat interests. His answers were vague and grand. He soon turned to the others to discuss beef matters. Gomez hung in for a bit, larded Vallejo with more compliments, then said, "We must leave you, Don Rafael, you are a busy man." Vallejo said to me, with mechanical largesse, "You must come to my stud-farm in Cundinamarca one day, señor. I will tell you *everything* about the meat business in Colombia." He laughed a gravelly laugh. "The meat business is very good. We are a nation of carnivores!" He made a grimace, gnashed his teeth comically. The others laughed fulsomely. Gomez cried, "It is true, Don Rafael, it is true!" Vallejo frowned for a moment. "In England you have these" — he searched for the word, and spoke it with distaste — "*vegetarianos*. Not in Colombia. It is not natural. For rabbits, maybe." There was a sudden bullying note in his voice. He covered it with a loud, false laugh, echoed once more by the entourage. Gomez writhed with delight, but I saw his eyes flick over to me to see how I was taking this slur on my homeland. I thought of making some smart-ass riposte, but the odds were against me. For a moment, though, I found myself staring straight into the little man's hard grey eyes.

"He's an important man, then?" I said to Gomez as we walked on.

"Millonario!" whispered Gomez, pouting with pleasure at the thought.

* * *

From a raised walkway we could view the entire corral. In the corner was a pen with a few steers lying awkwardly, some moving and struggling. These animals, immobilized by sickness or injury, would be dispatched *in situ*. All the other animals were progressing, hour by hour, pen by pen, towards the *corriente*, the narrow black-railed ramp that led up into the abattoir proper. There a man in white overalls and a safety helmet prodded them up, in single file, with an electric goad wired up to a live overhead cable. The ramp led to an opening, with steel half-doors, like saloon doors in a Western. The patient oxen plodded up. The leading one glimpsed the scene inside, beyond the steel doors. If there is a bovine notion of hell, this was surely it. It skidded back, but the animals behind blocked its retreat, and the prod goaded it on.

Without really meaning to, I said, "He doesn't want to go in."

Gomez laughed, as if I had made some polite little

joke. "It is sad, isn't it?" he said, unconvincingly. We walked on into the *matadero*, the killing place.

Just inside those swing doors, the steer came into a square well, about twenty feet long. A man stood high above it, wielding a long steel pole with a sharp spike at the end, like an elongated ski-stick. As the animal was released into the well, he held the *pica* vertical above him, two-handed, and brought it down in a swift, hard jab into the steer's neck, just behind the horns. The animal fell, stunned and helpless, eyes lolling, legs cavorting crazily. Another worker now nipped down into the well and slipped a heavy chain loop around its left hindleg. This was a deft operation, with half a ton of flesh and bones thrashing about on the floor. A third man, up on a level with the *picador*, pressed a button. The hoist clanked into action, winching the beast up, upside down. It hung swaying from the overhead rail. This rail ran on circuitously, like a ghost train, through the various departments of the slaughterhouse. With a brisk, practised slash the man next to the *picador* cut the upended animal's throat. Blood poured out like water from a pail, thick crimson blood, splashing and steaming on the wet concrete floor. The next man sliced off the head and feet, a surprisingly easy operation with those big, scoured knives. The whole process, from living creature to headless carcass, took no more than half a minute. At the San Felipe slaughterhouse eight hundred to one thousand cattle are dispatched every day. When the darkness comes they switch on floodlights over the corrals, and the sacrifice continues.

The carcass continued along the overhead rail till it

came to the skinners. Skinning is done with a kind of modified chainsaw. This sliced up the belly, and a hook was then passed through the skin at the back, and the chain-winch pulled upwards, bringing the whole hide with it. The skin was stretchy and pink on the inside, peeling off like a long pale glove. The guts piled out: strange coils and tubes, white, red and blue. The skins were carted off in one direction, the guts in another. In another room they were sorting great vats of the stuff — *viscera roja*, the offal; *viscera blanca*, the intestines, paunch, etc. Nothing will be wasted. The carcass now looked like a recognizable piece of butcher's meat, and off it went along the rail to the other half of the *matadero*, to be packed whole into cold-store trucks, or chopped and packaged ready for the butchers, restaurants, roadhouses and kitchens of this nation of carnivores.

Gomez was at my shoulder throughout, explaining it all, casual and precise, like Mephistopheles giving a guided tour of the inferno. When he judged I had seen enough, he took me to his office, up a few steps behind the gut room. When he closed the door I realized what a huge din had filled the slaughterhouse. The whole gory business had made such an impact on my eyes that I had hardly noticed the noise. I felt sick and tired. I saw my knuckles whiten as I leant on the metal desk. There was a pile of S-shaped hooks and a wooden-handled knife sharpener in the in tray.

Looking out of the barred window on to a small, enclosed yard outside, I saw two men talking. One was the little meat baron, Rafael Vallejo. He had his

79

back to me, but the tweed jacket and the white hair were unmistakable. The other was the white-coated minion he had been talking to when I first saw him. I watched with idle curiosity. Gomez was hunting out some statistics for me, tetchily complaining of the lack of a secretary to keep his papers in order. I heard a door opening into the yard. Vallejo turned. Another white-coated figure came into view, from some room next to Gomez's office. There was something vaguely troubling about his back view. The broad, slightly hunched shoulders, the square head of spiky black hair. I had seen it before. With a jolt, I realized. I had seen it walking out of The Place a couple of nights earlier, clad in sky-blue. It was Oddjob.

Rikki was right, Snow White was real, and I was right slap in the middle of it. Under no circumstances must Oddjob see me here. He did not look like a man who had much time for funny coincidences. I shrank back, grateful for the grimy film over the window.

Gomez had found the figures, the annual tonnages and percentage breakdowns so vital for my study of the meat business. He brought a few folders over to the desk and began to drone out the data. I mechanically wrote as he spoke, but all the while I was keeping an eye on the trio out in the yard. Vallejo was talking, with jabbed gestures of emphasis. Oddjob was listening, head still, occasional sulky monosyllables of agreement. The more I watched, the cosier it looked. Could it be possible? Had I stumbled right up the ladder all at once? Vallejo was no small-time spiv. If that was cocaine talk going on in that yard, then the distinguished millionaire and carnivore Don Rafael was something pretty big. The sun glinted on his white hair. Was he the *capo*? Was he Snow White himself?

In a pause between statistics, trying to sound casual, I said, "Look, there's Señor Vallejo again. He does a lot of business here, does he?"

"Oh yes. He has many cattle ranches in the *llanos*. We handle all his stock."

"And the meat itself? He has distribution networks, that sort of thing?"

"Of course. Transcarne. One of the biggest meat transportation companies in Colombia."

It was all falling into place. Out in the yard there was just Vallejo and Oddjob now. The third man had left. Oddjob's sleazy, slant-eyed, tom-cat's face was half-turned toward me. He was talking, with choppy, robotic gestures from his big paws. It was the first time I'd seen him utter a word. "Who's that Vallejo's talking to?" I asked.

Gomez had his glasses off for reading the figures and now had to fumble them out of his white coat. "That? Oh, that's one of our packing managers."

Somewhere a siren shrilled. Gomez looked at his watch, closed his folders. "Midday," he announced. "The end of the morning shift. You would like a beer?"

As in all the comedies, the booze was in the first-aid cabinet. He took out two bottles and two glasses. Vallejo and Oddjob were still conferring, but with a hasty, last-minute air now. Gomez was washing the glasses in a hand-basin. No: the glasses were on the desk — Gomez was washing two *more* glasses. He was walking to the door that led out into the yard. It opened with a squawk of metal on the stone floor. The two men outside wheeled around. Gomez bobbed in the doorway. "Don Rafael! Rodolfo! You will take a beer with us?" A curt wave from Vallejo. "How kind, Señor Gomez." A nod of assent from Oddjob, a.k.a. Rodolfo. Gomez fussed happily back into the room, polishing a glass on his coattail. "We will have a party," he chirped.

Fear is blank. Brain dazzled, body frozen, a rabbit caught in the headlights. I heard the fizz of beer, the thin clatter of bottle tops on the metal desk. You bloody idiot, I thought. You've really done it this time. Vallejo was walking slowly towards us, still talking. Oddjob glided resentfully beside him. In a few seconds he would be here. He would recognize me, he would start asking questions, he would go on asking till he didn't need any more answers. Then he would probably hook me up on the overhead rail and loosen my guts with one of those skinning saws.

There was only one way out: back into the slaughter-house. I hunched up, hand to my mouth, and blurted, *"Estoy enfermo! Voy a vomitar!"* Vallejo had just stepped in through the door as I rushed out of the office. The last thing I saw was Gomez's startled face, and the beer spilling past the glass as he looked up from pouring.

I sprinted down the steps, back into the mayhem of the killing-floor, through the gut-room, slowing to a trot, trying not to attract attention. I kept my hand over my mouth, so everyone would think the gringo *maricón* couldn't handle all the blood and death. I heard Gomez's voice behind me. "Señor Nee-col, this way!

Not there, señor!" I dodged down a corridor, passed through an empty room with a long line of severed calves' feet dangling from chains, crossed a yard, and came into what was evidently the pig section of the *matadero*. There were squeals without, but in this room all was quiet. A man in a rubber apron was thoughtfully prodding a few dead porkers in a vat of hot water. Another, wearing a cap with a cloth down the back of his head like a legionnaire's képi, was scraping the hairs off a strung carcass. I slowed to a walk. White coat on, notebook in hand, just an official on his way from this door to that.

I came out into another yard. Pigs milling in slatted stalls, but no one around that I could see. I tried to get some bearings. There was a sort of fenced runway through which the pigs were herded into the stalls. Beyond it I saw trucks and cars parked: the back of the *matadero*, I reckoned, the opposite side from the one I'd come in at. If I could just get myself out through some back gate. I edged along the side of the stalls and was just about to break cover when I heard footsteps and voices. I shrank back, but I was still in full view if they came into the yard. The stall nearest me was empty. I clambered over the side and dropped silently into a rich mulch of straw and pig shit. A few inches from my face, in the neighboring stall, a dozen fear-crazed pigs bumped and snuffled against the slats. I crouched shivering while the voices passed.

Skulking at the edge of the truck park I saw that there was indeed a rear gate. A few yards away a man was closing up the back of an old flat-bed truck.

He wore blue overalls and a battered straw hat: a pig-man, I supposed. He climbed into the cab and started the engine. He'll do, I thought. I stripped off my dung-smeared white coat, dumped it in a corner and trotted briskly up to the truck. "Excuse me, señor. Are you going? Can you give me a lift?"

The pig-man surveyed me, chewing on a toothpick. I was breathing heavily: fear at high altitude. There was muck on my hands, my tie, my notebook. He ran a hand over his grey stubble, amiable and puzzled. I tensed with impatience. Then he nodded slowly, and said something in a rich *campesino* brogue. It sounded like "I'm going to Zoggo."

"That'll do nicely," I said, and climbed up into the cab. He smiled a broad, toothless smile, fished out a crumpled pack of Pielroja, and offered me a cigarette. I fumbled for matches, trying to speed everything up. Any moment now Gomez and Oddjob were going to come round the corner and start the hue and cry. "My car won't start," I said. "I'm terribly late." He shook his head philosophically and said something else I couldn't understand. Lateness was not a concept that meant much to him. At last, clamping the cigarette in his mouth, he eased the pickup into gear. The truck chugged off lazily down along the red-brick back of the *matadero*. My eyes darted around, looking for the familiar little-and-large figures. The truck seemed to be firing on about half a cylinder. Optimum speed was reached at five miles an hour. The pig-man slumped comfortably in his seat, elbow resting on the window. Jesus, I thought, jiggling futilely, I've picked a real winner here.

I regretted my move even more when we reached the roadway, and instead of turning toward the rear gate he swung the truck right, heading for the front of the *matadero*. This brought us right into the central thoroughfare: offices, canteen, lunch-hour crowds of white coats, slaughterers, truckers. Almost immediately I spotted Gomez, talking to a security-looking man in a peaked cap. He was tugging at his little beard, puzzling away at the mystery of the vanishing journalist. Then, off to one side, I saw Oddjob, silently watching, his fat brown face ranging slowly round like a radar dish. From where he stood he could see both exits from the *matadero*. He was waiting for me to break cover. He was bound to see me as we passed.

We chugged serenely to my doom. I squeezed my hands in mute supplication. In doing so I felt the box of matches still cradled in my sweating palm. With a swift, purposeful movement I spilt the contents on to the rusty floor at my feet. *"Maldita sea,"* I cursed, "how clumsy," and bent myself double to retrieve them. In this position, I fervently hoped, I was just out of view below the line of the window. "It's all right, señor, I have matches," said the pig-man. "No, no," I called up from my jackknife position, "I'll get them." He shrugged. The truck hiccoughed on towards the gate. I scrabbled in the dust for the little waxy white matches. With this meagre camouflage I passed beneath and beyond the gaze of Oddjob.

When the truck stopped I straightened up, thinking we were at the gates. But we were still a good twenty yards short of them. The pig-man had stopped to talk to someone, another *campesino*, another crumpled hat. It was going to be one of those slow, mulled conversations full of pauses.

Craning around, I saw Gomez and the peaked-cap fellow walking purposefully up the roadway toward us. Clearly they were coming up to the gate. They were going to warn the security guard: a mad Englishman on the loose. The pig-man was talking about the price of pork, warming to his theme. I heard again the butcher's phrase Gomez had used, *"una arroba mas."*

Oh yes, we're all after that little bit extra, that one *arroba* over the top. Only sometimes it costs us more than we can pay.

It was now or never. "Thanks for the ride," I said, and jumped out of the cab. The truck shielded me from Gomez. Those twenty yards to the gate were a fast walk through eternity. I waited for the shout behind me but none came. As I passed through the gate the security man waved. I saw him jot something down on a clipboard. One consultant researcher, business done, leaves the slaughterhouse. He must be a busy man. Look how he's running. . . .

JONATHAN RABAN

Jonathan Raban was born in England in 1942, and has written about London in Soft City. *His travel books include* Hunting Mister Heartbreak, *which won the Thomas Cook Travel Book Award for 1991,* Arabia Through the Looking Glass, Coasting, *and* Old Glory, *which also won the Thomas Cook Award. He has also edited* The Oxford Book of the Sea. *He has published a novel,* Foreign Land, *and collected his journalism in* For Love & Money: A Writing Life, 1969–1989. *He is a Fellow of the Royal Society of Literature, and now lives in Seattle. The following excerpt includes the final pages of Raban's account of a three-month voyage alone in a sixteen-foot boat down the Mississippi in 1979.*

from OLD GLORY

In the morning the air was so still that I could feel the ripples of turbulence I caused by passing through it. A fine salt mist had put the water towers out of focus. They had lost their supporting pillars and looked like silver dirigibles adrift in the sky.

The earth felt like powdered glass underfoot. It was a mixture of black dirt and the shells of millions of tiny white mollusks. With every step, it crunched and snapped. There were mangled stalks of sugar cane on the road and on the bayou, and isolated stands of uncut cane as high as houses in the fields.

I eased the boat out onto the bayou. A faint tidal drift made the water hyacinths and the cane stalks wander sluggishly away from the direction of the sea. Following their lead, I ran up to the end of Lockport and turned left into Lake Fields: miles and miles of open water with the same veined, soapstony sheen. On the southern bank, someone had raised an improvised levee of crushed automobiles. The salt in the air had rusted them together so that they looked like an earthwork, oddly posted about with spots and scraps of their old, gaudy Ford and General Motors livery.

A muffled fisherman in a pirogue raised his hand in a salute as I went past. It was the kind of morning and the kind of place where it was important to acknowledge the existence of other people. The sheer, motionless space of sky and water tempted one into the hallucination that one had been given the world entirely to oneself. The intermittent reminders of human tenancy were unfailingly odd. There was a crumbling jetty sticking out of the mud. No road or track led to it. There wasn't a house in sight. Yet on the jetty there was a waterlogged sofa, its stuffing leaking from its sides. It was a queer foreign exile; it looked as if it were badly in need of the company of a coffee table, a television set, and a standing lamp. A mile farther on, a line of willows ran out across the water on a neck of land as narrow as a sidewalk. At the foot of the trees, three frame houses had been joined together and mounted on the hull of a barge. I rode up to the front door of one of them. The whole place was a ruin. The glass had gone from the windows; part of the roof had fallen in. I tied the boat to the porch and walked through the gutted rooms. Nothing had been left behind except for a few rags and some bits of old newspaper. The *New Orleans Times-Picayune*. June 1968. It had been preserved under a curling sheet of brown linoleum. I wondered what had driven the people from this ingenious and once beautiful house. The lonely vacancy of the view from its windows? Yet the hull of the barge alone must have been worth a fortune in scrap.

I made a long southwesterly loop and rejoined the Intracoastal Waterway, where towboats were busy stirring up the water and the morning. I was glad to see them. They were difficult companions to live with, but their general boisterousness came as a relief after the weird, evacuated stillness of the reach of swamp at my back.

At Houma, I turned up the arched Venetian canal of the Bayou Terrebonne and went to look for a bar. The one I found had the air of a place that scorned the daytime and had created its own perpetual night; it had a pool table and enough bare, dusty space to run several brawls in at once.

"Have you got anything to eat?" I asked the bartender.

"I can do you a shit on a shingle," she said.

It sounded interesting and disgusting in equal parts. My curiosity narrowly beat my feelings of incipient revulsion.

"Okay, I'll have a shit on a shingle," I said, trying to sound as if I'd been shitting on shingles for years.

Waiting for this object to appear, I played pool with a man who'd arrived in Houma five days before. He had come down to Louisiana from Connecticut and was looking for a job as a roustabout on a Gulf oil rig. Houma had scared him half out of his wits.

"Ain't this country something else, though? You should've been here last night. There was a guy came in the bar waving a three-five-seven Magnum and yelling that he wanted to shoot some niggers. I'm telling you, man: if there'd have been a black sitting here he would have been a dead man. That guy wasn't joking. I've only been here five days. It's crazy. What I need most in this town is a gun. If you're in Houma, you need a gun."

"That's pretty easy in Louisiana, isn't it? You only have to show your driver's license."

"Yeah. That's my problem. I don't have a driver's license."

My shit on its shingle was put out for me on the bar. It was only corned-beef hash on toast, but its revolting name had somehow worked its way into the flavor of the thing; it tasted foul.

I was trying to rid my mouth of the memory of it by smoking a pipeful of tobacco when I found Houma in person standing behind me. He was short and skinny, in his twenties; but his face had the creased and yellowed look of someone well past fifty. He had the shakes.

"What you think you tryin' to put over on me, man?"

"Me? Nothing."

"Why you come in here?"

I shrugged. "A drink . . . a game of pool . . . something to eat."

"What the fuck is *that*?"

He was pointing to the loose cellophane pouch in which my tobacco was wrapped.

"That's my tobacco. "

"Tobacco — shit!"

My pool partner came over. "Hey, what's the trouble?"

"And you keep *your* shit out of this, I'm warning you," Houma said. Connecticut backed off. His alarmed eyes were telegraphing *What did I tell you*? at me.

Houma's face was six inches away from mine. The top of his head came up to my nose. "I'm just asking you, polite, now, to get your fucking shit out of this bar."

"Would you mind telling me why?"

"I don't have to spell nothing out to you — Fed!"

"I'm not a Fed," I said.

"You don't fool nobody. You're a fucking Fed narc. You and your shit *bait*."

"Look —" I said, and started to reach inside my pocket to find my passport. I could hardly be an accredited Englishman and a Fed narc. My hand had been stopped and gripped almost before it had begun to move. I could feel the fierce trembling in Houma's wrist. He had a knife in his other hand.

"You pull your fuckin' gun on me, man, I'll cut you —"

"Look, please —" I said. The whole episode was so insane and sudden that I hadn't yet had time to

be frightened by it. "I haven't got a gun. I was trying to show you my passport. I'm British. I'm not
a policeman. I'm not an American. I'm not a Fed.
I'm not a narc. Now, please . . . look inside my
pocket. You'll find my passport with my wallet." I
could see Connecticut at the far end of the bar. He
had seen the knife and was watching shamefaced. I
thought: If I were in his position, all I'd do would be
watch too.

Houma's knife came up and flipped the lapel of my
jacket aside. He saw at least that I wasn't armed. His
fingers twitched at the contents of my pocket, and they
scattered in front of me on the bar floor: check-book,
wallet, passport, pen and, as I saw with real alarm, the
business card of Clarence Carter, superintendent of the
Shelby County Penal Farm in Memphis. I had visited his
jail. At this moment, he was the last person in the world
with whom I wanted any visible connection.

"You see my passport there? Now, look at it."

"*You* get it," Houma said. "I'm watching you, man."

I picked it up and showed it to him.

"What is this shit?"

"It proves that I'm an English citizen. I'm a foreigner.
I'm a visitor to this country."

"It don't prove fucking nothing —" The madness had
gone out of his voice, though. Connecticut, feeling the
tension slacken, came over to us again.

"He's just a goddamn tourist, man —"

Houma took my packet of tobacco from the bar and
sniffed at it. "Shit. Why you keeping it in this fucking
stuff, man? You want to get yourself killed?" His voice

had turned to a feeble whine. He was just a little runt with a knife in his belt and an addict's jitters. "Okay . . . so I made a mistake. I was wrong, okay? Will you shake my hand now?"

Absurdly, ceremonially, we shook hands.

"You're my friend now, okay, man?" He tried to put his arm around my shoulder, but it didn't quite reach. "You want another beer?"

"No, thanks."

"Come on — you and me, we'll shoot some pool, huh?"

"Okay."

His cue trembled in his hands; my cue trembled in mine. The balls on the table went everywhere except into the pockets. When Houma shambled jerkily off to the men's room, I fled the bar, and didn't stop running until I reached my boat.

* * *

A single-engined seaplane was coming in to touch down on the Waterway, and I had to pull over to the dock where a fleet of little planes rocked on their pontoons. A pilot came across to talk: he had spotted the Wisconsin registration on my boat and wanted to know what it was doing so far from home.

"God, that's something I'd like to do sometime. That's just the kind of thing I'm into myself."

He was a stranger here too. He had gone broke in the Florida Keys, flying a one-man passenger service. The day before, he had signed on as a pilot here, ferrying crewmen and supplies out to the drilling platforms offshore. He and his wife were living in a camper down the street. They had lost their house in Florida: Louisiana was their chance for a new start.

"So where are you going now?" he asked.

"I'm not sure. Morgan City, I think."

"Morgan City? I heard that place is a *real* dump."

"So did I."

I pushed on up the waterway as it cut from bayou to bayou: Bayou Cocodrie . . . Bayou Chene . . . Bayou Boeuf. Ahead of the boat, the water was like jade; behind, it was roiling cocoa. Wherever there was a bump of high ground in the swamp, someone had built himself a shack with a muddy yard full of chickens, a dock, a tethered boat. One could live like Crusoe here. The income-tax man would have to paddle out in a canoe to collect his revenue in crawfish, alligator skins, and the pelts of nutria rats; there'd be no mail, no telephone calls — just pelicans and vultures in the garden and the slow tidal swill of the water around one's house. Louis Beauregard's story of the froomids did correspond to something real: somewhere up the Bayou Capasaw or the Bayou Penchant there must be secret places where men have been living in hiding for years. I had heard rumors of a clandestine colony of Chinese shrimp fishermen who occupied a stilt city in the swamp and shot anyone curious enough to stumble on their hideout; the rumors weren't wholly unbelievable, and the pilots of the seaplanes must often have noticed things that were best left uninvestigated.

The Bayou Boeuf opened into the estuary of the Atchafalaya River, and Morgan City was a ramshackle patchwork of low roofs squatting on the junction. I cruised along its beach looking for a place to land. On the edge of the estuary there was a fisherman's jetty with two jonboats moored to its few remaining piles. I grounded on soft mud, and was met by an old man trailing a line of catfish hooks.

"What you want?"

"I wondered if I could tie up here for the night."

"You could lose your boat. Nothing's safe in this town."

"Why's that?"

"*Lot* of drifters about."

He took in my scuffed cases with a glance of scornful recognition.

"Oh. Why do *they* come here?"

"Looking for work." He looked at me again and gave an amused snort. "They don't get none, though. It'll cost you a dollar —"

"Fine."

"In advance."

Across the street there was a grocery with a pay phone. It took half an hour to raise a cab which was circling the town picking up passengers as it went along. The driver, a huge morose youth, introduced himself as Tiny; the elderly woman in the front seat was Miss Leonie.

"You new in town?" asked Miss Leonie.

"Yes, I've just arrived."

"You come to the armpit of the world," she said, making every vowel of the phrase last as long as it possibly could, like a particularly toothsome sweet.

We came to a scruffy little housing project, with piles

of old clothes flapping in yards of unplanted sand. Tiny hooted, and a black teenager came out dressed in a sharp dude suit and wearing pink-framed glasses. He sat beside me. "Know what I'm going to do?" he said. "I'm gonna buy me a machine gun."

"Why's that?" Miss Leonie said. "What you want with a machine gun?"

"Climb to the top of the highest building in Morgan City . . ." He swiveled in his seat, holding an imaginary carbine and spraying us all with bullets. "Rat-a-tat-a-rat-a-tat-a-rat-a-tat-a-rat-a-tat-a . . ." He rolled back and laughed, holding his knees.

I had asked to be set down at the best motel in Morgan City. This had driven Miss Leonie into a cigaretty coughing fit.

"*Best* motel in Morgan City? You ain't asking much, are you, mister?"

"Rat-a-tat-a-tat-a-tat-a . . ."

In the event, I was set down by a cluster of peeling cabins grouped around a courtyard with a dead banana plant in the middle. I was given a key to a room with a bare concrete floor. The sheets on the bed looked slept in; the single blanket was riddled with burns and stains. The floral shower curtain was cracked on every fold. I went back to the motel office to talk to two identically fat girls in tight stretch pants and Hawaiian blouses.

"Haven't you got a better room than that? One with a bath?"

"They don't none of them have *baths*."

"It's about the worst motel room I've ever seen."

"Oh, it ain't *good*. Ain't no worse than none of the others, though."

"Is there another motel in town where I could find a better room?"

"Nope. The rest of them, they're *worse*."

"Jesus." I was deeply impressed by Morgan City's pride in its own scabbiness. "What do people *do* in Morgan City?" I asked.

"Fight. Get drunk. Pick up women."

"You can get rolled around here," said the other girl tentatively, picking at a speck on her scarlet-panted buttock.

I wasn't sure whether "rolled" meant mugged or laid.

"I don't think I much want to get rolled."

"Okay," she said.

I went for a long walk around the town. It had a certain repetitive charm, since it consisted of acre after acre of exactly the same house. Half a dozen rough brick platforms, eighteen inches high, supported a shack with a corrugated-iron roof, a veranda draped in torn screening, a single, gray Grecian column made of wood, a broken rocker and a faded blue statue of the Virgin on the doorstep. There were many more cats than people on the streets, and the cats had the same glandular fattiness as the girls at the motel. They grazed on the little heaps of garbage that stood in front of almost every house, spilling appetizingly from leaky bags.

Three miles later I was back to where I'd started, on Brashear Avenue, which was as near as Morgan City seemed to come to possessing a Main Street. In the middle of the road there was one of the most arresting exercises in civic statuary that I had ever seen. It was called *The Spirit of Morgan City* and had been molded in some kind of lividly colored fiberglass. A life-size shrimp boat was in collision with something that at first I took to be the Eiffel Tower, but later decided was meant to be an offshore oil rig. The hideous glory of this marvel had been a little softened for Christmas: it had been wrapped up in tinsel ropes, stars and bangles, as if Morgan City were thinking of mailing it to someone as a surprise gift.

One building in Morgan City didn't fit at all. On the far side of the street beyond a high wall and a row of trees, a colonnaded mansion with a texas-deck front looked out over the Atchafalaya River. The rest of the town barely came up to the windows of its ground floor. This sugar planter's castle had once been all there was of Morgan City; now it was loftily marooned in a cheerful slum, so grand and tall that its owner might never have noticed the steady encroachment of the shanty-town around his feet. From his bedroom, he could probably see clear across to Texas and halfway down to Mexico; with luck, he might not even yet have set his eyes on Morgan City. Perhaps he took its tin roofs for a widening of the river and was wondering whether, granted this addition of a paddy field to his plantation, he might change from sugar cane to rice.

The bars on Front Street looked like places where I was certain to be ringed as a federal narcotics agent. I walked away up Brashear Avenue, searching for somewhere a little more salubrious, and ended up in a lounge crowded with other, bewildered strangers musing on their exile in Morgan City.

"What's *happening* here? I don't get it. I come from Chicago. In Illinois, or Missouri, you never see a dead dog on the highway. Here in Louisiana, Christ, you see more dead dogs than you can shake a stick at. What's happening? People here, they go out of their way to run a dog down. It's a goddamn sport!"

"Yeah, I'm from Tennessee. You don't see none of that there neither."

"Hell, when we was kids, we used to break off a car's antenna, make a zip gun out of it. But now it's *senseless*. Here, they take your antenna, no reason. Shoot! That's thirty-nine bucks!"

"But them dogs on the highway . . . Who are these people? People who'll kill a guy's dog just for fun . . . I never seen anything so crazy, not till I came down to Louisiana."

"Me neither."

Me neither.

*   *   *

The morning was a wide-open door, the sky empty except for a single violet-edged cloud in the far north. I took the boat across Bayou Boeuf and into the seaward neck of Bayou Shaffer, sliding past gleaming mud flats and reedbeds where the tide sucked and whispered in the grasses. Ahead, the color of the water ran from streaky green into an even blue.

It was rich water. Dark with peat, thickened with salt, it was like warm soup. When the first things crawled out of the water, they must have come from a swamp like this one, gingerly testing the mud with their new legs. I trailed my hand over the gunwale and licked my wet forefinger. It tasted of sea.

If the man at Lockport was right, there should be alligators still awake out on these salt flats. If there were, they weren't showing themselves. I made a slow circle around an inlet, watching for something to move on the bank. I took an oar and prodded at a bank of mud. It was as soft and greasy as black butter, and the oar went in as far as my hand. There was no alligator there.

Ain't nothing.

I had crossed, or thought I'd crossed, the line from green to blue.

I turned the motor off and let the boat drift out on the tide for a while, then pointed the bow back, in the same dumb, urban direction that the armadillos set their noses.

TED CONOVER

*Ted Conover was born in Japan in 1958. He gradu-
ated from Amherst College in 1981 and studied as
a Marshall Scholar at Cambridge University. His
adventures riding freight trains with hoboes all over
the United States is narrated in* Rolling Nowhere.
The more recent Coyotes *tells of his travels with
Mexican illegals on the underground railway into
and throughout the southern United States. His risky
travels remind us of Robert Louis Stevenson's anx-
iousness "to see the worst of emigrant life," and of
George Orwell's going down and out. Conover lives
in Denver.*

from ROLLING NOWHERE

We almost kept going when we reached Spokane. Often
I have wondered what might have turned out differently
if we had.

The idea of stopping in Spokane to work a day or
two had been discussed since Fargo. The St. Vincent
de Paul charity store there employed transients, paying
them partly in cash and partly in the necessities of life:
food, clothing, showers. Sleeping bags, in particular,
were the currency Pete and BB hoped to receive, for
though they each slept in two, one inserted inside the

101

other, often wearing all their clothes, the bags were too old and thin for the autumn nights ahead.

But just a few steps off the train, BB stopped. "Wait a minute," he said. "It's Friday night. Tomorrow's the weekend, and St. Vinnie's ain't open on the weekend. We'd have to wait till Monday."

"Forget it, then," said Pete. "Let's keep going."

They had already turned around when I spoke up. It was Thursday night, I asserted, and tried to prove it to them by counting back the days since the last weekend. But both of them refused to listen. Just then, however, a brakeman swung out from between two cars, not far from us, and I posed the question to him.

"'Course it's Thursday," he said, laughing. BB and Pete were humorless. Silently they changed directions again, and we arrived at a weedpatch not far from where they had jungled up just a few weeks before. The tramps had been traveling so much that they were the victims of their own kind of if-it's-Tuesday-this-must-be-Belgium syndrome.

I was up at dawn. Arrive at St. Vinnie's much later than that, BB said, and they might already have all the guys they needed. Because of his ever-worsening wound, Pete would not work; instead, I would donate the bedroll I earned to him, since I already had the best bedroll of the three, and BB would keep the one he earned. We were, after all, partners, and among partners, as Pete had said, it was "all for one and one for all."

But BB, strangely, lingered over his coffee, and then spent a lot of time helping Pete wrap his hand in a clean bandage "borrowed" from the first-aid kit of a caboose.

"You better get goin'," he said. "I'll finish this and be right over."

The work involved a lot of loading trucks and moving furniture. I was somewhat annoyed as the day progressed and BB failed to show, but other things kept my mind off it. One was the arrival of a police car and paramedics at the loading dock of a plant across the street. "Old Willy's been hurt," I heard one of the workers tell another. It seemed that Willy, a well-known personage around the yards, often slept under the dock. Apparently, the night before an eight-by-eight-inch wooden beam had fallen on him while he slept, pinning him and fracturing his ankle. It was midday now, and he had just been discovered. After learning Willy was still alive, though, nobody seemed worried: "He's got it good, now. Two or three weeks in the hospital, with clean sheets, a real roof over his head, new clothes, free food, nurses . . . I want to go there, too! Only there's no wine. Poor Willy!"

My salary, at day's end, was a small pouch of Bull Durham tobacco, rolling papers, two dollars, and the bedroll for Pete, consisting of a green blanket, comforter, and a length of twine.

Back at the jungle, BB and Pete were packed and ready to continue west, this time to Wenatchee, in central Washington. Pete grunted his thanks for the bedroll and then sat silently. After rekindling the fire, I reached for my knapsack to get out a can of chili I knew I had there. But . . . one of two straps on the knapsack had been left undone, and not by me. Odd. Maybe Pete or BB had needed some little cooking item, I thought, and had taken a quick look to see if I had it. It was a violation of etiquette — you *never* went in another tramp's pack without permission — but probably not serious.

Yet the chili was not where I had put it. And where were the old cotton gloves I used as hot pads when cooking? And my knit hat — that was gone, too. Suddenly I became alarmed. I looked over toward the campfire — BB was sitting there, chewing on a match and staring into the flames and Pete was gone. My railroad maps — the maps I had not told them about, which had been so hard for me to find, had been hidden at the bottom of the pack. Now they were gone, too. Apprehension grew in my stomach. To mention this or not to . . .

"Hey, uh, BB," I said, deciding. "Were both you and Pete around all day?"

"Well, yeah, I believe we were," said BB, closing the only route of escape from the impending conflict.

"That's funny. Stuff is missing from my pack."

"Oh, yeah? Like what?"

I recited the list, including the train maps.

"I didn't know you had no train maps."

"Well, I did."

BB chewed silently on the match, not looking at me. "So, you want to search my pack, right?"

"No, I don't want to, but I don't know any other way to go about this." The offer had caught me off guard.

"Well, there it is. Go ahead. I got nothin' to hide." He gestured toward his small carry bag. I looked at his bedroll, too, to which he had tied Brandy Lee. If he had offered to let me search his little bag, the stuff was probably in his bedroll.

"Okay if I look at your bedroll after that?"

"Sure."

I approached his pack, on the ground next to BB, my anger growing. I knew I had to ask this of them — if I didn't press it, what would be taken next? How far behind the loss of respect for my property would be the loss of respect for my person? Yet, as I reached into BB's bag, I was scared. BB, clench-fisted, hovered above.

"Careful — my knife's in there," said BB. It was an oblique threat.

My missing gear was not in the bag. I stood up. BB straightened, too, raising himself to his full height, a head above me. I gestured toward the bedroll.

"What should I do with Brandy Lee?" I asked.

"You'll leave her right fuckin' where she is, you son of a bitch!" snarled BB.

I stepped back. "You said I could look in your bedroll."

"Sure, you can look in it," he said, "but if you don't find your map I'm gonna bash your motherfuckin' head in."

It was just like with Roger. Everything fine one second, and then the next — bam. Complete changeover. But I was not drunk, and I had a dispute to resolve with BB.

BB advanced. I took another couple of steps backwards, out of the range of his fists, and put my hand in my pocket, on the canister of Mace.

"I don't want no trouble, BB — just my stuff back."

He wasn't even listening. BB, prison-trained, was sizing up the fight. He stopped walking toward me.

"I see you got your piece," he said, eyes on my pocket. "Well, I got mine, too."

He thought I had a gun, a mistake that would work in my favor. He claimed to have a gun, but I was almost certain he did not: few tramps did, because of a gun's high pawn value. Also, BB almost certainly would have told me about it before, in his own menacing way, if he did have it. But things were moving too fast. All I knew was that BB had stopped moving toward me. And his knife, in the pack, was closer to me than to him.

"Look, man, all I want is for us to be fair and square with each other. You don't want your ass whipped by me, and I don't want mine whipped by you. So play it straight with me."

"I tell you what, if I didn't have no faith in the sumbitches I was travelin' with, I wouldn't be travelin' with the motherfuckers," said BB, drawling at triple speed. "And if I lost somethin', I wouldn't go lookin' through your shit, I'd say, 'Yeah, I take your word for it, man,' and all that. And then I'd just go lookin' for the shit."

"If I didn't find it," I returned, "I'd owe you an apology, and I'd give it."

"I don't accept fuckin' apologies, I sure as fuck don't," said BB heatedly. "They ain't worth the fuckin' paper it's wrote on."

Pete, I noticed, had quietly returned to pick up his

gear, and was starting to leave. BB, still hollering, started to do the same. Along with his own bedroll, he picked up the one I'd gotten for Pete. I moved suddenly toward him as he did, my only offensive move of the night.

"You'll leave that," I said.

He drew back from the blankets, cursing me. He and Pete, with Brandy Lee trailing, began crossing the yard toward the tracks.

Pete's neutrality infuriated me. "Hey, Pete," I cried after him. "What ever happened to 'all for one and one for all'? Here we are, friends one minute and the next you split without a word. What happened, did you lose your voice?"

"You shut the fuck up, man," said BB, turning around and shaking a fist at me. "You ain't been straight with us."

"What the hell do you mean by that?" I said. But they disappeared into the strings of trains. I stood alone in the field, desolated and stunned. More than two weeks of round-the-clock companionship had just unraveled in about three minutes.

Gradually my heart slowed, and replacing the anger and adrenaline was fear. The field seemed suffused with BB's malice. I was afraid that he might circle around, trying to catch me unawares while I slept. I couldn't bring myself to eat anything at all. I repacked my gear and walked away, disposing of Pete's bedroll in a ditch as I headed toward the main road. I didn't want any tramp to have it.

To my disgust, two tramps walking in the opposite

direction approached me to ask about the jungle conditions. I answered curtly, but they kept talking, filling me in on life at the Spokane rescue mission, though I hadn't asked. Slowly, I began to listen; it sounded like a good destination. Then, to my surprise, I told them why I was leaving the jungle. They seemed genuinely sympathetic. "Town's about five miles from here," said one. "You oughta take the bus. Got change?"

I did not.

"Here," he said, and handed me a quarter, dime, and nickel. "That's handicapped fare, so just make sure you look it. And if that mission's full, you just come back and jungle up with us, okay?"

"Okay," I said. The moment I turned, my eyes flooded with tears. I waved them good-bye without looking.

PART TWO

WRITERS AND THE EFFECTS OF WAR

Standing in the aftermath of violent death is a numbing experience: the air about one feels torn, ripped and stretched.

—*Dirk Bogarde*

IRVING LAYTON

Author of many volumes of poetry, including The Improved Binoculars, The Collected Poems of Irving Layton, *and* Lovers and Lesser Men, *Irving Layton established his reputation in Montreal in the forties and fifties, winning the Governor General's Award for poetry in 1959. He has been prominent in the evolution of poetic sensibility in Canada, where he remains outspoken and prolific. A wide traveler, Layton was born in Romania and came to Canada at the age of one, in 1913. In 1982, he was nominated for the Nobel Prize.*

POSTCARD

For Aviva

In Venice
when it stormed
(ah, where have the years fled?)
you clasped me to you
in terror and love

Each thunderclap
was a fresh embrace
under the sheets;

we were never so close
as when the elements
seemed bent to destroy us

Tonight
as if another
War of Liberation
were in progress
thunderclashes
rock Budapest
and flares
light up the city
to direct fiery
salvos of rain
against roofs and bridges

Marauders
are hammering
on the windowpanes
and I cower
under my blanket
— but where are you, my love?

DIRK BOGARDE

Born in England in 1911, Dirk Bogarde was com-
missioned in the British army in 1941 and later
served in Europe and the Far East. The following
account describes his impressions of Normandy in
August 1944, where he found himself an "air
photographic interpreter attached to 39 Wing
of the Royal Canadian Air Force," and where
he also painted as an Unofficial War Artist
and kept a diary. Bogarde, who began his film
career in 1947 — appearing in over sixty films
— is more recently the author of several volumes
of autobiography, including A Postillion Struck by
Lightning *and* An Orderly Man, *as well as three*
novels. For the last twenty years he has lived in
Provence.

from BACKCLOTH

The sky was always blue, that strange intense blue of
northern France, sea-washed, wind-cleansed, limitless,
criss-crossed with lazy scrawls of vapour trails like the
idle scribbles of a child in a crayoning-book.

In the orchards the shade lay heavy beneath the trees,
spiked here and there with emerald blades of grass and
clumps of campion.

But everywhere the land was still. There was no birdsong.

Sometimes a bee would drone up and away, or a grasshopper scissor in the crushed weeds of the chalky soil, and then fall silent as if the effort had been too much, in the still heat, or as if, perhaps, reproved that there was no response in the ominous quiet.

No rabbits scuttled in the hedgerows, the corn stood high, ripe, heavy in the ear, unharvested, and in the meadows cows lay on their sides, stiff-legged, like milking stools, bellies bloated with gas.

Sometimes one of them would explode with a sound like a heavy sigh, dispersing memories of a lost childhood in the sickly stench of decay.

Death was monarch of that summer landscape: only the bee and the grasshopper gave a signal of life, or suggested that it existed. The familiar had become unfamiliar and frightening. A world had stopped and one waited uneasily to see if it would start again: a clock to be rewound in an empty room.

But that comforting tick-tock of normality, of the life pulse, had been provisionally arrested. In some cases it had been stopped for good, for a little farther back, toward the beaches, they were burying those who would remain forever in silence.

There was plenty of noise back there: of gears grinding, engines roaring, tracks rattling, metal groaning.

At the edge of an elm-fringed meadow, I stood against a tree watching, curiously unmoved, the extraordinary ballet between machines and corpses, which proved conclusively that the human body was nothing but a fragile, useless container without the life force.

For some reason it had never fully occurred to me before: I had seen a good number of dead men and had, as a normal reaction, felt a stab of pity, a creep of fear that perhaps it could be me next time, but I had become accustomed to them and got on with my own living.

But that afternoon in the shade of the elms I stood watching the bulldozers (a new toy to us then) shovelling up the piles of dead very much as spoiled fruit is swept into heaps after a market-day, and with as little care. Shuddering, wrenching, jerking, stinking of hot oil in the high sun, they swivelled slowly about with open jaws ripping at the earth to form deep pits, and then, nudging and grabbing at the shreds and pieces, rotting, bloody, unidentifiable, which heavy trucks had let slither from raised tailboards in tumbled heaps of arms and legs, they tossed them into the pits.

Back and forth they droned and crunched, swinging about with casual ease, manoeuvred by cheerful young men, masked against the stench and flies, arms burned black by the August sun.

"Tidying up," said someone with me. "One day they will turn this meadow into a war cemetery. Rows and rows of crosses and neat little walks; perhaps they'll erect a fine granite monument, a flagstaff will carry a proud flag to be lowered at the Last Post, they'll plant those bloody yew trees, and relatives will walk in silence through the toy-town precision and order, looking for their dead."

I remember what he said, because I wrote it all down later, but I can't remember who he was.

Fairly typical of me, I fear.

The words stayed with me for the simple reason that they moved me more than the things which I was observing. The dead lying there in putrid heaps among the sorrel and buttercups didn't move me at all: they were no more than torn, tattered, bloody bundles. The soul had sped; there could only be regret for those who had loved the individual bodies in this seeping mass: for everyone there had once belonged to someone. That was the sadness.

The absolute anonymity of mass death had dulled grief.

The silence didn't last long — silence in war never does. One gets to discover that very early on.

The ominous stillness which had reproved both grasshopper and bee simply preceded a gigantic storm: Caen fell, the Germans began their terrible retreat to the east. The battle for Normandy was over.

I use the word "terrible" advisedly, for the retreat, estimated at that time to be composed of at least 300,000 men plus vehicles and arms, crammed the dusty high-hedged roads and lanes, even the cart tracks through fields and orchards, in a desperate attempt to reach the ferries across the river Seine: the Allied armies surrounded them on three sides. We knew that all the main bridges had been blown, so it appeared evident to us that we contained the entire German fighting force in one enormous killing ground. Tanks and trucks, horse-drawn limbers, staff cars, private cars, farm carts and all kinds of tracked vehicles, anything in fact which could move, inched along the jammed lanes and roads in slow convoys of death.

Unable to turn back, to turn left or right, they had no alternative but to go ahead to the river, providing undefended, easy targets for Allied aircraft which homed down on them as they crawled along and blasted them to destruction: ravening wolves with cornered prey.

By 21 August it was over.

Across the shattered farms, the smouldering corn-fields, the smoking ruins in the twisting lanes, smoke drifted lazily in the heat and once again the frightening silence came down over a landscape of shattering carnage.

Those of us in the middle of things really thought that a colossal victory had been achieved. The Germans had been destroyed along with their weapons. There could be nothing left of them to fight, the Russians were about to invade their homeland, surely now victory was ours and war would finish before the end of the summer?

We were wrong. The people who are in the middle are nearly always wrong. The canvas of war is far too great to comprehend as one single picture. We only knew a very limited part — and even that part was not as it seemed. Gradually we began to realize that the war was not over, that it was going to go on, that the Germans were still fighting, still highly armed, stubborn and tougher than they had been before. Slowly "a colossal victory" faded from our minds and we accepted the fact that something must have gone a little bit wrong in our jubilant assessment of an early peace.

It had indeed gone wrong. But it was only some years later, when the generals who had squabbled, quarrelled, and bickered all the way through the campaign began to write their autobiographies, that one learned that, far from a victory, the retreat had been a catastrophe.

By that time it was far too late for thousands of men to worry.

They were laid out in neat rows under white crosses.

What had happened, quite simply, is that the Allied generals, by disagreeing among themselves, had left the back door open to the killing ground permitting thousands of Germans, and their arms, to escape and live to fight another day.

But we didn't know it, fortunately, at the time.

Standing in the aftermath of violent death is a numbing experience: the air about one feels torn, ripped and stretched. The cries of panic and pain, of rending metal, though long since dispersed into the atmosphere, still seem to echo in the stillness which drums in one's ears.

On the main road from Falaise to Trun, one of the main escape routes which we *did* manage to block, among the charred and twisted remains of exploded steel, dead horses indescribably chunked by flying shrapnel, eyes wide in terror, yellow teeth bared in frozen fear, still-smouldering tanks, the torn, bullet-ripped cars and the charred corpses huddled in the burned grass, it was perfectly clear that all that I had been taught in the past about hell and damnation had been absolutely wrong.

Hell and damnation were not some hellfire alive with dancing horned devils armed with toasting forks.

Nothing which Sister Veronica or Sister Marie Joseph has told me was true. Clearly they had got it all wrong in those early, happy Twickenham days. Hell and damnation were here, on this once peaceful country road, and I was right in the middle of it all.

My boots were loud on the gravel, oily smoke meandered slowly from smouldering tyres. Blackened bodies, caught when the petrol tanks of the trucks and cars had exploded, grinned up at me from crisped faces with startling white teeth, fists clenched in charcoaled agony.

Down the road in a haze of smoke stood a small boy of about seven; in his hand a tin can with a twisted wire handle.

I walked toward him and he turned quickly, then scrambled up the bank where a woman was bending over a body in the black grass, a hammer and chisel in her hand.

The boy tugged at her skirts, she stood upright, stared at me, shading her eyes with the flat of her hand, then she shrugged, cuffed the boy gently, and bent again to her task.

Hammering gold teeth from the grinning dead.

The boy raised the tin for me to see. It was almost a third full of bloody nuggets and bits of bridge-work.

Waste not, want not.

In the ditch below us a staff car lay tilted on its side, the bodywork riddled with bullet holes in a precise line as if a riveter had been at work rather than a machine gun from a low flying plane.

A woman was slumped in the back seat, a silver fox fur at her feet, her silk dress blood-soaked, a flowered turban drunkenly squint on her red head. A faceless man in the uniform of the SS lay across her thighs.

I kicked one of her shoes lying in the road, a wedge-heeled cork-soled scrap of coloured cloth.

The woman with the hammer shouted down, "Sale Boche! Eh? Collaboratrice . . . c'est plein des femmes comme ça! Sale Boche!"

I walked back to my jeep. My driver was sitting in his seat smoking.

"Where do they all come from?"

"Who?"

"Those blokes . . . wandering about having a good old loot. They just go through the pockets, get the wallets, pinch the bits of jewellery. There's a squad of women civilians in all this lot. Gives you a bit of a turn seeing dead women in this sort of set-up."

Here and there, pulling at the blackened corpses, wrenching open the doors of the bullet-riddled cars, a few elderly peasants clambered about the wreckage collecting anything of value. God knew where they had come from — every building nearby was destroyed, but like the woman on the bank with the boy, they had come to scavenge what they could.

As we drove away the first bulldozers began to arrive to clear the road. I didn't speak: the sight of the dead girl with the red hair had distressed me profoundly.

I was prepared for people to be dead in uniform, but my simple mind would not come to terms with the sight of a dead woman in a silk dress on a battlefield. That didn't seem to be right. They hadn't warned us about *that* on the assault course in Kent.

We had to pull aside to let a bulldozer grind past; I looked back and saw an old man dancing a little jig. In a fox fur cape.

JAMES FENTON

All the Wrong Places: Adrift in the Politics of the Pacific Rim includes the author's eyewitness accounts of the fall of Saigon, and of Ferdinand Marcos's overthrow in the Philippines. Fenton has reported from various countries, including Korea. He has also traveled in Borneo with Redmond O'Hanlon, where he almost drowned. (Asked by his fellow English author to accompany him on a second arduous journey, this time to the Amazon, Fenton is reported to have replied, "I would not come with you to High Wycombe.") His collections of poems include Children in Exile *and* Manilla Envelope. *He is a foreign correspondent for the* Independent *newspaper.*

from ALL THE WRONG PLACES

My first experience of Vietnam was quite different. I was impressed, overawed, by the scale and age of the subject: a war that had been going on for longer than I had been alive; a people about whose history and traditions I knew so little. I had read some books in preparation, but the effect of doing so was only to make the country recede further. So much had been written about Vietnam. I hadn't even had the application to finish *The Fire in the Lake*. The purpose of the book seemed to be to warn you off the subject.

De Quincey's "barrier of utter abhorrence, and want of sympathy" was up. I could well have believed that somebody was trying to tell me something when I came out of my room on the first morning in Saigon and stepped over the decapitated corpse of a rat. I was staying, as most British journalists did, in the Hotel Royale, but even there I felt myself to be something of an intruder. I had to find work, I had to sell some stories, but I was afraid of trespassing on somebody else's patch. There was an epidemic of infectious neurosis at the time: As soon as one journalist had shaken it off, another would succumb. It would attack without warning — in the middle of an otherwise amiable meal, in the bars, in your room. And it could be recurrent, like malaria.

The reason for this neurosis was not far to seek, indeed it sought you out, and pursued you throughout the day: Saigon was an addicted city, and we — the foreigners — were the drug. The corruption of children, the mutilation of young men, the prostitution of women, the humiliation of the old, the division of the family, the division of the country — it had all been done in our name. People looked back to the French Saigon with a sentimental warmth, as if the problem had begun with the Americans. But the French city, the "Saigon of the piastre" as Lucien Bodard called it, had represented the opium stage of the addiction. With the Americans had begun the heroin phase, and what I was seeing now were the first symptoms of withdrawal. There was a desperate edge to life. It was impossible to relax for a moment.

123

Saigon was a vast service industry clamoring for the attention of a dwindling number of customers: "Hey you! American! Change money, buy *Time* magazine, give me back *Time* magazine I sell you yesterday, buy *Stars and Stripes*, give me back *Stars and Stripes*, you number one, you number ten, you number-ten-thousand Yankee, you want number-one fuck, you want *Quiet American*, you want *Ugly American*, you give me money I shine shoes, number one, no sweat. . . ." On and on, the passionate pursuit of money.

The bar at the Royale was half open to the street. The coffee at breakfast tasted of diarrhoea. You washed it down with Bireley's orangeade ("Refreshing . . . and no carbonation!"). Through the windows peered the shoeshine boys — "Hey! you!" — it was starting up again. One morning I was ignoring a particularly revolting specimen when he picked up a handful of sand which he pretended to eat: "You! You no give me money, you want I eat shit!" His expression, as he brought the dirt to his mouth, was most horrible. It was impossible to imagine how a boy of that age had acquired such features: He was about ten years old, but his face contained at least thirty years of degeneration and misery. A few days later I did give him my boots to clean. He sat down in the corner of the bar and set to work, first with a matchstick and a little water, meticulously removing all the mud and dust from the welt, then with the polish. The whole process took about half an hour, and the barman and I watched him throughout, in fascination. He was determined to show his superiority to all other contestants in the trade. I was amused, and gave him a large sum. He was furious, it wasn't nearly enough. We haggled for a while, but I finally gave in. I gave him about a pound. The next day, at the same time, he came into the bar; his eyes were rolling back in their sockets and he staggered helplessly around the tables and chairs; I do not know what drug he had taken, but I know how he had bought it.

Of all the ingenious and desperate forms of raising money, the practice of drugging your baby and laying the thing on the pavement in front of the visitor seemed to me the most repulsive. It did not take long to see that none of these children was ever awake during the day, or to notice from the way they slept that something was amiss. Among the foreigners, stories circulated about the same baby being seen in the arms of five different mothers in one week, but the beggar who regularly sat outside the Royale always had the same child, a girl of eighteen months or so. I never gave any money either to the girl and her "mother," or to any other such teams.

One day, however, I was returning from a good lunch when I saw that a crowd had formed around the old woman, who was wailing and gesticulating. The child was more than usually grey, and there were traces of vomit around her face. People were turning her over, slapping her, trying to force her eyes open. At one point she and the old woman were bundled into a taxi. Then they were taken out again and the slapping was repeated. I went into the hotel and told the girl at reception to call a doctor. "No," she replied. "But the child is sick." "If baby go to hospital or doctor" — and here she imitated an injection — "then baby die."

125

"No," I replied, "if baby *don't* go to hospital maybe baby die." "No."

I took the girl out into the street, where the scene had taken on the most grotesque appearance. All the beggars I had ever seen in Saigon seemed to have gathered, and from their filthy garments they were producing pins and sticking them under the child's toenails. "You see," I said to the girl, "no good, number ten. Baby need number-one hospital." "No, my grandmother had same thing. She need this — number one." And the receptionist produced a small phial of eucalyptus oil. "That's not number one," I said, "that's number ten. Number ten thousand," I added for emphasis. But it was no good insisting or appealing to other members of the crowd. Everybody was adamant that if the child was taken to the hospital, the doctor would kill it with an injection. While I correspondingly became convinced that a moment's delay would cost the child's life.

Finally, after a long eucalyptus massage and repeated pricking of the fingers and toes had produced no visible results, I seemed to win. If I would pay for taxi and hospital, the woman would come. I pushed my way through the crowd and dragged her toward the taxi — a battered old Renault tied together with string. The baby was wrapped in a tarpaulin and her face covered with a red handkerchief. Every time I tried to remove the handkerchief, from which came the most ominous dry gaspings, the woman replaced it. I directed the taxi driver to take us to number-one hospital and we set off. But from the start everything went wrong. Within a hundred yards we had to stop for gas. Then a van stalled in front of us, trapping the taxi. Next, to my amazement, we came to what must have been, I thought, the only level crossing in Saigon, where as it happened a train was expected in the near future. And around here we were hit by the side effects of Typhoon Sarah, which at the time was causing havoc in the northern provinces. We also split a tire, though this was not noticed till later. Driving on through the cloudburst, the taxi driver seemed strangely unwilling to hurry. So I sat in the back seat keeping one hand on the horn and the other attempting to alleviate the restrictions around the baby's breathing apparatus. I also recall producing a third arm with which to comfort the old woman from time to time and I remember that her shoulder, when my hand rested on it, was very small and very hard. Everything, I said, was going to be number one, okay: number-one hospital, number-one doctor, babysan okay. We were traveling through Cholon, the Chinese quarter, on an errand of Western mercy.

All things considered, it took a long time for it to dawn on me that we were not going to a hospital at all. We even passed a first-aid post without the driver giving it a glance. In my mind there was an image of the sort of thing required: a large cool building dating from French times, recently refurbished by American aid and charity, with some of the best equipment in the East. I could even imagine the sententious plaques on the walls. Perhaps there would be a ward named after the former U.S. ambassador. It would be called the Bunker Ward.

It was when the old woman began giving directions that I saw I had been duped. We were now threading our way through some modern slums, which looked like the Chinese equivalent of the Isle of Dogs. "Where is the hospital? This is no hospital," I said. Yes, yes, the taxi driver replied, we were going to hospital, number-one doctor. We stopped by a row of shops and the driver got out. I jumped from the car and seized him by the arm, shouting: "I said number-one hospital. You lie. You cheap charlie. You number-ten-thousand Saigon." We were surrounded by children, in the pouring rain, the taxi man tugging himself free, and me gripping him by the arm. It was left to the woman, carrying the little bundle of tarpaulin, to find out exactly where the doctor lived. Finally I gave in, and followed her up some steps, then along an open corridor lined with tailors and merchants. At least, I thought, when the baby dies I can't be blamed. And once I had thought that, the thought turned into a wish: A little cough would have done it, a pathetic gurgle, then a silence, and my point about Western medicine would have been proved to my own satisfaction. I should have behaved very well; of course I should have paid for, and gone to, the funeral.

In retrospect it was easy to see how the establishment would command confidence: the dark main room with its traditional furnishings, the walls lined with photographs of ancestors in traditional Vietnamese robes, a framed jigsaw of the Italian lakes. And in the back room (it would, of course, have to be a back room) a plump, middle-aged lady was massaging the back of another plump, middle-aged lady. They paid hardly any attention when we came in. There was not the slightest element of drama. Indeed, I began to see that I was now the only person who was panicking. When she had finished the massage, the doctor turned her attention to the baby. First she took some ointment from a dirty bowl at her elbow, and rubbed it all over the little grey body. Then from another bowl she produced some pink substance resembling Euthymol toothpaste, with which she proceeded to line the mouth. In a matter of minutes, the child was slightly sick, began to cry, and recovered. I had never been more furious in my life. To complete my humiliation, the doctor refused any payment. She provided the old woman with a prescription wrapped in newspaper, and we left. We drove to the miserable shelter in which the old woman lived. "Sit down," she said, indicating the wooden bed which was the only feature of her home apart from the roof (there were no walls). In any other mood I might have been moved by the fact that the only English she knew beyond the terrible pidgin currency of the beggars was a phrase of hospitality. But I so deeply hated her at that moment that I could only give her a couple of pounds, plus some useless advice about keeping the baby warm and off the pavements, and go.

I left the taxi driver at a garage not far from the Royale, where I also gave him some money toward repairing the split tire. "You number one, Saigon," he said, with a slight note of terror in his voice. The weather had cleared up, and I strolled along past the market stalls. You could buy U.S. Army foot-powder in bulk, K-rations, lurp rations (for Long-Range Reconnaissance Patrols), souvenir Zippo lighters (engraved "Yea though I walk through the valley of the shadow of death I shall

129

fear no evil, for I am the evilest sonofabitch in the valley"), khaki toothbrushes and flannels, and model helicopters constructed out of used hypodermics. You could also buy jackets brightly embroidered with the words "When I die I shall go to heaven, for I have spent my time in hell — Saigon," and a collection of GI cartoons and jokes called *Sorry 'bout that, Vietnam.* As I approached the hotel, people began asking how the baby was, and smiling when I replied "Okay."

And I began to think, supposing they were all in it together? Suppose the old woman, the taxi driver, the man whose van stalled, the engine driver — suppose they were all now dividing out the proceeds and having a good laugh at my expense, congratulating the child on the way it had played its role? That evening I would be telling the story to some old Saigon hand when a strange pitying smile would come over his face. "You went to Cholon, did you? Describe the doctor . . . uh huh . . . Was there a jigsaw puzzle of the Italian lakes? Well, well, well. So they even used the toothpaste trick. Funny how the oldest gags are still the best. . . ."

Indeed I did have rather that conversation a few days later, with an American girl, a weaver. It began "You realize, of course, first of all that the taxi driver was the husband of the old woman. . . . But I do not think it was a conspiracy." Worse, I should rather conclude that the principals involved were quite right not to trust the hospital doctors with a beggar's child. It was for this reason that the hotel receptionist had countermanded my orders to the taxi man, I learned afterward, and many people agreed with her.

When the old woman came back on the streets, I hardly recognized either her or the child, who for the first time looked conscious and well. "Babysan okay now, no sick," she said, gazing at me with an awful adoring expression, though the hand was not stretched out for money. And when I didn't reply she turned to the child and told it something in the same unctuous tones. This performance went on for the rest of my stay: Whenever I was around, the child would be made to look at the kind foreigner who had saved its life. I had indeed wanted to save the child's life, but not in *that* way, not on the old woman's terms.

I was disgusted, not just at what I saw around me, but at what I saw in myself. I saw how perilously thin was the line between the charitable and the murderous impulse, how strong the force of righteous indignation. I could well imagine that most of those who came to Vietnam to fight were not the evilest sons-of-bitches in the valley. It was just that, beyond the bright circle illuminated by their intelligence, in which everything was under their control and every person a compliant object, they came across a second person — a being or a nation with a will of its own, with its own medicine, whether Fishing Pills or pink toothpaste, and its own ideas for the future. And in the ensuing encounter everything had turned to justifiable ashes. It was impossible in Saigon to be the passive observer. Saigon cast you, inevitably, into the role of the American.

P. J. O'ROURKE

P. J. O'Rourke was born in Toledo, Ohio, in 1947, and was educated at Miami University in Oxford, Ohio, and at The Johns Hopkins University. Currently the International Affairs Desk Chief at Rolling Stone, *where he took over from Hunter S. Thompson, he is the author of* Modern Manners, The Bachelor Home Companion, Republican Party Reptile, Holidays in Hell, *from which this piece is taken,* Parliament of Whores, *"a lone humorist's look at the US government", and* Give War a Chance. *He has also written for publications as diverse as* National Lampoon, Playboy, Esquire, Car and Driver, New Republic, *and* The American Spectator. *He now lives in New Hampshire and Washington, DC.*

THE PIECE OF IRELAND THAT PASSETH ALL UNDERSTANDING

MAY 1988

"Acceptable level of violence" — the phrase was coined in 1973 by a British official trying to be British about Northern Ireland. "There's an acceptable level

132

of violence," said the then Home Secretary Reginald Maudling. It's like the air quality index in an American city. During the week I spent in Ulster, that's what the violence level was, acceptable. Not excellent the way it was in 1972, 1916, 1798 or 1690 but fair to middling for a Connecticut-sized province with a population smaller than metropolitan Kansas City's.

On Sunday, the day before I arrived, two Protestant "paramilitaries" dropped into the Avenue Bar, a Catholic hang-out in Belfast, and let fly with indiscriminate automatic weapons fire, killing three tipplers and wounding six. This is called a "spray-job." On Monday a Protestant reservist in the British Army's Ulster Defence Regiment had a leg blown off by a bomb at his farm near Dungannon and, in Catholic West Belfast, a young man was "kneecapped," that is, shot in a limb by the IRA as punishment for something or other. Tuesday the police found a Protestant arms cache in Whiteabby. Wednesday the home of a Catholic family in Dunmurry was attacked with what the newspapers called "a device," Thursday a bomb exploded in the middle of the Royal Ulster Agricultural Show, injuring four policemen and ten civilians including two children. Friday there was another kneecapping in West Belfast and a British soldier was burned by pre-teens throwing Molotov cocktails. Saturday an Army bomb disposal expert and his explosives-sniffing dog were blasted to pieces in South Armagh and a part-time policeman was injured when his car was hit by three "drogue bombs," which are large, exploding versions of the parachute things every boy used to make out of tin soldiers and dad's hankies. And, on Sunday, to begin the new week, a sniper attacked a Belfast police station and two Londonderry Protestants were wounded by a car bomb (car bombs, incidentally, being an Irish invention).

* * *

You probably think Belfast looks like those photographs of Belfast you always see. Not at all. It's a charming port, one of the world's great deep-water harbours, cupped in rolling downs on the bight of Belfast Lough. Cave Hill rises to the north like Sugar Loaf Mountain above Ipanema beach, causing some to go so far as to call Belfast "an Hibernian Rio" (not that anybody really wants to see an Irish girl in a string bikini). The city is built in the best and earliest period of Victorian architecture with delicate brickwork on every humble warehouse and factory. Even the mill hand tenement houses have Palladio's proportions in a miniature way and slate roofs you couldn't buy for money now.

The Belfast pictured in *Time* magazine, the rubble and barbed wire, litter and graffiti Belfast is, in fact, a patch of highly photogenic impoverishment no more than a mile long and a half a mile wide. It is as though *Architectural Digest* came to "do" a house and took pictures of the closet in the teenager's bedroom. The rubble is from slum clearance not bombs (though which is worse may be argued by critics of the modern welfare state). And the barbed wire is on top of the "Peace Wall," a kind of sociological toddler gate erected by the British to keep the ragamuffin Protestant homicidal maniacs of Shankill Road away from the tatterdemalion

Catholic murderers in Falls Road two blocks over. The graffiti and litter are real.

People who live in this heck's half-acre have been worked over by social scientists until there's hardly one of them who's not a footnote on somebody's master's thesis. And they're so thoroughly journalised that urchins in the street ask, "Will you be needing a sound bit?" and criticise your choice of shutter speeds.

Photographer Tony Suau and I had hired a Belfast driver, whom I'll call Dick Cullen — an experienced wheelman for the Grub Street crowd. Cullen took us straight from the airport to the heart of the Falls Road Catholic ghetto without even being asked. Here was one filthy low-income high-rise complex, the notorious Divis Flats, built in the Sixties before city planners discovered that you can't stack poor people who drink. But Divis was on its way to being demolished and the rest of the area was filled with small, new "town houses" and "garden apartments" — some jerry-built and fairly depressing, some faced with brick and verging on pleasant.

As in all the world's poor places, there were plenty of idle young men with beer and tattoos. (Unemployment in the district is about 125 percent, if you accept the locals' figures.) These neighborhood toughs greeted Tony and me with friendly waves and lengthy chats about political economy, international law, theoretical analysis of Irish history since the Battle of the Boyne and about how they couldn't talk to us at all until we'd checked in with the Sinn Fein, the reasonably legal, political arm of the IRA.

"You Irish have got a lot to learn about slums," I told Cullen when we got back in the car. "Where's your incoherent rage? Where's your homeless living in Hefty Bags? Where's your crack vials, your gang colors, your six-foot hairy-legged transvestites with knives? Slum, *hah*. I could take you down streets in New York where you'd be mugged in broad daylight three times in a block and that's the good part of town."

"Well, you wouldn't want to leave your car unlocked around here," said Cullen, a bit on the defensive, "not with expensive camera equipment lying on the seat."

"I hope you've at least got some heroin addicts?"

"Well, no," said Cullen, "the IRA shoots them."

The rest of Belfast consists of tidy lower-middle-class neighborhoods, tidy middle-class neighborhoods, a few rich neighborhoods — also very tidy — and tidy commercial and industrial zones. The local economy is suffering a mild upswing. A nascent trendiness is spreading south from the old town center, along the "Golden Mile" of Dublin Road — here a hanging plant, there a bare brick wall and here and there a restaurant with a foreign word in its name. (Though you still get potatoes with every meal. Even the Chinese joint had boiled, baked and fried potatoes on the menu.)

The people of Northern Ireland, however, have escaped a fate of suburban tedium and petit bourgeois anomie.

"MURDER" it says in black block letters in the upper corner of the *Belfast News* front page, where "weather" or "Today's Chuckle" would be in an American paper:

MURDER

If you know anything about terrorist activities — threats, murders or explosives — please speak *now* to the CONFIDENTIAL TELEPHONE . . .

Take a walk down the most humdrum residential street and there will come, thundering like the juggernaut of Vishnu, a huge British Saracen personnel carrier with soldiers bobbing in and out of its hatches, leveling their weapons on all and sundry.

And the boring and commonplace downtown shopping district is enclosed by an exciting spiked fence. Armed guards watch your every move as you shop.

Tony Suau and I were hanging around Divis Flats one afternoon, looking for photos of woe and injustice. The day was warm and clear. Kids were playing soccer in the parking lots and women were sunning their babies and having their tea all over the lawns. The scene was entirely too cheery for journalism. We were just about to give it up and go have a drink when an Army patrol in head-to-toe jungle camouflage materialised from behind a trash dumpster. They moved in combat formation through the picnickers, Enfields at the ready, crouching low. One soldier walked backward, sweeping his rifle from side to side, keeping the soccer team covered while the squad's point man picked his way between perambulators.

The patrol reached safety under cover of a swing set and dropped into prone firing positions. The soldiers were sighting through their rifle scopes at anything suspicious — which in this case happened to be Tony and me. We also seemed to be the only people who could see these guys. The Irish didn't even ignore the Brits, they looked and talked straight through them. Perhaps jungle camo works better than you'd think it would in a Belfast slum, a place where the best protective coloration would be a stiff drink to get the right wobble in your walk.

Anyway, there we were, standing in a balmy greensward midst tableaux of domestic felicity, staring down the gun barrels of a guerrilla warfare unit which looked like it got lost on the way back from the 1948 Malay States Emergency and which was maybe invisible, too. Finally a child of eighteen months or so wandered over and tried to give his ball to a soldier. The soldier gently turned the kid around, gave him a pat and sent him back to his mother who never glanced up from her knitting. It was a perfect "photo op" but Tony, who's been strafed in Ethiopia, besieged in Afghanistan and nearly shot to pieces in Sri Lanka, Angola, and Haiti, was too rattled to snap a single frame.

Northern Ireland's countryside has also been rescued from banality. The worst Robert Frost poem couldn't conjure a landscape so tiresomely pretty, so unrelentingly restful to the eyes. And the deeper you go into the Catholic counties, the more soporific the scenery becomes until you arrive in South Armagh, close by the Irish Republic's border, in the most narcoleptically bucolic spot on the face of earth. This is "Bandit country." There are places around here where the British Army cannot move by land at all, and the soldiers have to be helicoptered in and out as though it were Khe Sahn.

The chopper pad at Bessbrook military base is the busiest in the world. It sits behind corrugated metal walls in the middle of a perfect eighteenth-century town like an oil rig in a gallery of the Louvre. The local sheep and people have grown oblivious to the din.

Elsewhere in South Armagh, the cow pastures are decorated with extraordinary British observation towers — gangling, soaring contraptions of guy wire and pipe that look like building scaffolds had cross-bred with the Martian war machines of H. G. Wells.

The town of Crossmaglen, where the demolition expert and his dog were blown up, is as cute as anything on a train layout. The people are cheerful and garrulous. There's a sweet town square lined with chip shops and pubs. And smack in the middle of Main Street is a huge black edifice of corfam steel and cement, forty feet high, with a dinosaur spine of radio masts out of the top and sides covered in lappings and layers of anti-bomb mesh. This is the police station in Mayberry IRA.

Tony and I were only a few miles from Crossmaglen when the bomb went off. We rushed to the scene though there was nothing to see, just some dirt and branches scattered across a lane. The jungle fighters were there again, pointing their guns at us from a hedgerow. Their camouflage still didn't work. Ireland is so lush and trim, you'd swear it was laid out in fairways by Robert Trent Jones. The only uniform that would blend with this wartorn landscape would be orange pants, a purple sweater, white, tasseled shoes, and a five iron.

Tony and I also visited the Avenue Bar where Protestant gunmen had shot up Catholics for no reason. It took us a few days to get up the nerve. The same bar had been bombed in 1976 and again in 1983, and how friendly could the regulars be? And would the place be open at all?

Of course it was. The Friday after the killings, the Avenue Bar was jammed. There was a guard at the door, but when he saw Tony's cameras he all but pulled us inside. "Sure, you're American reporters, you are," said somebody, thrusting pints of beer into our hands before we'd had a chance to try the subtle conversational gambits we'd composed to break the ice with the hostile and suspicious Avenue patrons. "An O'Rourke, you say?" And I got to hear the entire history of my clan.

It seems we were kings in the olden days. But who wasn't? It must have been interesting, the Ireland of Zero AD: "I'm the king — from this rock down to the creek and from that cow to the tree. And this is my wife the Queen and our dog Prince." And it must have been every bit as peaceful as it is today, with a million or two kings on one island.

Would anybody be willing to talk about the horrible crime that took place last Sunday? No, no, they all said, it was too horrible to speak about, "the way the Protestant animals came in the front door just there, looking as normal as day and one pulls out a AK-47 from beneath his long coat and shoots up this corner here where Damien Devlin and Paul McBride died, and then he shoots down the length of the bar this way, killing poor Stephen McGaghan and bullets going right into the women's loo — if there'd been anyone in there, they'd have died certain."

Most of the sixty or eighty people in the bar on Friday had been among the twenty customers there at the time of the slaughter. "I was here," said one, patting his seat. "I thought I was dead. I said a Hail Mary and jumped over the back of the booth."

The barmaid was urged out from behind the taps to hold the lead that had been dug out of the walls, her hand still shaking from terror. The customers stood Tony on a chair, to get the proper dramatic photo angle on the flattened slugs, and they held lamps to make sure his exposure was right. Two or three dozen people retold the story of the massacre. Some things are too awful for words, they agreed.

"This murder was, oh, a terrible, low and disgusting thing." "The work of crazy-minded men." "A foul deed, senseless and cowardly, too." "Only the Protestants do things like that." "The IRA would never." "No." "They're selective, they are." "And the three lads mown down, not political at all, innocent as lambs." "Not a political thought in their heads." "The Avenue isn't a political place." "No, indeed." "Protestants are welcome here." "They are." A dozen hands pointed to pictures framed on the walls — Protestant Orange Lodge members holding fêtes at the Avenue Bar. "Could have been anyone killed." "Why, mothers and babies had been in here earlier that very day."

The evening news came on the bar's TV with more reports of the bomb at the Royal Ulster Agricultural

Show. "Now *that's* selective, you see." "Only a 7½ pound bomb." "In a police recruiting booth." "People should know to stay away from there." "Yes." "That's certain."

"If I was arrested and in a police station. I'd be proud to die in an IRA bomb," announced one young man drinking two beers at once.

Tony and I stayed at the Avenue Bar until we were nearly too stewed to walk. No one would let us buy a drink. It took a full half hour of handshakes and back slaps for us to get out of the door. It was one of the most pleasant evenings I've spent in years.

* * *

The best thing about the violence in Northern Ireland is that it's all so ancient and honorable. And I'm proud to say it began in the household of my own relative Tighernan O'Rourke. Prince of Breffni. In 1152 Tighernan's comely wife Dervorgilla ran off with Diamuid MacMurrough, King of Leinster. Cousin O'Rourke raised such a stink (and army) that MacMurrough had to call King Henry II of England for help. The Brits arrived, somewhat tardily, in 1169 and proceeded to commit the unforgivable sin of having longbows and chain mail. For the next 819 years (and counting) the English stole land, crushed rebellions, exploited the populace, persecuted Catholics, dragged a bunch of Scottish settlers into Ulster, crushed more rebellions, held potato famines, hanged patriots, stamped out the language, taxed everybody's pig, crushed more rebellions yet, and generally behaved in a manner much different than the Irish would have if it had been the Irish who invaded England and the shoe was on the other foot (assuming the Irish could afford shoes).

At any rate, the Irish are in the same terrific position as the Shiites in Lebanon, the peasants in El Salvador, the blacks in America, the Jews in Palestine, the Palestinians in Israel (and everybody everywhere, if you read your history) — enough barbarism has been visited on the Irish to excuse all barbarities by the Irish barbarians.

Not that the Irish seemed like barbarians to *me*. The Sinn Fein office on lower Falls Road was the very picture of the Sixties "Movement" crash pads where I spent my own uncivilised years. The walls were decorated with leftist slogans and two Birkenstock-shod women with the kind of dirty hair that serious political thought seems to cause were designing a poster and discussing how to avoid using "wives" or "girlfriends" or other nouns that might offend feminists. They settled on the phrase "partners of political prisoners".

The Sinn Fein spokesman, whom I'll call Tom, looked like an art teacher. He was a small, sweatered man of about thirty-five with wire-rim glasses and a friendly air. He had, however, been interned by the British for four years and sent to a British prison for another four and there was a flak jacket in the kneehole of his desk.

"Isn't there something," I ventured, "that you could try besides violence?"

"There's *no* other course of action — no other *possible course*," said Tom as though he were Churchill and England were Nazi Germany and I were an American pacifist fool (a group of similes that rings true enough to any real Irish patriot). "We're completely isolated," said Tom. "We have no allies. The leftists in Britain don't care. There's no other liberation situation like ours left in Europe except perhaps the Basque ETA."

"Tony Suau, here, actually *is* a Basque," I said. But Tom kept on. It was obviously more interesting to be alone in noble resistance, bloody but unbowed, ever beaten but ne'er defeated, etc.

"Even if you do become part of the Republic of Ireland, the IRA is just as illegal down there," I said.

"'The real war begins when the Brits pull out,' as they say," said Tom with a smile. "I don't want the country unified under the system it has now in the Republic. I wouldn't expect the Shankill Road people to accept that either." By which I gather he meant that not only does Ireland get to have British fighting Irish and Irish fighting Irish but a class war, too. Tom then gave me a load of socialist cant. What seemed to bother him most about private property was Englishmen owning exclusive fly-fishing rights on Irish trout streams. "I'm a keen fisherman myself," he said.

I don't mean to give the impression that it's only the Catholic "nationalist" or "republican" Irish who are perfectly justified in their maiming and slaughter. The Protestant "orange" or "loyalist" Irish have plenty of excuses themselves. They're patriots after all. "We'll fight anybody to stay British, even the British," they like to say. What could be more patriotic than that? And they've been in Ulster since the 1600s and have nowhere else to go. It's not like our New York City gentrification where the poor can move out and get new homes under bridges and in the bus station. And the Protestants are very frightened of popery which might seep into their houses through cracks beneath the doors and suddenly quadruple their number of dirty, unemployable children.

I talked to Sammy Wilson, former Lord Mayor of Belfast and a figure in the Democratic Unionist Party, a hard-line "Prod" political faction led by nuthatch Ian Paisley. Sammy, 34, also looked like a teacher which, in fact, he is although he used to be a policeman; just like Tom, at Sinn Fein, used to be a policeman's opposite number. And just like Tom, Sammy was forthright and gregarious.

Sammy gave me a line of capitalist bumf. But he and Tom didn't disagree about anything you'd kill anybody over unless you really wanted to, and, if you're Irish, you do.

According to my notes:

SAMMY:	. . . admitted there was prejudice against Catholics in Northern Ireland but said it was less than it had been.
TOM:	"The bigotry isn't as hard as it was."

SAMMY:	. . . complained that the people of Northern Ireland were ruled directly from London and needed a bill of rights.
TOM:	"The Brits can't afford a bill of rights; the whole origin of this statelet was not democratic."

SAMMY:	"I would have no objection to Catholics bearing their fair share in the burden of policing Northern Ireland."
TOM:	. . . said there were Protestants in the IRA.
SAMMY:	"Loyalists and republicans could both argue that police and Army are directed towards them."

But agreement is something the Irish can always overcome.

And what about the Brits? This is legally part of their country. Shouldn't they have as much right as anyone to kill, cripple, and imprison the population here? I had lunch with Brian Mawhinney, the Thatcher government's Northern Ireland Under Secretary of State for Education. He was every bit as amiable as Sammy and Tom and laid on a fine spread with three wines.

Mawhinney explained how folding your tent and pulling a sneak is not the done thing in the nation-state game. He expressed bewilderment about why Americans are so proud of their own civil war and so indignant about Ireland's. Simple British withdrawal from Northern Ireland would be, he said, equivalent to a unilateral expulsion of Hawaii without consulting the Hawaiians (though anyone who's been to Waikiki lately might consider it). Mawhinney didn't want me to think he was letting principle run away with itself. If the Brits just left there'd be a "lot of blood," he said. I might have replied, "What's this you've got now?" But that would have been rude with my mouth full. Besides, Mawhinney and his press secretary Andy Wood both said that working in Northern Ireland was "incredibly interesting" and "never dull," and I think more people should have jobs they enjoy.

*   *   *

Of course there are some spoil-sports and wet blankets who think enough's enough and say things like "let's get on with our lives." I talked to one businessman, a Catholic from the "hard" neighborhoods who'd made his millions in computers and thought the whole "troubles" thing was a crock. He pointed out that you could never unite the North with the rest of Ireland because the Irish Republic couldn't afford the welfare system that keeps the gunmen's families fed while the boyos are out shooting and bombing each other. He thought unemployment was the whole cause of the fighting. Well, he admitted, *almost* the whole cause. He had a plan. He wanted to send the entire population of Northern Ireland overseas, 5,000 at a time, so the Irish could see how normal people led quiet, harmonious, industrious lives — New York on St Patrick's Day, for example, he suggested. "I've been there five or six times, now. It's a helluva thing."

A student leader at a Belfast peace rally had a similar plan. He, too, was from West Belfast and admitted he'd got a kick from the riots when he was a boy. "But the kids in Northern Ireland," he said, "should be sent out to see the world, expand their horizons, understand that the world does not revolve around shooting on Shankill Road to achieve some mystical, magical end." The peace march had attracted all of forty people. "Maybe a good natural disaster would solve this problem," said the student leader.

And the women who'd lost their sons and lovers in the Avenue Bar shootings didn't look like they were deriving any thrill from the brilliant Irish struggle and its age-old glorious history.

I went to Damien Devlin's funeral. His mother had already had another son killed, shot by the IRA for "hooliganism." She looked as good as dead as she followed the coffin from the church to the cemetery and watched her second boy buried in the same grave as the first.

Six hours later, after another of the Avenue Bar funerals, I went back to the cemetery with Stephen McGaghan's body. Damien Devlin's girlfriend was still there, alone on the other side of the graveyard, sitting, head in hands, among the flower arrangements.

People walked out of both these funerals because the priests denounced paramilitary violence.

* * *

Tony and I spent our last day in Northern Ireland with the police, who are much like the police anywhere in the world — apprehending shoplifters, tracing stolen VCRs, quieting domestic tiffs — except they perform these duties wearing flak vests, carrying submachine guns and riding in armored cars.

"It's not such a bad job," said the police sergeant as we rode in the cramped olive-drab interior of a "pig" — an eight-man vehicle specially designed for duty in Northern Ireland, with bomb skirts, run-flat tyres and a device for clearing paint bombs off the bullet-proof, mesh-covered windscreen. "It's basically a law-abiding community," said the sergeant, peering out of a gun port. "We have the highest detection rate in the UK." A stone bounced off the armor-plate roof.

The sergeant gave us the official version of the "security situation." It's the same info you get at Army briefings or from the government in London — hardly anybody's involved in the violence. "It's 3 percent of the population, 1½ percent on each side, that carry this thing on," the sergeant said. The authorities always tell you there are only a few hundred actual Protestant and Catholic gunmen. Though these few somehow manage to keep 10,000 regular Army soldiers, 6,500 members of the Ulster Defence Regiment, 8,000 police officers and 4,500 members of the police reserve pretty busy. "You're dealing with smart fellows here," said the sergeant. The authorities also say it's nothing more than gangsterism when you get right down to it. "Go into a republican bar," said the sergeant, "and you'll see Protestant gunmen. They divide up territories. They're doing business. You go into some of these fellows' homes, and there are three or four colour TVs — I've only got one. You're ankle deep in carpet. Drinks cabinets over there. Three- or four-bedroom bungalows with beautiful views." He sighed. "It's the wee fellows who pay. Always the wee fellows take the risks. They pay . . ."

"With their lives," I almost said.

". . . higher car insurance," said the sergeant. It seems the paramilitaries steal a lot of cars to use in their "actions."

We got out of the pig to have a smoke in a Protestant neighborhood near the Peace Wall. All around us were little pin-neat houses with weedless, butch-cut rug-sized lawns and ceramic bunnies in the marigold beds. "We're not usually attacked in the loyalist neighborhoods," said the sergeant, "we're more likely to get tea over here." But the first cop killed in the current round of Northern Ireland troubles was shot, in 1969, in the Shankill Road, one block away.

"Come on," I said to the sergeant, "there's got to be more to this than an organised crime spree or, for that matter, than a debate over governance or hurt feelings about what King Billy did four hundred years ago."

"Oh, it's not hard to give a poor man a cause," said the sergeant. "Why, you read about it in poems and plays and books, and it almost convinces *me*."

"You don't see any end to it?"

He looked slightly puzzled. "This is an acceptable level of violence," he said.

GAVIN YOUNG

As foreign correspondent for the Observer *Gavin Young covered at least fifteen wars and revolutions around the world. Many of his experiences are recounted in* Worlds Apart: Travels in War and Peace (1987), *from which the following extract is taken. He has written about living with the Marsh Arabs of southern Iraq in* Return to the Marshes *and of his journey through Mesopotamia in* Iraq: Land of Two Rivers. *The story of his improvisational voyage around the world in whatever would float is told in* Slow Boats to China *and* Slow Boats Home. *He has also published* In Search of Conrad, *which is part biography, part travel book.*

THE MURDER OF HUÉ

Hué, 3 March 1968

It is hideously unreal, yet you can feel real rubble underfoot; put a handkerchief to your nose and you can still smell the corpses. I visited Hué first in 1965, and came to know and love it. Now, between them, in the name of the people's salvation, General Giap and the U.S. High Command have killed the flower of Vietnamese cities. Today Hué is no more the city I knew than a friend lying in a street, charred and ripped by a bomb, is the human being one talked or made love to. You can disguise it in whatever military terms you like but in Hué murder has been arranged.

Along the airport road to Hué, which I used to travel in a minibus full of cheerfully chattering Vietnamese, I was made to feel like one of General Patton's soldiers storming across occupied France in 1944. I came, of necessity, in a convoy of fifteen vehicles, huge petrol tankers, trucks full of GIs, lewd or comic slogans painted on the camouflaged covers of their helmets, crouching with Lucky Strikes clamped in dusty and unshaven jaws, guns at the ready for ambushes, tanks spewing up the dust, their drivers' feet stepping hard on the gas.

Fear of the enemy and the enemy's persistent power is everywhere evident. By little bridges, blown and hastily repaired, Americans crouch in sandbagged strong points. Jets and helicopters scream overhead without cessation, airstrikes and artillery barrages send napalm and bombs down on the surrounding green countryside. Impassive Vietnamese villagers line the road in the dust and stare at the pandemonium, the clanking machinery, the big-nosed foreign soldiers. Are these the saviours?

Coming into Hué is like a dream in which you turn a corner expecting to see a familiar scene and find that it has undergone a sudden and hideous change. You twist and turn through deep mud roads between blighted gardens and skeleton houses and shops, looking for the makeshift pontoon bridge the Americans have thrown across the canals. Bewildered Vietnamese carrying bundles of possessions press into the roadside to avoid being crushed by the trucks. There are soldiers everywhere, Americans in helmets and bulky in flak jackets, tense Vietnamese fingering sub-machine gun triggers. Huge armoured personnel carriers are waiting down side alleys like gangsters in ambush. There is no transport; you walk, and that is better because you can escape with the Vietnamese from a military machine that is more and more irritable now that its omnipotence has turned to myth.

Always in the past I had stayed with a rather poor Vietnamese family who live in an old-fashioned, rambling building on the north bank of the Perfumed River between the river bank and the Citadel, where the North Vietnamese and Vietcong held American mobility and firepower at bay for three weeks. From the south bank it seemed as if they could not possibly have survived. The north bank area looked like the worst parts of London after the Blitz. Formerly, I had always hired a bicycle in Hué and ridden across the great-girdered bridge over the river. Now the central span plunges into the water, dynamited by the Vietcong who held it for a time. I had to push my way through a horde of Vietnamese struggling desperately across the one narrow gangway. When too many people force themselves on it you wade calf-deep. Machine guns and mortars cracked and thumped in the river bank trees not far away, where the Vietnamese used to take me on picnics. The Citadel has fallen, but the Americans are still fighting in Hué. The family's street is a blackened shambles of gutted houses. The market and teashops across the road on the river bank have ceased to exist. Miraculously, my Vietnamese friends were there, standing outside their door, running through the rubble to meet me. Their house is one of the very few that has not been razed.

They led me in excitedly. One or two were crying. They began to explain that they had gathered as usual in the house for the Tet (New Year) holiday, ten of them, uncle, aunts, cousins, sons, and daughters, with two small babies, and Mimi, the old dog with stubby legs. Since then they had had three weeks of unimaginable nightmare. The upstairs rooms no longer exist. They were torn apart by American fire during the Buddhist "struggle group" demonstrations against the Ky Government. In 1966 I stayed in the front upper room and we watched the angry torchlight processions parading through the street shouting: "Peace." Now there are four walls and no roof. The floor is littered with broken tiles and burned beams. The American mortar bombs had thrown the family's little Buddhist shrine into a mass of coloured tatters in the dust; a piece of shrapnel had embedded itself in a French translation of *The Grapes of Wrath*; the braided, ceremonial uniform cap of the eldest son, who was shot in action last year, lay on the wreckage of the balcony.

We sat downstairs in a room pocked with bullet holes and a floor littered with tiles from the roof. There was a small mortar crater in the cement floor. Madame Dinh, a tiny, frail and very wise woman of about forty-five, who runs the house, explained: "When the first fusillades began we were all asleep. The Vietcong were firing across the river at U.S. headquarters. We thought it was like any other bombardment, and would stop. But then we all got up and came downstairs and saw the Vietcong in the street outside. There were about twenty of them, then sixty. They made for the bridge. The first ones to come wore shorts and khaki shirts and no caps. They were very young — seventeen or eighteen. They didn't come into the houses here because everyone had barred their shutters. I knew then that in the end the government would drive them out. But I didn't know when, and I knew we would suffer."

Madame Dinh has lost a husband and her eldest son in war. Tam, the eldest surviving son, who studies Government administration in Saigon, said: "One Vietnamese soldier lay wounded and bleeding outside our door all the morning. Nobody dared come out and help him. Then one of a Vietcong patrol walked up and just shot him. He was harmless, but he just shot him."

What about the bombing?

"That happened after the Vietcong had left — at least in this street. When the Americans shelled us the Vietcong had retreated toward the Citadel," said Tam. "Can you imagine, shelling twenty-four hours for fourteen days?"

For all that time this family huddled together with no link to the outside world except the radio. They listened avidly to the BBC or Saigon Radio. At U.S. headquarters in Hué an American colonel, phlegmatically contemplating his artillery shelling a suburb, said next day: "You know what BBC stands for? British Communist Broadcasting Corporation." Only hawks are really welcome in the North now among the military.

Behind Madame Dinh's house, outside the colonel's field of vision, the teeming residential and commercial areas resemble something out of Goya. Whole streets are laid waste. Rubble chokes the sidewalks. There are craters in the streets and blackened shells of cars. A truck is embedded in a wall. At two points I saw crowds who scrabbled and clawed at the grilles of stores where rice was being sold. The lucky ones — paying four times the normal price — quickly loaded the sacks onto bicycles and scurried away. They looked, if one approached too close, as if they would turn and defend the rice like famished dogs with a bone. The Americans had dropped huge bombs — 750 and 500 pounders — on what they imagined were the Citadel walls. Where they fell is one of the more fearful parts of a fearfully shattered city. It was a residential area packed with families like Madame Dinh's gathering for Tet. Now, like the Vietnamese, you walk there with a handkerchief to your nose.

A wispy Vietnamese teacher of French came up. He was trembling, and looked as though he might cry. What did he think of all that had passed?

"We don't think any more, *monsieur*. We are like dogs. We live by instinct. Instincts are all that are left to us." He pointed to a monstrous pile of rubble. "The man who lived in there was shot by the Vietcong. Now his house has been destroyed by the Americans. Curious, eh?" He stopped in front of another. There were plenty to choose from. "There are thirty people under this one." Vietnamese were digging in another mound of bricks and mortar. "They are still bringing the bodies out of there. Two families, about twenty people, eight survivors."

Here the stench of the dead was overpowering. In an open space between the houses mutilated corpses were being wrapped in sheets. Three men in nose masks dug graves. Women and children stood around keening, and shaking with sobs. A woman flung herself on a new mound of earth, hammering on it with her fist, and rolling on it in a paroxysm of grief.

We stepped through fragments of glass, pathetic muddied wrappings of Tet holiday gifts, filth and dead rats, to where a crowd of Vietnamese were passing under the great ornamental gate to the Citadel stormed by the U.S. Marines. They shuffled through quickly, holding their noses because here three rotting bodies of Vietcong soldiers lie as yet unburied. The Citadel's solid walls are punctured by shells, and the gate itself riddled by everything from bullets to rockets. Inside the Citadel there seems to be no shop nor house that is not wholly or partially destroyed. The Americans used tanks here, after the airstrikes. The Vietcong and North Vietnamese used rockets from the camouflaged foxholes you see everywhere.

In a dazed way the people are friendly. There is no doubt they are glad the Communists were driven out — a number of civil servants live in the Citadel. In another quarter of Hué inhabited largely by army officers and civil servants they are still digging up the bodies of relatives, men, women, and children, who had their hands tied behind their backs and then were shot by the Vietcong. There are still many families missing. Mothers stand about weeping as the diggers work, and rush forward to try to recognize relatives as the bodies are taken out of the earth. This is in a secondary school garden used by the invaders as a command post. Thirty bodies have been recovered so far. But scores more may be there.

There are thought to be three hundred to six hundred government employees buried in two mass graves somewhere in the city, but no one has been able to find them yet. In any event, Government here is like the city itself — in ruins. Officials have disappeared for the most part, kidnapped or killed. Official records were destroyed by the invading Vietcong and North Vietnamese when they occupied the municipal buildings, which are themselves in ruins.

No one knows how many civilians were killed. Perhaps they never will. Some were killed deliberately by certain Vietcong, others by American bombing and mortaring. Two French priests were shot by a Vietcong patrol at eleven o'clock one morning in a crowded street, and their grave now stands in the grounds of their house near the Collège de la Providence in West Hué. Yet other priests were not molested, the Father Superior told me. "The North Vietnamese — they were from Tonkin — occupied the college. I would describe them as very well disciplined and ferocious."

In the Citadel an old Vietnamese with a wispy beard said: "They came into the house but didn't harm us. They said they were winning the war and we should support them. They were forty percent Tonkinese, the rest Vietcong from this region." So they behaved well in some areas, badly in others.

In Madame Dinh's house one evening, a family came

in which had had to put up with Vietcong units in their house for eighty days. "They blew down part of our walls and fired out through them, and they knocked down walls into neighbouring houses all down the street, linking them all up," said one.

A student called Minh said: "They tried to organize young people like me to study their doctrines, carry arms for them. They sat about singing communist songs." He sang one to illustrate the point. The Dinh family rocked with laughter, out of sheer relief that the worst is temporarily over.

The song was the souvenir of a monstrous experience. Did many young Vietnamese respond to Vietcong propaganda? "Only a few spivs and the very poor — some trishaw drivers, people like that."

What did students like Minh think?

"Well, the Vietcong told us they were fighting for the independence of Vietnam from the Americans. I don't like the Americans, but I don't like the Vietcong either. I am sure some students went with the Vietcong, but, believe me, not many."

These student attitudes are extremely significant. All the student friends I have made in Hué were militant "struggle group" members in the days when Hué and Da Nang rebelled against the Government of General Thieu and Air Vice-Marshal Ky. Minh and Tam both took carbines down to Da Nang and manned the barricades against Ky's troops. They wanted then — and they want now — an end to the Thieu-Ky Government and really free elections, which can throw up, they think, a representative government with which the National Liberal Front would bargain. They say they are true nationalists. They feel the Vietnamese nationality is being swamped by a massive American presence, which rules Vietnam against its better interests through unrepresentative people like the generals. They did not even like the Buddhist monk, Thich Tri Quang, who played a leading part in the struggle movement. They suspect he might be playing along with the Vietcong. They did like the dynamic General Nguyeu Chanh Thi, who commanded the Vietnamese armies in Hué, where he was born, and was opposed to Thieu and Ky, and who is now living in Washington where the government exiled him. All this Minh and Tam and other students have explained to me in Madame Dinh's house many times. They did not want the Vietcong. They wanted honest government. They did not want American domination. Yet few American officials in Saigon have ever been convinced that the struggle movement *en masse* was not pro-Vietcong. They thus approved Ky's dispatch of troops to Hué and Da Nang, and the bloodshed that followed.

But now the battle for Hué has highlighted something of considerable political significance. The Vietcong occupation of Hué provided the ultimate test of the students' real feelings. Since Tet they have had every opportunity to go with the Vietcong. Apart from an extreme leftwing minority, they did not, even when it was much safer for them to go than to stay and risk a bullet from angry Vietcong soldiers. Perhaps now the Americans will realize their grave political misjudgement over the struggle groups. In any event the Vietcong, too, must have had a sharp surprise.

Another student in the Dinhs' house that night lives in a suburban area where the Vietcong tried to organize a temporary administration. "A tailor down the road was appointed chairman for youth. Only a few peasants were enthusiastic," he said. And several friends were obliged to carry Vietcong wounded up into the hills during the fighting. "We were sixty — four of us to each wounded man. We marched at night because the Vietcong officers said we must get past the villages and U.S. flares and helicopters before dawn. We must have gone fifty kilometres, with no food and no water. They seemed to have no medicine. They did not seem to know the way very well either. At certain crossroads we had to stop and wait for other soldiers to come and show us which track to take. We didn't wait long, there were lots of Vietcong soldiers coming and going. When we got to a rough shelter on a hill we were made to sign a paper saying that we had delivered so many wounded for the soldiers of the National Liberation Front — they got very angry if anyone referred to them as Viet Minh or Vietcong. In my village they shot one man for saying 'Viet Minh.' Then they asked each of us to stay with them, saying they had already won in Hué and everywhere else, and that now was the time to make a choice. But we said we would go home. And we went all alone back through the dark."

Not every Vietnamese in Hué was so lucky. "Before they left our village they took a lot of young men with them," I was told. And Madame Dinh's chief concern is to get her sons and nephews out of Hué in case the

Vietcong return and take them off. In one quarter of Hué hundreds were led off with bandaged eyes and hands tied.

"They seemed to think that because we were Buddhist students and were in the struggle movement we would welcome them here."

I asked my student what his attitude and that of his friends was now.

"I think you know what we have always told you. That has not changed. We think — I mean the educated people, more or less, from university and secondary school, like us — that the Vietcong is no good; that the Americans are not good for us, because they destroy our houses and our souls; that the present government is no good because it doesn't represent anyone much, and its Army destroys whole streets because of four snipers."

Once I said to them in Madame Dinh's shattered living room, while she and some women friends were playing cards: "What a catastrophe for you."

Tam leaned forward intently: "Not a catastrophe," he answered. "It's normal, it's war, and this is normal. . . . Well then," he cried, with a rising note of great anguish unusual for a Vietnamese. "Well, we must have peace, mustn't we? Oh yes, yes, yes!" At that moment a violent explosion rocked the already weakened building and a shower of loose tiles fell into the room. I discovered later that it was a U.S. ammunition ship blowing up after two direct hits from a Vietcong mortar. It was about six hundred yards away.

Because things like that can happen, and are likely to continue to happen for some time, Hué is almost totally isolated from the outside world. The Vietcong are strong on both sides of the river that is Hué's main lifeline. The airport is open only to military aircraft. The road south is hopelessly insecure. With an almost non-existent local government, the refugees, about 30,000 of them officially, are likely to get only the bare necessities for the time being, and their numbers are likely to increase. This week I watched thousands more scrambling to safety from a thickly populated suburb in which there were said to be Vietcong snipers and which the Americans and Vietnamese preferred to mortar rather than invade. Shops are still largely closed. Prices are up and there is a black market. Many families have suffered from the looting, of which there are unending complaints. The Vietnamese Army units undoubtedly took what they could, wherever they found it. Nor are the U.S. troops above suspicion. A local French resident says he found his house denuded after U.S. troops had occupied it. The safes were blown open, he claims, and everything that could not be taken was destroyed, including his desk.

So far American aid to the chief of the Vietnamese province is stymied because of a lack of men who know the region's problems. Perhaps twenty to thirty Americans were killed in Hué — nobody will say — and certainly several were taken off by the Vietcong. The local U.S. administrator, a man of long Vietnam experience, is now, it seems, suffering from nervous exhaustion and can hardly be much good on his own. Most American civilians in the northern sector work in a cloud of foreboding. It is obvious that pacification and development programmes are in ruins. Today there are large American, Vietnamese, and North Vietnamese, and Vietcong forces in the neighbourhood of Hué. Military casualties are heavy and still rising. I watched U.S. jets striking with napalm and rockets a few hundred yards away from Hué's stadium. American dead were being brought in there, wrapped in green plastic shrouds and loaded into helicopters. Cartloads of captured Vietcong weapons, many as good as anything the Americans have, were being stacked. There was a growing pile of uniforms of American dead, their water bottles, rifles, pathetic letters ending, "With love, and try and write soon, Mom."

And what has the battle of Hué meant? Tragically, it has symbolized the entire war. The people have been raped by two forces which they have come to distrust and fear. The Americans have regained Hué at the cost of destroying it. They will be blamed for that. General Giap's men thought they could win over people they wrongly considered ripe for conversion, simply because they have opposed the Saigon government. In the main they, too, have had to learn that there are three political forces in South Vietnam, not two, and that the third one, the one that rejects the big-stick images of Hanoi and Saigon, is both large and, when opportunity arrives, courageous. Militarily, the holocaust that enveloped this beautiful city and its thousands of Madame Dinhs, Vinhs, and Tams has ended in stalemate after the initiative with the North Vietnamese and Vietcong. Neither side has won any appreciable number of Vietnamese hearts and minds.

And standing in the stench of Hué's streets, contemplating the ruins of the university and schools — there will be no education in Hué for upwards of a year from now — and foreseeing the inevitable exodus from this cultural centre and former imperial capital of central Vietnam when travel from it is again possible, one can see only one thing very clearly: that a criminal act has been committed here since Tet. One is tempted to refer to other ruined cities: Warsaw or Budapest. But there is only one Hué, victim of cynical ideologists who talk with unctuous arrogance of nationalism and democracy from their loudspeaker vans and who between them have destroyed perhaps the most purely nationalist city in either North or South Vietnam.

Madame Dinh said one evening: "You know, during the bombardment I sat thinking, 'Suppose President Ho Chi Minh and President Johnson visited Hué at the same time and saw all this, and they said to each other: "Why are we doing this?" and shook hands.'" She added shyly: "You think that's very stupid. Of course, I am not serious. It was only my dream."

BRUCE CHATWIN

In 1968 Bruce Chatwin began his study of nomads, travelling widely from Afghanistan to Mauretania. He was co-organiser of the 1979 "The Animal Style" exhibition at the Asia Society in New York. From 1972 to 1975 he worked as a journalist for the Sunday Times. *His first book was* In Patagonia, *a study of "the uttermost part of the earth" at the tip of South America, which won the 1978 Hawthornden prize and the 1979 E. M. Forster Award of the American Academy of Arts and Letters. He is also the author of* The Viceroy of Ouidah, The Songlines, *and* What Am I Doing Here, *and his novels* On the Black Hill, *which won the 1982 Whitbread Literary Award for Best First Novel, and* Utz, *which was shortlisted for the 1988 Booker Prize. He died in 1989.*

A COUP

The coup began at seven on Sunday morning. It was a grey and windless dawn and the grey Atlantic rollers broke in long, even lines along the beach. The palms above the tidemark shivered in a current of cooler air that blew in off the breakers. Out at sea — beyond the surf — there were several black fishing canoes.

166

Buzzards were spiraling above the market, swooping now and then to snatch up scraps of offal. The butchers were slaughtering, even on a Sunday.

We were in a taxi when the coup began, on our way to another country. We had passed the Hôtel de la Plage, passed the Sûreté Nationale, and then we drove under a limply flapping banner which said, in red letters, that Marxist-Leninism was the one and only guide. In front of the Presidential Palace was a road-block. A soldier waved us to a halt, and then waved us on.

"*Pourriture!*" said my friend, Domingo, and grinned.

Domingo was a young, honey-coloured mulatto with a flat and friendly face, a curly moustache and a set of dazzling teeth. He was the direct descendant of Francisco-Félix de Souza, the Chacha of Ouidah, a Brazilian slaver who lived and died in Dahomey, and about whom I was writing a book.

Domingo had two wives. The first wife was old and the skin hung in loose folds off her back. The second wife was hardly more than a child. We were on our way to Togo, to watch a football game, and visit his great-uncle who knew a lot of old stories about the Chacha.

The taxi was jammed with football fans. On my right sat a very black old man wrapped in green and orange cotton. His teeth were also orange from chewing cola nuts, and from time to time he spat.

Outside the Presidential Palace hung an overblown poster of the Head of State, and two much smaller posters of Lenin and Kim Il-Sung. Beyond the road-block, we took a right fork, on through the old European

167

section where there were bungalows and baulks of bougainvillaea by the gates. Along the sides of tarmac, market women walked in single file with basins and baskets balanced on their heads.

"What's that?" I asked. I could see some kind of commotion, up ahead, towards the airport.

"Accident!" Domingo shrugged, and grinned again.

Then all the women were screaming, and scattering their yams and pineapples, and rushing for the shelter of the gardens. A white Peugeot shot down the middle of the road, swerving right and left to miss the women. The driver waved for us to turn back, and just then, we heard the crack of gunfire.

"*C'est la guerre!*" our driver shouted, and spun the taxi round.

"I knew it," Domingo grabbed my arm. "I knew it."

The sun was up by the time we got to downtown Cotonou. In the taxi-park the crowd had panicked and overturned a brazier, and a stack of crates had caught fire. A policeman blew his whistle and bawled for water. Above the rooftops, there was a column of black smoke, rising.

"They're burning the Palace," said Domingo. "Quick! Run!"

We ran, bumped into other running figures, and ran on. A man shouted "Mercenary!" and lunged for my shoulder. I ducked and we dodged down a sidestreet. A boy in a red shirt beckoned me into a bar. It was dark inside. People were clustered round a radio. Then the bartender screamed, wildly, in African, at me, and the boy. And then I was out again on the dusty red street, shielding my head with my arms, pushed and pummeled against the corrugated building by four hard, acridly sweating men until the gendarmes came to fetch me in a jeep.

"For your own proper protection," their officer said, as the handcuffs snapped around my wrists.

The last I ever saw of Domingo he was standing in the street, crying, as the jeep drove off and he vanished in a clash of colored cottons.

* * *

In the barracks guardroom a skinny boy, stripped to a pair of purple underpants, sat hunched against the wall. His hands and feet were bound with rope, and he had the greyish look Africans get when they are truly frightened. A gecko hung motionless on the dirty whitewash. Outside the door there was a papaya with a tall scaly trunk and yellowish fruit. A mud wall ran along the far side of the compound. Beyond the wall the noise of gunfire continued, and the high-pitched wailing of women.

A corporal came in and searched me. He was small, wiry, angular, and his cheekbones shone. He took my watch, wallet, passport, and notebook.

"Mercenary!" he said, pointing to the patch-pocket on the leg of my khaki trousers. His gums were spongy and his breath was foul.

"No," I said, submissively. "I'm a tourist."

"Mercenary!" he shrieked, and slapped my face — not hard, but hard enough to hurt.

He held up my fountain pen. "What?"

"A pen," I said. It was a black Mont Blanc.

169

"What for?"

"To write with."

"A gun?"

"Not a gun."

"Yes, a gun!"

I sat on a bench, staring at the skinny boy who continued to stare at his toes. The corporal sat cross-legged in the doorway with his submachine gun trained on me. Outside in the yard, two sergeants were distributing rifles, and a truck was loading with troops. The troops sat down with the barrels sticking up from their crotches. The colonel came out of his office and took the salute. The truck lurched off, and he came over, lumpily, towards the guardroom.

The corporal snapped to attention and said, "Mercenary, Comrade Colonel!"

"From today," said the colonel, "there are no more comrades in our country."

"Yes, comrade Colonel," the man nodded; but checked himself and added, "Yes, my Colonel."

The colonel waved him aside and surveyed me gloomily. He wore an exquisitely pressed pair of paratrooper fatigues, a red star on his cap, and another red star in his lapel. A roll of fat stood out around the back of his neck; his thick lips drooped at the corners; his eyes were hooded. He looked, I thought, so like a sad hippopotamus. I told myself I mustn't think he looks like a sad hippopotamus. Whatever happens, he mustn't think I think he looks like a sad hippopotamus.

*   *   *

"Ah, *monsieur!*" he said, in a quiet dispirited voice. "What are you doing in this poor country of ours?"

"I came here as a tourist."

"You are English?"

"Yes."

"But you speak an excellent French."

"Passable," I said.

"With a Parisian accent I should have said."

"I have lived in Paris."

"I, also, have visited Paris. A wonderful city!"

"The most wonderful city."

"But you have mistimed your visit to Benin."

"Yes," I faltered. "I seem to have run into trouble."

"You have been here before?"

"Once," I said. "Five years ago."

"When Benin was Dahomey."

"Yes," I said. "I used to think Benin was in Nigeria."

"Benin is in Nigeria and now we have it here."

"I think I understand."

"Calm yourself, *monsieur.*" His fingers reached to unlock my handcuffs. "We are having another little change of politics. Nothing more! In these situations one must keep calm. You understand? Calm!"

Some boys had come through the barracks' gate and were creeping forward to peer at the prisoner. The colonel appeared in the doorway, and they scampered off.

"Come here," he said. "You will be safer if you stay with me. Come, let us listen to the Head of State."

We walked across the parade-ground to his office where he sat me in a chair and reached for a portable radio. Above his desk hung a photo of the Head of State, in a Fidel Castro cap. His cheeks were a basketwork of scarifications.

"The Head of State, " said the colonel, "is always speaking over the radio. We call it the *journal parlé*. It is a crime in this country *not* to listen to the *journal parlé*."

He turned the knob. The military music came in cracking bursts.

Citizens of Benin . . . the hour is grave. At seven hours this morning, an unidentified DC-8 jet aircraft landed at our International Airport of Cotonou, carrying a crapulous crowd of mercenaries . . . black and white . . . financed by the lackeys of international imperialism. . . . A vile plot to destroy our democratic and operational regime.

The colonel laid his jowls on his hands and sighed. "The Sombas! The Sombas!"

The Sombas came from the far north-west of the country. They filed their teeth to points and once, not so long ago, were cannibals.

". . . launched a vicious attack on our Presidential Palace . . ."

I glanced up again at the wall. The Head of State was a Somba — and the colonel was a Fon.

". . . the population is requested to arm itself with stones and knives to kill this crapulous . . ."

"A recorded message," said the colonel, and turned the volume down. "It was recorded yesterday."

"You mean . . ."

"Calm yourself, *monsieur*. You do not understand. In this country one understands nothing."

Certainly, as this morning wore on, the colonel understood less and less. He did not, for example, understand why, on the nine o'clock communiqué, the mercenaries had landed in a DC-8 jet, while at ten the plane had changed to a DC-7 turbo-prop. Around eleven the music cut off again and the Head of State announced a victory for the Government Forces. The enemy, he said, were retreating *en catastrophe* for the marshes of Ouidah.

"There has been a mistake," said the colonel, looking very shaken. "Excuse me, *monsieur*. I must leave you."

He hesitated on the threshold and then stepped out into the sunlight. The hawks made swift spiraling shadows on the ground. I helped myself to a drink from his water flask. The shooting sounded further off now, and the town was quieter. Ten minutes later, the corporal marched into the office. I put my hands above my head, and he escorted me back to the guardroom.

* * *

It was very hot. The skinny boy had been taken away and, on the bench at the back, sat a Frenchman.

Outside, tied to a papaya, a springer spaniel was panting and straining at its leash. A pair of soldiers squatted on their hams and were trying to dismantle the Frenchman's shotgun. A third soldier, rummaging in his game-bag, was laying out a few brace of partridge and guinea fowl.

"Will you please give that dog some water?" the Frenchman asked.

"Eh?" The corporal bared his gums.

"The dog," he pointed. "Water!"

"No."

"What's going on?" I asked.

"The monkeys are wrecking my gun and killing my dog."

"Out there, I mean."

"*Coup monté.*"

"Which means?"

"You hire a plane load of mercenaries to shoot up the town. See who your friends are and who are your enemies. Shoot the enemies. Simple!"

"Clever."

"Very."

"And us?"

"They might need a corpse or two. As proof!"

"Thank you," I said.

"I was joking."

"Thanks all the same."

The Frenchman was a water-engineer. He worked up-country, on artesian wells, and was down in the capital on leave. He was a short, muscular man, tending to paunch, with cropped grey hair and a web of white laugh-lines over his leathery cheeks. He had dressed himself *en mercenaire*, in fake python-skin camouflage, to shoot a few game-birds in the forest on the outskirts of town.

"What do you think of my costume?" he asked.

"Suitable," I said.

"Thank you."

The sun was vertical. The color of the parade-ground

had bleached to a pinkish orange, and the soldiers strutted back and forth in their own pools of shade. Along the wall the vultures flexed their wings.

"Waiting," joked the Frenchman.

"Thank you."

"Don't mention it."

Our view of the morning's entertainment was restricted by the width of the doorframe. We were, however, able to witness a group of soldiers treating their ex-colonel in a most shabby fashion. We wondered how he could still be alive as they dragged him out and bundled him into the back of a jeep. The corporal had taken the colonel's radio, and was cradling it on his knee. The Head of State was baying for blood — *Mort aux mercenaires soit qu'ils sont noirs ou blancs. . . ."* The urchins, too, were back in force, jumping up and down, drawing their fingers across their throats, and chanting in unison, *"Mort-aux-mercenaires. . ! Mort-aux-mercenaires. . !"*

Around noon, the jeep came back. A lithe young woman jumped out and started screeching orders at an infantry platoon. She was wearing a mud-stained battledress. A nest of plaits curled, like snakes, from under her beret.

"So," said my companion. "The new colonel."

"An Amazon colonel," I said.

"I always said it," he said. "Never trust a teenage Amazon colonel."

He passed me a cigarette. There were two in the packet and I took one of them.

"Thanks," I said. "I don't smoke."

He lit mine, and then his, and blew a smoke-ring at the rafters. The gecko on the wall hadn't budged.

"My name's Jacques," he said.

I told him my own name and he said, "I don't like the look of this."

"Nor I," I said.

"No," he said. "There are no rules in this country."

Nor were there any rules, none that one could think of, when the corporal came back from conferring with the Amazon and ordered us, also, to strip to our underpants. I hesitated. I was unsure whether I was wearing underpants. But a barrel in the small of my back convinced me, underpants or no, that my trousers would have to come down — only to find that I did, after all, have on a pair of pink-and-white boxer shorts from Brooks Brothers.

Jacques was wearing green string pants. We must have looked a pretty couple — my back welted all over with mosquito bites, he with his paunch flopping over the elastic, as the corporal marched us out, barefoot over the burning ground, and stood us, hands up, against the wall which the vultures had fouled with their ash-white, ammonia-smelling droppings.

"*Merde!*" said Jacques. "Now what?"

What indeed? I was not frightened. I was tired and hot. My arms ached, my knees sagged, my tongue felt like leather, and my temples throbbed. But this was not frightening. It was too like a B-grade movie to be frightening. I began to count the flecks of millet-chaff embedded in the mud-plaster wall. . . .

* * *

176

I remembered the morning, five years earlier, my first morning in Dahomey, under the tall trees in Parakou. I'd had a rough night, coming down from the desert in the back of a crowded truck, and at breakfast time, at the *café-routier*, I'd asked the waiter what there was to see in town.

"Patrice."

"Patrice?"

"That's me," he grinned. "And, *monsieur*, there are hundreds of other beautiful young girls and boys who walk, all the time, up and down the streets of Parakou."

I remembered, too, the girl who sold pineapples at Dassa-Zoumbé station. It had been a stifling day, the train slow and the country burnt. I had been reading Gide's *Nourritures terrestres* and, as we drew into Dassa, had come to the line, *Ô cafés — où notre démences s'est continuées très avant dans la nuit . . .* No, I thought, this will never do, and looked out of the carriage window. A basket of pineapples had halted outside. The girl underneath the basket smiled and, when I gave her the Gide, gasped, lobbed all six pineapples into the carriage, and ran off to show her friends — who in turn came skipping down the tracks, clamouring, "A book, please? A book? A book!" So *out* went a dog-eared thriller and Saint-Exupéry's *Vol de nuit*, and *in* came the "Fruits of the Earth" — the real ones — pawpaws, guavas, more pineapples, a raunch of grilled swamp-rat, and a palm-leaf hat.

"Those girls," I remember scribbling in my notebook, "are the ultimate products of the *lycée* system."

* * *

And now what?

The Amazon was squawking at the platoon and we strained our ears for the click of safety catches.

"I think they're playing games," Jacques said, squinting sideways.

"I should hope so," I muttered. I liked Jacques. It was good, if one had to be here, to be here with him. He was an old Africa hand and had been through coups before.

"That is," he added glumly, "if they don't get drunk."

"Thank you," I said, and looked over my shoulder at the drill-squad.

"No look!" the corporal barked. He was standing beside us, his shirt-front open to the navel. Obviously, he was anxious to cut a fine figure.

"Stick your belly-button in," I muttered in English.

"No speak!" he threatened.

"I won't speak." I held the words within my teeth. "But stay there. Don't leave me. I need you."

Maddened by the heat and excitement, the crowds who had come to gawp were clamoring, *"Mort-aux-mercenaires . . ! Mort-aux-mercenaires . . !"* and my mind went racing back over the horrors of Old Dahomey, before the French came. I thought, the slave-wars, the human sacrifices, the piles of broken skulls. I thought of Domingo's other uncle, "The Brazilian," who received us on his rocking-chair dressed in white ducks and a topee. "Yes," he sighed, "the Dahomeans are a charming and intelligent people. Their only weakness is a certain nostalgia for taking heads."

No. This was not my Africa. Not this rainy, rotten-fruit Africa. Not this Africa of blood and laughter.

The Africa I loved was the long undulating savannah country to the north, the "leopard-spotted land," where flat-topped acacias stretched as far as the eye could see, and there were black-and-white hornbills and tall red termitaries. For whenever I went back to that Africa, and saw a camel caravan, a view of white tents, or a single blue turban far off in the heat haze, I knew that, no matter what the Persians said, Paradise never was a garden but a waste of white thorns.

"I am dreaming," said Jacques, suddenly, "of *perdrix aux choux*."

"I'd take a dozen Belons and a bottle of Krug."

"No speak!" The corporal waved his gun, and I braced myself, half-expecting the butt to crash down on my skull.

And so what? What would it matter when already I felt as if my skull were split clean open? Was this, I wondered, sunstroke? How strange, too, as I tried to focus on the wall, that each bit of chaff should bring back some clear specific memory of food or drink?

*   *   *

There was a lake in Central Sweden and, in the lake, there was an island where the ospreys nested. On the first day of the crawfish season we rowed to the fisherman's hut and rowed back towing twelve dozen crawfish in a live-net. That evening, they came in from the kitchen, a scarlet mountain smothered in dill. The northern sunlight bounced off the lake into the bright white room. We drank akvavit from thimble-sized glasses and we ended the meal with a tart made of cloudberries. I could taste again the grilled sardines we ate on the quay

179

at Douarnenez and see my father demonstrating how his father ate *sardines à la mordecai*: you took a live sardine by the tail and swallowed it. Or the elvers we had in Madrid, fried in oil with garlic and half a red pepper. It had been a cold spring morning, and we'd spent two hours in the Prado, gazing at the Velasquezes, hugging one another it was so good to be alive: we had canceled our bookings on a plane that had crashed. Or the lobsters we bought at Cape Split Harbour, Maine. There was a notice-board in the shack on the jetty and, pinned to it, a card on which a widow thanked her husband's friends for their contributions, and prayed, prayed to the Lord, that they lashed themselves to the boat when hauling in the pots.

How long, O Lord, how long? How long, when all the world was wheeling, could I stay on my feet . . ?

* * *

How long I shall never know, because the next thing I remember was staggering groggily across the parade-ground, with one arm over the corporal's shoulder and the other over Jacques's. Jacques then gave me a glass of water and, after that, he helped me into my clothes.

"You passed out," he said.

"Thank you," I said.

"Don't worry," he said. "They *are* only playing games."

It was late afternoon now. The corporal was in a better mood and allowed us to sit outside the guardroom. The sun was still hot. My head was still aching, but the crowd had simmered down and fortunately, for us, this particular section of the Benin Proletarian Army had found a new source of amusement — in the form of three Belgian ornithologists, whom they had taken prisoner in a swamp, along with a Leica lens the shape and size of a mortar.

The leader of the expedition was a beefy, red-bearded fellow. He believed, apparently, that the only way to deal with Africans was to shout. Jacques advised him to shut his mouth; but when one of the subalterns started tinkering with the Leica, the Belgian went off his head. How dare they? How dare they touch his camera? How dare they think they were mercenaries? Did they look like mercenaries?

"And I suppose they're mercenaries, too?" He waved his arms at us.

"I told you to shut your mouth," Jacques repeated.

The Belgian took no notice and went on bellowing to be set free. *At once! Now! Or else! Did he hear that?*

Yes. The subaltern had heard, and smashed his fist into the Belgian's face. I never saw anyone crumple so quickly. The blood gushed down his beard, and he fell. The subaltern kicked him when he was down. He lay on the dirt floor, whimpering.

"Idiot!" Jacques growled.

"Poor Belgium," I said.

* * *

The next few hours I would prefer to forget. I do, however remember that when the corporal brought back my things I cursed, "Christ, they've nicked my traveler's checks," — and Jacques, squeezing my arm very tightly, whispered, "Now *you* keep your mouth shut!" I remember "John Brown's Body" playing loudly over the radio, and the Head of State inviting the population, this time, to gather up the corpses. *Ramasser les cadavres* is what he said, in a voice so hoarse and sinister you knew a great many people had died, or would do. And I remember, at sunset, being driven by minibus to the Gezo Barracks where hundreds of soldiers, all elated by victory, were embracing one another, and kissing.

Our new guards made us undress again, and we were shut up, with other suspected mercenaries, in a disused ammunition shed. "Well," I thought, at the sight of so many naked bodies, "there must be some safety in numbers."

It was stifling in the shed. The other whites seemed cheerful, but the blacks hung their heads between their knees, and shook. After dark, a missionary doctor, who was an old man, collapsed and died of a heart attack. The guards took him out on a stretcher, and we were taken to the Sûreté for questioning.

Our interrogator was a gaunt man with hollow temples, a cap of woolly white hair and bloodshot slits for eyes. He sat sprawled behind his desk, caressing with his fingertips the blade of his bowie-knife. Jacques made me stand a pace behind him. When his turn came, he said loudly that he was employed by such and such a French engineering company and that I, he added, was an old friend.

"Pass!" snapped the officer. "Next!"

The officer snatched my passport, thumbed through the pages and began blaming me, personally, for certain events in Southern Africa.

"What are you doing in our country?"

"I'm a tourist."

"Your case is more complicated. Stand over there."

I stood like a schoolboy, in the corner, until a female sergeant took me away for fingerprinting. She was a very large sergeant. My head was throbbing; and when I tried to maneuver my little finger onto the inkpad, she bent it back double; I yelled "Ayee!", and her boot slammed down on my sandalled foot.

* * *

That night there were nine of us, all white, cooped up in a ramshackle office. The President's picture hung aslant on a bright blue wall and, beside it, were a broken guitar and a stuffed civet cat, nailed in mockery of the Crucifixion, with its tail and hindlegs together, and its forelegs splayed apart.

In addition to the mosquito-bites, my back had come up in watery blisters. My toe was very sore. The guard kicked me awake whenever I nodded off. His cheeks were cicatrized, and I remember thinking how remote his voice sounded when he said, *"On va vous fusiler."* At two or three in the morning, there was a burst of machine-gun fire close by, and we all thought, This is it. It was only a soldier, drunk or trigger-happy, discharging his magazine at the stars.

None of us was sad to see the first light of day.

It was another greasy dawn and the wind was blowing hard onshore, buffeting the buzzards and bending the coco palms. Across the compound a big crowd was jamming the gate. Jacques then caught sight of his houseboy and when he waved, the boy waved back. At nine, the French Vice-Consul put in an appearance,

183

under guard. He was a fat, suet-faced man, who kept wiping the sweat from his forehead and glancing over his shoulder at the bayonet points behind.

"*Messieurs*," he stammered, "this situation is perhaps a little less disagreeable for me than for you. Unfortunately, although we do have stratagems for your release, I am not permitted to discuss your liberty, only the question of food."

"*Eh bien!*" Jacques grinned. "You see my boy over there? Send him to the Boulangerie Gerbe d'Or and bring us sandwiches of *jambon, paté*, and *saussisson sec*, enough croissants for everyone, and three *petits pains au chocolat* for me."

"*Oui*," said the Vice-Consul weakly.

I then scribbled my name and passport number on a scrap of paper, and asked him to telex the British Embassy in Lagos.

"I cannot," he said. "I cannot be mixed up in this affair."

He turned his back, and waddled off the way he'd come, with the pair of bayonets following.

"Charming," I said to Jacques.

"Remember Waterloo," Jacques said. "And, besides, you may be a mercenary!"

Half an hour later, Jacques's bright-eyed boy came back with a basket of provisions. Jacques gave the guard a sandwich, spread the rest on the office table, sank his teeth into a *petit pain au chocolat*, and murmured, "Byzance!"

The sight of food had a wonderfully revivifying effect on the Belgian ornithologists. All through the night the three had been weepy and hysterical, and now they were wolfing the sandwiches. They were not my idea of company. I was left alone with them, when, around noon, the citizens of France were set at liberty.

"Don't worry," Jacques squeezed my hand. "I'll do what I can."

He had hardly been gone ten minutes before a big German, with a red face and sweeps of fair hair, came striding across the compound, shouting at the soldiers and brushing the bayonets aside.

He introduced himself as the Counsellor of the Germany Embassy.

"I'm so sorry you've landed in this mess," he said in faultless English. "Our ambassador has made a formal protest. From what I understand, you'll have to pass before some kind of military tribunal. Nothing to worry about! The commander is a nice chap. He's embarrassed about the whole business. But we'll watch you going into the building, and watch you coming out."

"Thanks," I said.

"Anyway," he added, "the Embassy car is outside, and we're not leaving until everyone's out."

"Can you tell me what *is* going on?"

The German lowered his voice: "Better leave it alone."

* * *

The tribunal began its work at one. I was among the first prisoners to be called. A young zealot started mouthing anti-capitalist formulae until he was silenced by the colonel in charge. The colonel then asked a few perfunctory questions, wearily apologized for the inconvenience, signed my pass, and hoped I would continue to enjoy my holiday in the People's Republic.

"I hope so," I said.

Outside the gate, I thanked the German who sat in the back of his air-conditioned Mercedes. He smiled, and went on reading the *Frankfurter Zeitung*.

It was grey and muggy and there were not many people on the street. I bought the government newspaper and read its account of the glorious victory. There were pictures of three dead mercenaries — a white man who appeared to be sleeping, and two very mangled blacks. Then I went to the hotel where my bag was in storage.

The manager's wife looked worn and jittery. I checked my bag and found the two traveler's checks I'd hidden in a sock. I cashed a hundred dollars, took a room, and lay down.

I kept off the streets to avoid the vigilante groups that roamed the town making citizens' arrests. My toenail was turning black and my head still ached. I ate in the room, and read, and tried to sleep. All the other guests were either Guinean or Algerian.

Around eleven next morning, I was reading the sad story of Mrs Marmeladov in *Crime and Punishment*, and heard the thud of gunfire coming from the Gezo Barracks. I looked from the window at the palms, the hawks, a woman selling mangoes, and a nun coming out of the convent.

Seconds later, the fruit-stall had overturned, the nun bolted, and two armored cars went roaring up the street.

There was a knock on the door. It was the manager.

"Please, *monsieur*. You must not look."

"What's happening?"

"Please," he pleaded, "you must shut the window."

I closed the shutter. The electricity had cut off. A few bars of sunlight squeezed through the slats, but it was too dark to read, so I lay back and listened to the salvoes. There must have been a lot of people dying.

There was another knock.

"Come in."

A soldier came into the room. He was very young and smartly turned out. His fatigues were criss-crossed with ammunition belts and his teeth shone. He seemed extremely nervous. His finger quivered round the trigger-guard. I raised my hands and got up off the bed.

"In there!" He pointed the barrel at the bathroom door.

The walls of the bathroom were covered with blue tiles and, on the blue plastic shower-curtain, was a design of tropical fish.

"Money," said the soldier.

"Sure!" I said. "How much?"

He said nothing. I glanced at the mirror and saw the gaping whites of his eyes. He was breathing heavily.

I eased my fingers down my trouser pocket: my impulse was to give him all I had. Then I separated one banknote from the rest, and put it in his outstretched palm.

"*Merci, monsieur!*" His lips expanded in an astonished smile. "*Merci,*" he repeated, and unlocked the bathroom door: "*Merci,*" he kept repeating, as he bowed and pointed his own way out into the passage.

That young man, it struck me, really had very nice manners.

* * *

The Algerians and Guineans were men in brown suits who sat all day in the bar, sucking soft drinks through straws and giving me dirty looks whenever I went in. I decided to move to the Hôtel de la Plage where there were other Europeans, and a swimming-pool. I took a towel to go swimming and went into the garden. The pool had been drained: on the morning of the coup, a sniper had taken a pot-shot at a Canadian boy who happened to be swimming his lengths.

The frontiers of the country were closed, and the airport.

That evening I ate with a Norwegian oil-man, who insisted that the coup had been a fake. He had seen the mercenaries shelling the palace. He had watched them drinking opposite in the bar of the Hotel de Cocotiers.

"All of it I saw," he said, his neck reddening with indignation. The palace had been deserted. The army had been in the barracks. The mercenaries had shot innocent people. Then they all went back to the airport and flew away.

"All of it," he said, "was fake."

"Well," I said, "if it was a fake, it certainly took me in."

It took another day for the airport to open, and another two before I got a seat on the Abidjan plane. I had a mild attack of bronchitis and was aching to leave the country.

* * *

On my last morning I looked in at the "Paris-Snack," which, in the old days when Dahomey was Dahomey, was owned by a Corsican called Guerini. He had gone back to Corsica while the going was good. The bar-stools were covered in red leather, and the barman wore a solid gold bracelet round his wrist.

Two Nigerian businessmen were seated at lunch with a pair of whores. At a table in the corner I saw Jacques.

"*Tiens?*" he said, grinning. "Still alive?"

"Thanks to you," I said, "and the Germans."

"*Braves* Bosches!" He beckoned me to the banquette. "Very intelligent people."

"*Braves* Bosches!" I agreed.

"Let's have a bottle of champagne."

"I haven't got much money."

"Lunch is on me," he insisted "Pierrot!"

The barman tilted his head, coquettishly, and tittered. "Yes, Monsieur Jacques."

"This is an English gentleman and we must find him a very special bottle of champagne. You have Krug?"

"No, Monsieur Jacques. We have Roerderer. We have Bollinger, and we have Mumm."

"Bollinger," I said.

Jacques pulled a face: "And in Guerini's time you could have had your oysters. Flown in twice a week from Paris . . . Belons . . . Claires . . . Portugaises . . ."

"I remember him."

"He was a character."

"Tell me," I leaned over. "What *was* going on?"

"Sssh!" his lips tightened. "There are two theories and, if I think anyone's listening, I shall change the subject."

I nodded and looked at the menu.

"In the official version," Jacques said, "the mercenaries were recruited by Dahomean émigrés in Paris. The plane took off from a military airfield in Morocco, refuelled in Abidjan . . ."

One of the whores got up from her table and lurched down the restaurant towards the Ladies.

"'66 was a wonderful year," said Jacques, decisively.

"I like it even older," I said, as the whore brushed past, "dark and almost flat . . ."

"The plane flew to Gabon to pick up the commander . . . who is supposed to be an adviser to President Bongo . . ." He then explained how, at Libreville, the pilot of the chartered DC-8 refused to go on, and the mercenaries had to switch to a DC-7.

"So their arrival was expected at the airport?"

"Precisely," Jacques agreed. "Now the second scenario . . ."

The door of the Ladies swung open. The whore winked at us. Jacques pushed his face up to the menu.

"What'll you have?" he asked.

"Stuffed crab," I said.

"The second scenario," he continued quietly, "calls for Czech and East German mercenaries. The plane, a DC-7, takes off from a military airfield in Algeria, refuels at Conakry . . . you understand?"

"Yes," I said, when he'd finished. "I think I get it. And which one do you believe?"

"Both," he said.

"That," I said, "is a very sophisticated analysis."

"This," he said, "is a very sophisticated country."

"I know it."

"You heard the shooting at Camp Gezo?"

"What was that?"

"Settling old scores," he shrugged. "And now the Guineans have taken over the Secret Police."

"Clever."

"This is Africa."

"I know and I'm leaving."

"For England?"

"No," I said. "For Brazil. I've a book to write."

"Beautiful country, Brazil."

"I hope so. "

"Beautiful women."

"So I'm told."

"So what is this book?"

"It's about the slave-trade."

"In Benin?"

"Also in Brazil."

"*Eh bien!*" The champagne had come and he filled my glass. "You have material!"

"Yes," I agreed. "I do have material."

JOHN RYLE

John Ryle's Warriors of the White Nile *is a popular ethnography of the Dinka of eastern Bahr-el-Ghazal, and his* An Unfinished Country *is a book on Brazil. In late 1988 he and two other relief workers drove to the southern Sudan, a week's journey from Khartoum, to report for a relief agency on its operations there among Dinkas displaced by famine and the five-year civil war between the Sudan People's Liberation Army and the government's National Army. The following excerpt is from an article about this journey that first appeared in* Granta. *Ryle lives in London.*

from "THE ROAD TO ABYEI"

SUPPING WITH THE DEVIL IN EL MUGLAD

The next day we drove to El Muglad, the heart of Humr Misseriya territory. Here the road to Abyei meets the road to El Meiram. It was the last place where there was any semblance of civil, as opposed to military, administration. As in Babanusa there was a large camp of displaced Dinkas by the railway. In Babanusa we had been forbidden to speak to them; in El Muglad we were not even allowed to visit the camp.

There was one relief agency in El Muglad. We arrived

there at an awkward moment. The agency had arranged a supper party for local dignitaries, but that morning an order had come from Khartoum expelling all foreign relief workers from Southern Kordofan. It looked as though their soirée might turn out to be an envoi — for us too. But their field officer, a genial Irishman, was unphazed, and, by lunchtime, the expulsion order had been revoked.

The field officer had a certain fame. At a time when no one was able to enter Abyei, he had succeeded in getting five hundred sacks of dura into the town — in the rainy season, on donkeys, having hired local militiamen to ride shotgun. He made no bones about it: nothing moved between El Muglad and Abyei without their say so. The priest in Abyei had sent him a message: dozens of Dinkas were dying every day. The only way to help them was to employ the same militias who had driven them from their homes. It was a heightened version of the dilemma facing all the relief organizations. The field officer knew where he stood.

"They're killers, aren't they, the militias?" I asked.

"Of course," he said, stroking his beard. "So are the SPLA."* And then he added: "I'd sup with the devil to get food to Abyei."

At dusk the guests arrived for the field officer's party.

In the yard of the house, under the mango trees, a long table was laid with food and flowers, and easy chairs made of bright nylon cord were arranged in a square.

*Sudan People's Liberation Army

On one side of the square sat the Misseriya elders in snow-white *jallabias*, with fine cotton scarves thrown over their shoulders and turbans perched on their heads like whipped cream. They clutched heavy walking sticks and murmured to their neighbours while waiting to eat. On the other side sat the agency staff. Government officials in western dress were on the third side — the chiefs of police from Babanusa and Abyei, the army commander and the head of military security in El Muglad. Next to the head of military security, and engaged in intimate conversation, was a small man in a pale-coloured safari suit. He was also clutching a walking stick. The field officer pointed him out to me. "That is the head of the Misseriya militia," he said. "Al Capone. Mr. Big. If he says 'Kill,' they kill."

Between Mr. Big and the head of military security was an Arab trader with a gold tooth and an ingratiating smile. This was Mr. Fixit, the go-between with the militiamen. Majak recognized him. Gold-tooth had grown up in Abyei. "He was just a truck driver then," said Majak. But it seemed he had grown rich on famine. It was he who had arranged the agency donkey train to Abyei. He owned many houses in El Muglad, including the one we were sitting in. We were, in a sense, his guests. Mark mentioned to him that we were planning to go to Abyei the next day, and soon Gold-tooth was arranging an escort for us. There was a whispered conversation and a nod from Mr. Big.

"We'll protect you against the SPLA," he said warmly. But we knew the SPLA was not the problem on the road to Abyei — it was not from them we needed protection: it was from the militiamen themselves. Nevertheless, Gold-tooth was very persuasive, and by the end of the conversation Mark and I found we had arranged to meet him for breakfast the next day to pick up an escort.

A nervous young northerner was circulating among the guests, a journalist on a Khartoum paper, *Senabil*, the voice of the fundamentalist Islamic Front. He wandered about with a Nikon camera round his neck, but never used it. He was a Misseri from Tibbun, where the slave market was supposed to be, and since he was a journalist, I felt it was reasonable to ask him about the market. He moved aside so that no one could hear.

"What is going on is *bad*," he said. "But you have to remember we are tribal people. All of us — Arab, Dinka — everyone. Even I — I am a Muslim, but I am also a Misseri. I practice *rituals* that are not Muslim at all. There is a tradition to everything we do, a *subtext*, a tribal subtext."

"Really?" I said, startled by the salon language, but aware that he had not answered my question.

"Yes," said the journalist, "my people are Arabs. But they are Africans also. It is their way. They come out of the forest on horses. They think everyone is their slave. When they take cattle it is not just for them, it is for the good of the tribe. They are not thieves, they are — what is the phrase?"

"Social bandits?" I said.

"Yes, yes," said the journalist. "Sociable bandits."

At that moment the only other expatriate in El Muglad arrived, a British employee of Chevron, the oil company that has the lion's share of the concessions in the southern Sudan. He was wearing a white T-shirt with a red inscription. In the twilight I could not quite make it out. One of the Misseriya elders gave it an uncomprehending glance.

The journalist studied it intently. "What does that say?" he asked.

I looked again. On the chest of the man from Chevron were the words "Fuck the World with Yuppie Condoms."

I said something about it being a tribal subtext, but I wasn't sure if the journalist got the joke. I wasn't sure if I got it myself. In the circumstances literary theory and the delinquent language of T-shirts both seemed obscene. Words had come unhinged from events; people took refuge in subtexts and incomprehensible slogans. I thought about our car with its bloody handprints, about the Misseriya elders with their beautiful white clothes, about slaves and social bandits, yuppie condoms, gold teeth. Bloodstains. The milk of birds. I felt stoned. I thought about what was happening in the South, just south of here, behind this screen of lies. Burning, looting, pillage, killing, torture, rape, starvation. I thought about the massacre in Ed Da'ein the year before. Such things could happen again. I tried to remember why I had come, why I had imagined there was anything I could usefully do or say about these terrible things.

THE ROAD TO ABYEI

In the morning Mark and I woke with the same feeling. We had gone too far: we felt ashamed in front of Majak;

arriving in Abyei under the protection of the militia was not the right way to begin. We drove to breakfast discussing how we could get out of the arrangement, but in the event the trader was all smiles and shrugs. On our heads be it. It was clear he reckoned that any transport operation we set up would require his services in the end. He wrote a letter of recommendation for us to a fellow-trader in Abyei. As we talked, a police sergeant stepped into his shop, looked around and exchanged a word with him. The policeman left with a fifty-pound note. Gold-tooth winked and sighed. "Their salaries are so low," he said. As we got up to leave we saw the leader of the militia, the sociable bandit, crossing the street; we moved away rapidly and drove out of town.

We followed the railway south of Abyei past pools of lotus flowers. To cross the watercourses, still deep with mud, we had to straddle the tracks and bump along the cross-ties. After a few miles, we branched west, hoping we had chosen the right road. There were no other vehicles. An Arab rode ahead of us on a donkey, a huge rusty spear under his arm. He looked like Don Quixote, an anachronism from the age before automatic weapons changed the rules of the game.

The road worsened and our progress was slow. There were Dinka boys herding cattle and goats. One was malnourished and needed a stick to walk. He was about six years old. We stopped to speak to him. His mother, he said, had given him to an Arab because she had no food. We drove on. Two boys in rags froze when they saw our car. We stopped and Majak got out and spoke to them in Dinka. They told him they were brothers;

the elder was nine, the younger five; they were running away from their Arab master and trying to rejoin their mother in El Muglad. They did not know what had become of their father. We gave them food and money, but their chances of making it without being recaptured were not too good.

Farther ahead, we saw another group of men under some trees. They also were on donkeys, but instead of spears they carried GM3 rifles, a type used by the army. They were not in uniform.

They motioned us to stop and we did so. I stowed my camera. Mark kept his foot poised over the accelerator. They asked where we had come from but they did not ask about the boys we had just spoken to. They peered in the back of the car and stared at the bloody handprints on the body-work. Then they waved us on.

We were entering what had once been Dinka territory. There were deserted villages with rusting water tanks and unused pumps; there were charred huts, and fields reclaimed by the bush. The vegetation was lusher and the woods thicker but many trees had been burned in forest fires. The evening sky grew dark, and we entered Abyei. The town looked eerie, swathed in smoke from cooking fires, with a faint glow on the trees as though the undergrowth was alight.

Just as we passed the first buildings, a soldier in camouflage ran from the shadows. *"Sebit!"* he shouted, "Halt!" He crouched down in the road with his rifle pointing at the windscreen. Mark doused the headlights and switched on the cabin light. The sentry demanded a password that we did not have. He asked where we had come from. There was only one place we could have come from. And there was only one place he could take us to. We drove on with him to the police post.

In Kordofan you are not supposed to arrive anywhere after dark. In Abyei it was rare for anyone to arrive at all. We did not know if the authorities had been advised of our departure from El Muglad, but it would not have been unusual if the message had not got through. In the event the police were perfectly civil. They took us to a nearby compound where the medical team were staying. Most of the team were asleep outside. Their mosquito nets shone in the moonlight like sails in harbour. The policemen, off-duty in their long white *jallabias*, glided like pleasure craft among them. For the moment we were glad to anchor there.

THE HARVEST OF SKULLS

In the morning Mark and I registered formally with the chief of police. To our surprise, he gave us permission to move around the town. A soldier accompanied us.

The army had burned the huts to the south of the town to discourage infiltration by the SPLA, and we were not allowed to go there. We could see a bare mound under a tree, the grave of a former Paramount Chief of the Ngok. Close to the airstrip there was the army compound, and beyond the airstrip were the ruins of the Harvard Project, an ill-fated scheme that was supposed to have made Abyei into a model of integrated rural development for the Sudan.

Abyei is a small town in normal times: a market

place, a street of shops, three schools, the airstrip and a sprawl of grass huts. It has a dry season population of about five thousand. That five thousand is composed of Dinka villagers, government administrators, and Arab traders. It is the administrative centre for the Ngok — in normal times. It is also a market town for other Dinka tribes from the South. It was these tribes who now formed the majority of the displaced population of the town. The dry season is the busy time in a place like Abyei: the harvest is over and people move between the surrounding villages and the cattle camps near the rivers; the rivers are low and travelling is easier. People come and go from October until April when the rains come again and planting begins.

But 1988, of course, had not been a normal year. Plenty of people left their villages to come to Abyei, but few went back. The seasonal movement had become one-way. The buildings of the town had diminished — the army having burned whole sections to the ground — but the population itself had tripled or quadrupled. It had been even larger in the months before we arrived, but malnutrition and disease had taken their toll. The rains had been plentiful, but the harvest had been pitiful — no one dared risk attacks from the militia. The only good thing was that the rains had brought fish. The dry season is the fishing season, and, in Abyei, fish had very likely saved more lives than relief agencies.

* * *

We walked through the centre of the town. There was a scattering of brick and cement buildings — schools commandeered by the army. The *suq*, the food market, was virtually empty; there were a few traders. In the crowded huts behind the *suq* lived the famine victims. Not everyone looked hungry: the worst cases were hidden. In many of the huts were sick children and old people, their skin in folds. One struggled to rise to her feet to greet us but she failed. They could not get to the hospital; the medical workers were forbidden to go to them.

In the hospital we found the medical team. It was administering the MUAC test — measuring children's middle and upper arm circumference — to discover the incidence of malnutrition. The children were given coloured wristbands to identify them as participants in the supplementary feeding programme. They got a mixture of dried skimmed milk, sugar and cereal called Unimix, brewed up in oil drums over charcoal fires in the hospital grounds. The hospital had no water supply. That also came in drums from the pump near the airstrip.

All over the town were children with pencil legs and balloon bellies wearing those tiny wristbands. They wore them like jewellery. Some had nothing else to wear. Some of them were too weak to walk and had to be carried by their siblings a mile or more from their huts to the hospital. Many had perpetual diarrhoea. Weak children are wiped out very quickly by diarrhoea. In the hospital they were given rehydration fluid, with one measure of salt to half-a-dozen of sugar; the measuring spoon bore this inscription: DO NOT USE IF MORE SALTY THAN TEARS.

There were few men under the age of forty in Abyei.

Among the Dinkas there were only women and children and old men to be seen. The young men had been killed by soldiers or by militiamen, or they had stayed deep in the bush with the remaining cattle, or they had joined the SPLA. But as we walked among the huts near the *suq* we were startled by half-a-dozen tall youths, bare-chested, sleek and healthy, with red berets and guns, who strode past us looking straight ahead. The youths did not acknowledge us or return our greeting — until we spoke to them in Nuer, the language of a Nilotic tribe to the east of Ngok. They were, we established, members of another government-backed militia, Anyanya II. Most of Anyanya II had abandoned the government side and gone over to the SPLA, but not these ones. They had been driven out by the SPLA and had fallen back on Abyei. The Nuer and their families had safe passes from the government. In one section of the town they had even set up a machine gun emplacement. It was pointing directly into the market place. The Nuer boys had exploited their position to loot the displaced Dinka. They had stolen all the fishing nets. In the whole town only the Nuer and a few Arab traders had cattle. It was a complicated war.

We were forbidden from visiting the church in Abyei, but in the open space in front of the barracks we met a Catholic father, the Italian priest who had alerted the relief people in El Muglad to the situation in Abyei earlier that year. At the height of the famine, he told us, he had fed seven thousand people in one day. "Beats Jesus," I murmured. Then I felt ashamed, because the priest was old and ill. Luckily he was also very deaf. He told us that the local church representative on the food distribution committee in Abyei had been arrested and the church, which arranged the relief supplies, was now prevented from distributing them.

* * *

We spent the night with the medical team again, and in the morning accompanied members of the Red Crescent on a burial detail. On the northeast side of the town there was a field of skulls. Corpses had been thrown there in the last months of the rains when the grass was tall. Now the grass was pale and dry. It had died down to reveal the shame of people too weary and ill to bury their dead. Vultures and hyenas had spread the remains far and wide. The Red Crescent volunteers, northerners, collecting the scattered bones to bury them in a single grave, made much of this. "We even gave them money to bury their dead," said the team leader, a doctor, "but they took the money and left the corpses in the grass."

"What would you have done?" I asked, "if you got money when you were starving? Wouldn't you feed the living first?"

The Red Crescent doctor turned back to the bones. The volunteers had dug a very shallow pit. The bones would soon be gnawed out of their graves again.

I walked across the plain with Majak counting skulls and noting the size of the skeletons. Adults and children seemed to be represented in equal numbers; on one skull the tribal marks of the Dinka tribe to the south were faintly visible — four lines across the forehead in a broad V-shape, gouged to the bone in early adolescence.

Tiny zig-zag cracks flickered across the cranium like streambeds on an extinct volcano. Everywhere there were bones. In the distance women came out of the woods with bundles of grass and firewood on their heads. It was a glimpse of normality in the charnel house. Famine or no famine, in Africa it is women who do the work.

* * *

A glimpse was all we got of the situation in Abyei. Someone had been talking to the chief of police and overnight he became distinctly sour. "Why are you here?" he kept asking us. "We do not know why you are here." In the end he turned to me. "You will have to leave on the next plane," he said. Majak, born and bred in Abyei, might have asked the chief of police the same question — why was he there? — but he did not. He had come back to find his hometown half-burned to the ground and under military occupation.

He told me he was trying to think of Abyei as another place altogether; a place where he had not been before.

"Why are you here?" As for me I couldn't really answer the question in a way that would have satisfied the police chief. I was there to assess the effectiveness of the relief programme. But the authorities in Abyei did not seem to think that it was a relief agency's job to assess its own programme, or, for that matter, even to administer it. In particular they did not think it was an agency's job to know anything about the people it was trying to help — especially if those people were Southerners, causing the government so much grief and dying in such embarrassing numbers.

More and more in the Sudan the most valuable function of relief agencies has come to be to protect people from their own government. The government does not take kindly to this.

CAROLYN FORCHÉ

In the foreword to Carolyn Forché's first book, Gathering the Tribes, *Stanley Kunitz wrote: "In her search for poetry, in her effort to understand it, she has bent over the potter's wheel, climbed mountain ranges, ventured into the Mojave Desert." In her second book,* The Country Between Us (1981), *Forché has traveled out of her own country into El Salvador, as may be observed in the following poem. Born in 1950, she was raised in Michigan and now teaches at George Mason University in Virginia. She has traveled widely and lived in Paris, Beirut, El Salvador, and South Africa. She is currently at work on a collection of essays, a novel, and a third book of poetry,* The Angel of History.

RETURN

for Josephine Crum

Upon my return to America, Josephine:
the iced drinks and paper umbrellas, clean
toilets and Los Angeles palm trees moving
like lean women, I was afraid more than
I had been, even of motels so much so
that for months every tire blow-out

was final, every strange car near the house
kept watch and I strained even to remember
things impossible to forget. You took
my stories apart for hours, sitting
on your sofa with your legs under you
and fifty years in your face.
                                        So you know
now, you said, what kind of money
is involved and that *campesinos* knife
one another and you know you should
not trust anyone and so you find a few
people you will trust. You know the mix
of machetes with whiskey, the slip of the tongue
that costs hundreds of deaths.
You've seen the pits where men and women
are kept the few days it takes without
food and water. You've heard the cocktail
conversation on which their release depends.
So you've come to understand why
men and women of good will read
torture reports with fascination.
Such things as water pumps
and co-op farms are of little importance
and take years.
It is not Che Guevara, this struggle.
Camillo Torres is dead. Victor Jara
was rounded up with the others, and José
Martí is a landing strip for planes
from Miami to Cuba. Go try on
Americans your long, dull story
of corruption, but better to give

them what they want: Lil Milagro Ramirez,
who after years of confinement did not
know what year it was, how she walked
with help and was forced to shit in public.
Tell them about the razor, the live wire,
dry ice and concrete, grey rats and above all
who fucked her, how many times and when.
Tell them about retaliation: José lying
on the flat bed truck, waving his stumps
in your face, his hands cut off by his
captors and thrown to the many acres
of cotton, lost, still, and holding
the last few lumps of leeched earth.
Tell them of José in his last few hours
and later how, many months later,
a labor leader was cut to pieces and buried.
Tell them how his friends found
the soldiers and made them dig him up
and ask forgiveness of the corpse, once
it was assembled again on the ground
like a man. As for the cars, of course
they watch you and for this don't flatter
yourself. We are all watched. We are
all assembled.
               Josephine, I tell you
I have not rested, not since I drove
those streets with a gun in my lap,
not since all manner of speaking has
failed and the remnant of my life
continues onward. I go mad, for example,
in the Safeway, at the many heads

of lettuce, papayas and sugar, pineapples
and coffee, especially the coffee.
And when I speak with American men,
there is some absence of recognition:
their constant Scotch and fine white
hands, many hours of business, penises
hardened by motor inns and a faint
resemblance to their wives. I cannot
keep going. I remember the American
attaché in that country: his tanks
of fish, his clicking pen, his rapt
devotion to reports. His wife wrote
his reports. She said as much as she
gathered him each day from the embassy
compound, that she was tired of covering
up, sick of his drinking and the loss
of his last promotion. She was a woman
who flew her own plane, stalling out
after four martinis to taxi on an empty
field in the *campo* and to those men
and women announce she was there to help.
She flew where she pleased in that country
with her drunken kindness, while Marines
in white gloves were assigned to protect
her husband. It was difficult work, what
with the suspicion on the rise in smaller
countries that gringos die like other men.
I cannot, Josephine, talk to them.

And so, you say, you've learned a little
about starvation: a child like a supper scrap

filling with worms, many children strung
together, as if they were cut from paper
and all in a delicate chain. And that people
who rescue physicists, lawyers and poets
lie in their beds at night with reports
of mice introduced into women, of men
whose testicles are crushed like eggs.
That they cup their own parts
with their bedsheets and move themselves
slowly, imagining bracelets affixing
their wrists to a wall where the naked
are pinned, where the naked are tied open
and left to the hands of those who erase
what they touch. We are all erased
by them, and no longer resemble decent
men. We no longer have the hearts,
the strength, the lives of women.
Your problem is not your life as it is
in America, not that your hands, as you
tell me, are tied to do something. It is
that you were born to an island of greed
and grace where you have this sense
of yourself as apart from others. It is
not your right to feel powerless. Better
people than you were powerless.
You have not returned to your country,
but to a life you never left.

1980

PEREGRINE HODSON

Peregrine Hodson read Oriental Studies at Oxford. In 1984 he left his career as a barrister to travel to Afghanistan as a free-lance for The Sunday Times. *With the* mujahedin, *he walked into Afghanistan with arms and ammunition for the rebels, and his narrow escapes from drowning and ambushes are recounted in* Under a Sickle Moon. *In the following excerpt he has just eluded Russian commandos and is hoping to make his way back to Pakistan with two other free-lance journalists. (Within a week of his return to London he was hospitalized with hepatitis.) Hodson lived for five years in Japan, where he was employed as an investment banker, and his resulting book is* Circle Around the Sun. *He is a Fellow of the Royal Asiatic Society.*

from UNDER A SICKLE MOON

Nuristan

The cave was our home for the next few days. There were two or three families in the vicinity and the men used to visit us. Yaqub, the man who had given us handfuls of nuts and berries when we first arrived, visited us every day and once his elderly father accompanied him. There was also a lapis trader on his way to Pakistan and a middle-aged man who, it was said, had two beautiful wives in a cave on the other side of the river and a Kalashnikov to protect them.

The days were bright and clear but autumn was already in the air and the leaves of a nearby spinney of beech trees were turning gold. From eight or nine o'clock in the morning till six o'clock in the evening the jets attacked in waves; the sound of bombs exploding reverberated up the valley and every few hours spotter planes flew over.

"Bombing and spotter planes getting a bit oppressive," I wrote in my diary. "Cold days being in cave, but dangerous to be outside. Makes men feel like mice under the unpredictable eye of savage birds of prey. Washing socks and hearing the sounds of jets sweeping through the roar of the water and the wind through the booming rocks. The scene like a Shell calendar but everything somehow discoloured."

The syntax reflects my state of mind when I wrote the passage: time was fractured and suspended in a vacuum, events were isolated and had no connection with one another. It required a considerable mental effort to think beyond our immediate situation and we were struggling to ignore an undermining sense of fatalism. I wrote my diary. Julian listened to Bob Marley tapes. In desperation we took turns reading my pocket Bible.

Peter was very quiet. He spent most of the time in his sleeping bag at the back of the cave and I noticed that the whites of his eyes had a yellowish tinge, suggesting hepatitis. Every evening we tuned in to the World Service but there was no mention of any new offensive in the Panjshir valley.

It was disturbingly unreal to be caught in the middle of a forgotten war. At times it was like being in the grip of a massive hallucination: living on nuts and berries in a cave, being bombed by Soviet jets. The outside world acquired another meaning.

Early in the morning, when the mountains were still dark against the dawn, I used to go to the torrent, splash its icy water on my face, then watch the sunlight gradually cover the peaks high above the cave. But before the chill of the night had faded from the rocks, the bombing began once more and I returned to the gloom of the cave.

The uncertainty was weighing on our minds and our tempers began to fray: Julian complained bitterly when I lit a cigarette in the cave; I accused him of wasting the batteries of my Walkman; Peter sulked in his sleeping bag. There were long silences between one conversation and the next. To stop our morale deteriorating further, we tried once more to find a guide, but most of the men we asked were ignorant of the way or unwilling to go with us. Once it seemed as if we had succeeded when Yaqub reluctantly agreed to take us; but he qualified his promise with *"Insha'allah"* in a wilting tone of voice and I realised we would not be able to rely on him.

We also needed food for the journey into Nuristan, and spent hours negotiating with two shepherds to buy a sheep. One of them was a slow-witted youth of seventeen with a sun-darkened face and clumsy movements, wrapped in the folds of a torn petou. His companion was the owner of the sheep, a small, wizened man with a shrewd eye for business. Unfortunately, a speech impediment rendered him virtually dumb and the bargain was pursued through a bewildering sequence of gestures, sharp inarticulate moans and shaking of heads, while the simpleton made dismal attempts to mediate. In the end, several days and numerous meetings later, the deal fell through.

Without food, we could not rely on the kindness of our neighbours indefinitely. Entries in my diary got shorter and I could not conceal my misgivings about our future: "Our situation in a nutshell: we only have one escape route, we don't have much time or strength — and we don't have a reliable guide. We have to get the trip right. If not we will be too weak to do it a third time."

I decided to go down the valley once more to find a guide. On the way down I made enquiries of groups of villagers camped under rock overhangs or in the shelter of sheepfolds, but none of them knew of a guide to take us over the pass. I arrived at the *kargah* at twilight; there was heavy fighting in the village and there were only a few *mujahedin* present. I wrote another letter to Commander Kohzad outlining our probable route into Nuristan and gave it to one of the *mujahedin*. He was against our departure.

"Wait another few days. The Shuravi will go and then it will be easy. We will find your horses and equipment and there will be no problem." But his optimism seemed misplaced and did nothing to reassure me. Once he realised we were determined to go his manner changed.

"If you go now, you go without the permission of Commander Kohzad. Your safety is no longer his responsibility. If you meet with bad men that is your affair." He warned me of the unreliable character of the Nuristanis. "Some say they are not true Muslims, but *kafir*. They are a stupid and lazy people: the women work in the fields and the men do nothing but drink chai. If they want something they steal it from travellers. Only a fool travels in Nuristan without a gun."

He went on to describe notorious acts of brigandage, each more bloodthirsty than the last, until he was in a more cheerful mood. "But if you must go it is God's will, *Mosafer aziz khodast* — the traveller is beloved of God. I will give you some food for your journey; you'll be lucky if you can buy an egg in Nuristan." We tied bundles of sugar, tea, bread and meat into my petou and said good-bye to one another. It was now dark and I still had no guide.

I descended a path and came to a shadowy collection of buildings; closer to them I saw that most of the houses lacked roofs and tarpaulins had been stretched across the walls. Here and there the gleam of a lamp shone in the darkness. I went from one to the next in search of a guide. Once again I was unsuccessful, but several times the name "Mustapha Khan" was mentioned as a man who might help me. A group of men invited me to join them for a glass of chai and one of them set off in search of the elusive Mustapha Khan.

It was almost like a homecoming to be alone once more among Afghans and for the first time in several days my spirits lifted. But the conversation was solemn.

215

"Tell your people what is happening here. Tell them what you have seen with your own eyes," were the constant refrains. "If your people believe the Shuravi we are lost."

Half an hour later Mustapha Khan stepped into the circle. He was older than I had expected, a man of sixty or so with a slight stoop.

"Who is seeking Mustapha Khan the hunter?" he called out. "I know every pathway, every stream and every cave in this valley. I can guide a man anywhere, for a price."

We shook hands and studied each other's faces in the lamplight. His eyes were quick and knowing and when he smiled I saw his two lower front teeth were missing. He looked a rogue, but I liked his confident lack of modesty and we quickly agreed a price.

We set off back to the cave with Mustapha Khan leading the way, staff in hand. He moved over the rough stones at a good steady pace, and only an occasional rattle of loose pebbles marked his passing. The moon rose, bathing the rocks and trees in still, shining light. We climbed without a rest until we came to an icy spring hidden in the shadow of the cliffs.

As we moved through the crystalline night air the subdued roar of water tumbling in the darkness beneath us, the war was unimaginably distant. Mustapha Khan beckoned to me to leave the path and I followed him down to the torrent's edge. He knelt down and removed a small tin box from underneath a boulder and poured its contents on to a flat rock. From a waistcoat pocket he produced another packet of powder and carefully measured out some of it on to the rock beside the first mound. He mixed the mounds together in a practised rhythm, several times dipping his hand into the stream and shaking sparkling drops of water over the darkened surface. Then he chose a smooth pebble from the water's edge and ground the mixture in a swift circular motion until it was spread in a thin layer. Up till then he had said nothing, but after patting the substance and sprinkling it with a few more drops of water from the river he turned to me. "Take some, Abdul," he said, "it will do you no harm." By now I had guessed that the mysterious substance was naswar and I put a pinch under my tongue. A satisfying heat radiated under my tongue, my pulse quickened and the heaviness vanished from my legs.

We had just begun to cross the river when there was the sharp whistling sound of a mortar to our right and we glimpsed a bright light disintegrate with a bang a few hundred feet below us. Mustapha Khan muttered something and launched himself across a makeshift bridge of branches paved with stones. Halfway across he stumbled, dislodging two large rocks which slipped into the hissing water with a heavy splash, and he only just managed to scramble to the other side. The branches were still in place and I teetered across them towards the staff which Mustapha Khan held out towards me. There were no more mortars and we continued on in silence. But the spell of the moonlight was broken.

When we reached the cave it was in darkness and Peter and Julian were asleep: I lit the lamp and introduced them to Mustapha Khan. We talked briefly of the journey and decided to climb the pass the following day. Mustapha seemed completely unperturbed by our company and when we arranged our blankets for the night he lay down between Julian and myself as if spending the night with three Englishmen was the most natural thing in the world for him.

It was still dark when Mustapha Khan woke us and for the next few hours we climbed without a break, except for pauses when jets or spotter planes passed over. By mid-morning we had crossed the minefield and reached the edge of the plateau where we had camped previously. We stopped for a rest and shared our meat and bread with Mustapha Khan who in turn produced generous supplies of dried mulberries and *qu'rut* and told us of his exploits as a hunter. One of his closest companions, a skilful hunter like himself, lived in the village over the mountains. On arrival we should ask for a man whose name sounded like "Muddy Sore" who would surely help us.

We reached the top of the pass by mid-afternoon: Mustapha Khan pointed down into the neighbouring valley several thousand feet below at some dark specks at the foot of a grey mountain.

He was eager to return before nightfall so we paid him at once and thanked him for his help. Then we shook hands and he kissed us farewell.

The way down led across a scree of jagged black boulders. It was one of the most uncomfortable and desolate stretches of country I have encountered. Scott's description of the Antarctic — "God this is an awful place!" — fitted it perfectly and when the first flecks of sleet began to sting through the air, my misery was complete.

We found a herd of goats sheltering in a fold of the hills and some villagers watching over them. The man had dispiriting news for us: a few hours earlier Soviet troops had attacked and overrun the village and surrounded the *mujahedin* in their *kargah*. The people had fled to the north of the village and taken refuge in caves and sheepfolds. The men were slow-witted with the cold and the shock of the past few hours, and were unable to help us further. To our right, a cloud of smoke was rising over the crest of a hill. It seemed unwise to spend any more time in conversation so we took the path to our left which the men assured us led toward Nuristan. Half an hour later we came to a huddle of buildings and a boy led us to a small, windowless hut where we slumped down on a straw-covered floor. After a few minutes he returned with some blankets and a lamp which he set in a niche in the wall.

"You are safe here," he said; "the Shuravi are two or three miles away and will not be here before morning, *Insha'allah*. Now I will try to find you something to eat. But we have very little food. Most of our possessions are in the village. We only live here in the summer, when the sheep are in the higher pastures — or when the Shuravi come."

The boy vanished into the night and we settled down to wait. The warmth of the little room and the gentle light of the lamp were deeply soothing. Peter lay down and went to sleep immediately, while Julian and I sat in silence, listening to the wind rustling in the roof of thorns and leaves. There was nothing to be said.

I was woken by the arrival of an old man bringing a plate of eggs and bread which he placed on the floor in front of us. He had the slanting eyes and wispy beard of an Uzbek. He introduced himself as the village headman; his son was the local *mullah* and the building we were staying in was the village mosque. The boy was his grandson and would guide us over the next pass into Nuristan.

While eating we heard the sound of a plane circling overhead and the old man became agitated, wringing his hands and moaning softly to himself.

"Taking infra-red photographs," said Peter. "The *muj* still haven't got used to them. Even if they're undercover, heat concentrations reveal their position. Nothing much they can do about it, except stop lighting fires."

We gave the old man some money for the meal, turned down the lamp and settled down to sleep. I considered briefly what might happen if we were captured, but I was too tired to give it much thought. For the moment it was good to be wrapped in a blanket listening to the wind buffeting outside the door.

* * *

"Quickly! Quickly! Get up! Get up!" The lamp was lit and the old man was standing over us, wrapped in a coat and wearing thick leather boots. In his anxiety, he lapsed from Dari into another dialect which I could not understand, but it was clear from his shaking hands and voice that there was no time to lose. We threw our things together, pulled on our boots and followed the swaying lamp into the darkness.

Outside the boy was waiting for us. The old man handed him the lamp then bent down to hoist a huge bundle of clothes and blankets on to his shoulders; he extinguished the lamp and tied it to the old man's pack, then we set off. At first the old man went ahead, but after a quarter of an hour the path rose more steeply and he began to fall behind. Several times he stopped to ease the pack on his shoulders and finally he came to a halt by the side of the path and unhitched the pack on to a boulder. I offered to take it but when I put my arms through the carrying cords and took the weight of the pack on my back I could hardly stand. My weakness shocked me but there was nothing I could do: it was too heavy for me. The old man tied a few items into a blanket and hid the remainder of the pack under a thorn bush.

We stumbled on through the darkness. Now and again flares shot up over the village behind us, and mortars and artillery reverberated in the hills around us. "*Ay khoda, khoda*," the old man groaned. "The Shuravi are terrible, terrible, terrible." Half an hour later he left us. We stood in silence and watched the dawn filter into the east: mist and clouds hung suspended against the mountain walls. A thick column of smoke was drifting up from the floor of the valley and the morning air was bitter with the smell of ash. A wind blew across the rocky slope, rattling the branches of some thorn bushes and, in between gusts, there was the sound of a small child crying. The boy was telling me to wait until his grandfather returned when he clutched at his stomach and slipped away behind some boulders. Some time later he staggered into view, still adjusting the cord of his trousers, and mumbled, *"mariz* — sick."

The sun cast a pale yellow light from behind a bank of grey cloud and the high-pitched wailing of the child echoed across the wet stones. The old man reappeared with a bundle of dried mulberries and bread which he pressed into Julian's pack. We gave him as much money as we could afford, and set off after the boy who had already started walking up the pass.

The path was still in shadow and the ground was frozen hard beneath our feet. The boy stopped repeatedly to relieve himself. Eventually he sat down on a rock and called out that he could go no further. We tried to persuade him to go on but it was hopeless: his cheeks were hollow and his eyes were half-closed with exhaustion. We waited for him to recover his strength and the sun grew hot on our shoulders. The boy was lying on a rock: his clothes were in rags and his feet were encased in thin brown plastic shoes, split at the heels, crudely patched with strips of green plastic and tied together with strips of torn cloth. He turned his back to the wind which twitched the loosely wrapped petou from his body, displaying a shirt tail and trousers, streaked with blood and feces.

We ate a few handfuls of mulberries and I bent down to drink at a glistening rivulet of water running between narrow margins of close-cropped grass. It was numbingly cold and the grass and weeds at the water's edge were encased in shining beads of ice.

A helicopter flew over the mountains further down the

valley. For a minute or two it hovered on the edge of the cloud of smoke from the burning village, then an explosion erupted beneath it and, as it wheeled away, another darker cloud of smoke and dust climbed into the sky.

"Must have been a big one," said Peter, "probably a thousand-pound bomb."

The boy was still asleep on the rock and I had to shake him by the shoulder to wake him. We had no idea where the pass crossed over into Nuristan: only the boy knew where it was. He was on the verge of unconsciousness and for a quarter of an hour I had to shout and bully him into giving us directions. His mouth was thick with saliva and several times I had to ask him to repeat himself. At last I understood enough to have a reasonable idea of the direction we needed to take. His eyes had closed again and when I put some money into his hand his fingers remained motionless.

Our progress up the pass was heartbreakingly slow. Peter was very weak and we stopped every fifteen minutes. I kept looking back at the place where we had left the boy and finally, to my relief, I saw that he had disappeared from the rock.

The peaks seemed to grow sharper in the bright frosty air and the sky was a cloudless blue. In the middle of the morning several MiG 27s and Su 17s howled overhead in a plunging attack and began bombing the valley below. The attacks went on, intermittently, for the next two hours. But we reached the top of the pass, and sat watching the planes race over the mountains, listening to the monstrous thumping of their bombs. The roaring of demons in the sky and the mountains trembling, fire and terror: how could the people who lived in these remote hills and valleys possibly begin to understand what was happening to them?

From where we were, safe on the heights overlooking the valley, the bombing was so much noise and smoke: just as the battlefields of Troy must have appeared to the inhabitants of Mount Olympus. For a few minutes I ignored the dangers of hubris and considered the similarities between those all-too-human deities and ourselves. Observers from another world, we had passed among the people, seen their suffering and heard their prayers, received their kindness and momentarily known the turbulence of war. But all the while we had been wearing an invisible armour: the knowledge of another life to which we could eventually return.

In front of us, the desolate beauty of Nuristan stretched out toward the majestic range of Hindu Kush and freedom. Behind us were the mountains and valleys and plains of Afghanistan, and a people who remained captives in their own country. As we began the descent into Nuristan I felt like an escaped prisoner: relief and exhilaration, mixed with guilt and regret for those that could not come with me. We crossed another, mine-strewn plateau and descended into a barren valley where an icy river tumbled past a few, abandoned shelters made of stone and timber. It was late afternoon, the sun had dropped below the mountains and a sharp wind was picking up. The boy had told us of a village an hour's journey over the pass into Nuristan, but we had been walking for three or four hours already and there was still no sign of it. We briefly considered spending the night in one of the shelters but then decided to press on.

An hour later we rounded a bend in the river and saw a thread of smoke drifting from between some large rocks at the bottom of a cliff. The fire belonged to a family from Khunduz who assured us that there was, indeed, a village another hour's walk down the river.

We walked until it grew dark. A figure on horseback approached us out of the twilight. Again we asked how far it was to the next village and again the reply was an hour, or even a little longer. The journey had become unreal and I toyed with the whimsical idea that travellers in search of Shangri-La might well have received the same answer, always the same answer, "Yes, keep on, it isn't far from here, only another hour, another day, you may get there by candlelight . . ." spurring them on toward an unknown end.

The moon was high in the sky by the time we came to the glow of a lamp hanging inside a tent. Some men, refugees from the Panjshir, invited us inside to share their meal and stay the night. We accepted gratefully: we had been travelling almost continuously for more than eighteen hours and were glad to be able to rest at last. As we sat drinking chai I asked one of them, out of idle interest, how far he thought it might be to the next village. I had already guessed the answer and I was not disappointed.

"With a good horse — maybe an hour. *Insha'allah*."

PART THREE

CLASSIC QUESTERS IN EXTREMIS

We snapped the branch into three pieces, laid them together on the snow, and stood over the twigs until, with the aid of Gibbon's noble prose, they began to burn.

—*John Mills*

AL PURDY

Al Purdy has traveled to various parts of the world, but his extensive travels throughout Canada, ever since riding freight trains to the west coast in the thirties, have helped map the country for younger poets influenced by his sense of place and history. Among his books are The Cariboo Horses, North of Summer: Poems from Baffin Island, *and* The Collected Poems of Al Purdy, *which recently earned him a second Governor General's Award. In the following Baffin poem from 1967, the mock-heroic tone discloses none of the three-day illness that he suffered there with "no one to give me a pill or needle."*

WHEN I SAT DOWN TO PLAY THE PIANO

He cometh forth hurriedly from his tent
and looketh for a quiet sequestered vale
he carrieth a roll of violet toilet tissue
and a forerunner goeth ahead to do him honour
yclept a snotty-nosed Eskimo kid
He findeth a quiet glade among great stones
squatteth forthwith and undoeth trousers

"The Irrational Man" by Wm. Barrett in hand
while the other dismisseth mosquitoes
and beginneth the most natural of natural functions
buttocks balanced above the boulders
Then
     dogs[1]
          Dogs[3]
              DOGS[12]
                    all shapes and sizes
all colours and religious persuasion
a plague of dogs rushing in
having been attracted by the philosophic climate
and being wishful to learn about existential dogs
and denial of the self with regard to bitches
But let's call a spade a shovel
therefore there I am I am I think that is
surrounded by a dozen dozen fierce Eskimo dogs
with an inexplicable (to me) appetite
for human excrement
                  Dear Ann Landers
what would you do?
                  Dear Galloping Gourmet
what would you do
                  in a case like this?
Well I'll tell you
NOT A DAMN THING
You just squat there cursing hopelessly
while the kid throws stones
and tries to keep them off and out from under
as a big black husky dashes in
swift as an enemy submarine

white teeth snapping at the anus
I shriek
> and shriek
> (the kid laughs)
> and hold onto my pants
> sans dignity
> sans intellect
> sans Wm. Barrett
> and damn near sans anus

Stand firm little Eskimo kid
it giveth candy if I had any
it giveth a dime in lieu of same
STAND FIRM
Oh avatar of Olympian excellence
noble Eskimo youth do your stuff
Zeus in the Arctic dog pound
Montcalm at Quebec
Horatius at the bridge
Leonidas at Thermopylae
Custer's last stand at Little Big Horn
"KEEP THEM DAMN DOGS OFF
YOU MISERABLE LITTLE BRAT!"

Afterwards
Achilles retreateth without honour
unzippered and sullen
and sulketh in his tent till next time appointed
his anus shrinketh
he escheweth all forms of laxative and physick
> meanwhile
and prayeth for constipation

addresseth himself to the Eskimo brat miscalled
"Lo tho I walk thru the valley of
the shadowy kennels
in the land of permanent ice cream
I will fear no huskies
for thou art with me
and slingeth thy stones forever and ever
thou veritable David
Amen"

P.S. Next time I'm gonna take a gun
Kikastan Islands

RUSSELL BANKS

Born in the United States in 1940, Russell Banks is the author of eleven books of fiction, including Searching for Survivors, Success Stories, Affliction, *which was shortlisted for the International Fiction Prize, and* The Sweet Hereafter. *He has lived and worked in Florida, Jamaica, and other parts of the Caribbean, and now teaches at Princeton. In the following passage from his novel* Continental Drift, *the two main themes, one about New Englander Bob Dubois and the other about Vanise Dorsinville, now fleeing Haiti with her nephew and baby, have converged aboard a fishing boat smuggling aliens into Florida. This horrifying account is the imagined fate of would-be citizens who put their lives in unconscionable hands. The worst journeys today are doubtless the journeys of refugees — movements of the persecuted and unfortunate poor, which remain largely untold but for occasional writers who find it morally imperative to give voice to such migrations.*

from CONTINENTAL DRIFT

Their first sight of land is the flash of the lighthouse below Boca Raton, which tells them that the *Belinda Blue* has come out of the Gulf Stream farther to the north than they intended, miles from where they planned to drop off the Haitians and so far from Moray Key that they can't hope to get home before dawn. Tyrone grumbles and blames Bob, who blames the southeast wind and his not being used to running the *Belinda Blue* with so much weight aboard.

It's dark, thickly overcast this close to shore, and the sea is high. The boat rides the swells, and when she crests, they can see the beach stretching unbroken from the pink glow of Miami in the south to the lights of Fort Lauderdale in the north. Then, when the boat slides down into the belly between the huge waves, they see nothing but a dark wall of water and a thin strip of sky overhead.

Frightened, the Haitians have crawled aft from their lean-to, and peer wide-eyed at the sea. The pitch and roll of the boat tosses them against one another, and several of them begin to cross themselves and pray. The old woman, hiding behind the others, has started to sing, a high-pitched chanting song that repeats itself over and over. The boy Claude is still up on the bridge with Bob, where Tyrone has joined them. Claude, too, is frightened, but he watches the white man's face closely, as if using it to guide his own emotions. Right now, the white man, who is at the wheel, seems angry with his mate, and the mate seems angry also, for they are scowling and shouting at one another in the wind.

"For Christ's sake, we drop them off at Hollywood or Lauderdale now, they won't know where the hell they are! They'll get busted in an hour! They'll stick out like sore thumbs, for Christ's sake! If we take them down to

Coral Gables, like we said we'd do, they'll get to cover in Little Haiti right away."

"Too far, Bob! Dem too heavy in dis sea, mon! Got to leave 'em up here, let 'em find dere own way!"

Bob argues a little longer, but he knows the man is right. "All right. Hollywood, then. Be midnight by then, we can drop them by the A-One-A bridge at Bal Harbour. The water's calm there once you get around the point. Christ only knows how they'll get down to Miami from there, though."

"Not our problem, Bob."

"Go down and talk to them," Bob says to Tyrone. "Tell them what's happening, you know? Maybe one of 'em's got family or something can come out with a car. Who knows? At least let 'em know where they're going to get dropped off. Draw a map or something for 'em."

Tyrone shrugs his shoulder and turns away. "Don't make no never mind to dem, mon. Long's dem in America."

"Yeah, sure, but do it anyway." Bob brings the boat around to port, facing her into the waves, and moves the throttle forward. The boat dips and slides down and hits the gully, yaws into the sea and starts to climb again. Tyrone motions for Claude to follow, and the two of them start down from the bridge. When the boat reaches the crest and hangs there for a second before beginning the descent again, Bob looks off to his starboard side and sees the beach like a taut, thin white ribbon and believes that he can hear the waves crashing not a half mile distant. Beyond the beach he can see the lights of houses between the sea and the road to Palm Beach,

where here and there cars move slowly north and south
— ordinary people going about their night's ordinary
business.

Again, the boat rolls a second and starts the drop,
pitches across the smooth trough, yaws between waves
and rises, and this time, when it reaches the crest of the
wave, Bob looks out over the dripping bow and sees
the lights of another boat. It's less than two hundred
yards off the portside and headed north, and it's a large
boat, twice the size of the *Belinda Blue* — that's all
Bob can see of her, before the boat disappears from
sight, and Bob realizes that they have pitched again and
are descending. He yells for Tyrone, who's under the
tarpaulin talking to the Haitians, and frantically waves
him up to the bridge. "Boat!" he shouts. "Boat!"

Tyrone scrambles up the ladder to the bridge, and
when the *Belinda Blue* crests again, Bob points out the
lights of the stranger.

"Coast guard," Tyrone says. "Cut de lights."

Bob obeys at once. "Oh, Jesus H. Christ!" he says.
"The fucking coast guard." He can hear the twin diesels
that power her and can see that, yes, it is a cutter, ninety
or a hundred feet long, with the high conning tower and
the fifty- and sixty-caliber machine guns bristling at the
stern and bow. "I don't think they spotted us," Bob says.
But then he realizes that the cutter is turning slowly to
port. "Oh, fuck, here they come!"

Tyrone reaches out and cuts the throttle back.

"What the fuck you doing?"

"Bring 'er around, gwan get dem Haitians off,"
Tyrone says.

"What? What're you saying?" Bob grabs Tyrone's shoulder and flips the man around to face him.

"Dem can get to shore from here, mon!" Tyrone shouts into the wind. "It's not far!"

"Not in this sea, for Christ's sake! We can't *do* that! We can't!"

"Got to, Bob!" The Jamaican turns away and starts to leave.

"Wait, goddammit! *I'm* the fucking captain, you're not!"

Tyrone looks at Bob with cold disgust. "We cut dem fuckin' Haitians loose, den *maybe* we get home tonight. Captain."

"Otherwise?"

Tyrone does not answer.

Bob shouts, "They've got us anyhow, the coast guard! We're caught anyhow!"

"No, dem got to stop to pick up de Haitians. Wid dem gone, de boat fast enough to get us out of here first maybe!"

"Or else we end up in jail, and they go back to Haiti! Right? Right, Tyrone?"

Again, Tyrone says nothing.

Bob says, "All right. Go ahead." Tyrone leaps away and down the ladder.

Bob looks over the rail to the deck below, where the Jamaican frantically, roughly, yanks the Haitians out from under the tarpaulin. He's shouting at them in Creole and Jamaican patois, making it very clear that they must jump into the water, and they must do it now. Every few seconds he points out to where

237

they spotted the coast guard cutter, though Bob can no longer see her, for they're down in the trough between waves again, and Tyrone pulls at their arms, shoving the Haitians toward the starboard rail, but they shake their heads no, and a few start to cry and wail, no, no, they will not go. They cling to one another and to the chocks and cleats and gunwales and look wild-eyed about them, at the towering sea, at Bob up on the bridge, at Tyrone jumping angrily about, at each other, and they weep and beg, No, no, please don't make us leave the boat for the terrible sea.

The *Belinda Blue* rises to the ridge of water, and Bob sees the cutter again, now clearly turning back toward them, and they've got searchlights whipping wands of light across the water. "They're turning, they're gonna try to board us!" he yells down, and he sees Tyrone step from the cabin with a rifle in his hand, the shark gun, a 30-06 with a scope, and Bob says quietly, "Tyrone, for Christ's sake."

The Haitians back swiftly away from Tyrone, horrified. With the barrel of the gun, he waves them toward the rail and tells them once again to jump, but they won't move. The babies are screaming now, and the women and several of the men are openly weeping. Claude's face is frozen in a look of amazed grief.

Tyrone pulls the trigger and fires into the air, and one of the Haitians, the boy Claude, leaps into the water and is swept away. A second follows, and then a woman. Tyrone screams at the rest to jump, and he fires again.

Bob bellows from the bridge, "Tyrone! For Christ's sake, stop! They're drowning!" But the Jamaican is now bodily hurling the Haitians into the sea, one after the other, the old man, the woman with the two small children, Vanise and her child, the old woman. He's clearing the deck of them. They weep and cry out for help from God, from the loas, from Bob, who looks on in horror, and then they are gone, lifted up by the dark waves and carried away toward the shore.

Tyrone scrambles back up to the bridge, the rifle still in his hand, and he wrenches the wheel away from Bob and hits the throttle hard, bringing the boat swiftly around to port and away. Off to the north a few hundred yards, its searchlights sweeping over the water, the cutter has slowed and stopped, for they have apparently spotted the Haitians bobbing in the water. Bob sees that they are dropping a lifeboat from the stern. He follows one of the beams of light out to where it has fixed on a head in the water, one of the young men, and then he sees the man go down. The light switches back and forth, searching for him, then seems to give up and move on, looking for others. "They're drowning!" he cries. "They're drowning!"

Tyrone doesn't answer. He shoves the rifle at Bob and takes the wheel with both hands, bucking the *Belinda Blue* into the waves, driving her against mountains of water and quickly away from shore, heading her straight out to sea.

Bob holds the gun for a moment, looks at it as if it were a bloody ax. Then he lifts it over his head with two hands and hurls it into the sea.

Tyrone looks over his shoulder at Bob and says, "Good idea, mon. Dem prob'ly heard de shootin'.

Nobody can say we de ones doin' de shootin' now. Got no gun, got no Haitians," he says, smiling. Then he says, "Better clear de deck of anyt'ing dem lef' behind, mon."

Slowly Bob descends to the deck, and kneeling down, he crawls under the tarpaulin, reaching around in the dark, until he comes up with several battered suitcases, a cloth bundle, a woven bag, and he tosses them overboard one by one, watches them bob on the water a second, then swiftly sink.

* * *

It's a pink dawn, the eastern sky stretched tight as silk on a frame. Overhead, blue-gray rags of cloud ride in erratic rows, while in the west, over southern Florida, the sky is dark and overcast. A man with white hair leads a nosy, head-diving dog, a blue-black Labrador, from his house and down the sandy walkway to the beach.

The man and the dog stroll easily south, and now and then the man stops and picks up a piece of weathered beach glass for his collection. The dog turns and waits, and when the man stands and moves on, the dog bounds happily ahead.

A quarter mile from where they started, the dog suddenly darts into the water, and the man stops and stares, as a body, a black woman's body, passes by the dog and with the next wave is tossed onto the beach. A few yards beyond, a child's body has been shoved up onto the beach, and beyond that, a pair of men lie dead on the sand.

The man counts five bodies in all, and then he turns and runs back up the beach, his dog following, to his home, where he calls the local police. "Haitians, I'm sure of it. Washing up on the sand, just like last time. Women and children this time, though. It's just awful," he says. "Just awful."

*   *   *

A mile south of where the other bodies came to shore at Golden Beach, and five miles south of Hollywood, while ambulance crews are lugging the bodies away from the water and up the beach to the ambulances, a woman struggles through the last few waves to the shore. She is alone, a young black woman with close-cropped hair, her dress yanked away from her by the force of the water, her limbs hanging down like anchors, as she staggers, stumbles, drags herself out of the water and falls forward onto the sand. Her name is Vanise Dorsinville; she is the only Haitian to survive the journey from New Providence Island to Florida on the *Belinda Blue*.

*   *   *

At the same time, possibly at the same moment, for these events have a curious way of coordinating themselves, Bob Dubois brings the *Belinda Blue* in from the open sea, passes under the bridge at Lower Matecumbe Key and heads for the Moray Key Marina. He cuts back the throttle as he enters the marina, letting the boat drift around to starboard so he can reverse her into the slip next to the *Angel Blue*, and he notices that Ave's boat is gone from the slip.

He puts the boat into reverse, and his Jamaican mate jumps onto the deck in the bow, ready to tie her up. Bob is backing the boat skillfully into the slip, when he sees, standing on the pier, apparently waiting for them, two Florida state troopers.

The Jamaican looks up at Bob on the bridge. "Get out, Bob! Reverse de fuckin' boat, mon, and get 'er out of here!"

Bob simply shakes his head no and calmly backs the boat into the slip.

J. M. COETZEE

Born in Cape Town in 1940, J. M. Coetzee was educated in South Africa and the United States and now teaches at the University of Cape Town. Among his novels are Age of Iron, Foe, In the Heart of the Country, *and* Dusklands. *The following fictional journey through a harsh hinterland is taken from* Waiting for the Barbarians. *Coetzee seems able to fashion landscape into archetype without any loss of details, and travel into moral allegory without losing human idiosyncrasy — an ability he would deploy again in his succeeding novel* Life & Times of Michael K, *which won the Booker Prize. The narrator here, the Magistrate, who is returning his native consort to her people, comes to see this girl in a new light as she adapts well to the hard conditions of travel.*

from WAITING FOR THE BARBARIANS

The air every morning is full of the beating of wings as the birds fly in from the south, circling above the lake before they settle in the salty fingers of the marshes. In the lulls of the wind the cacophony of their hooting, quacking, honking, squawking reaches us like the noise of a rival city on the water: greylag, beangoose, pintail, wigeon, mallard, teal, smew.

The arrival of the first of the migrating waterfowl confirms the earlier signs, the ghost of a new warmth on the wind, the glassy translucence of the lake-ice. Spring is on its way, one of these days it will be time to plant.

Meanwhile it is the season for trapping. Before dawn, parties of men leave for the lake to lay their nets. By mid-morning they are back with huge catches: birds with their necks twisted, slung from poles row upon row by their feet, or crammed alive into wooden cages, screaming with outrage, trampling each other, with sometimes a great silent whooper swan crouched in their midst. Nature's cornucopia: for the next weeks everyone will eat well.

Before I can leave there are two documents to compose. The first is addressed to the provincial governor. "To repair some of the damage wrought by the forays of the Third Bureau," I write, "and to restore some of the goodwill that previously existed, I am undertaking a brief visit to the barbarians." I sign and seal the letter.

What the second document is to be I do not yet know. A testament? A memoir? A confession? A history of thirty years on the frontier? All that day I sit in a trance at my desk staring at the empty white paper, waiting for words to come. A second day passes in the same way. On the third day I surrender, put the paper back in the drawer and make preparations to leave. It seems appropriate that a man who does not know what to do with the woman in his bed should not know what to write.

To accompany me I have chosen three men. Two are

young conscripts to whose services on secondment I am entitled. The third is an older man born in these parts, a hunter and horse trader whose wages I will pay out of my own pocket. I call them together the afternoon before we leave. "I know this is not a good time of year to travel," I tell them. "It is a treacherous time, the tail end of winter, spring not yet here. But if we wait longer we will not find the nomads before they start on their migration." They ask no questions.

To the girl I say simply, "I am taking you back to your people, or as near as I can, seeing that they are now dispersed." She gives no sign of rejoicing. I lay at her side the heavy fur I have bought her to travel in, with a rabbitskin cap embroidered in the native fashion, new boots, gloves.

Now that I have committed myself to a course I sleep more easily and even detect within myself something like happiness.

We depart on the third of March, accompanied through the gate and down the road to the lakeside by a ragtag escort of children and dogs. After we pass the irrigation wall and branch off from the river road, taking the track to the right used by no one but hunters and fowlers, our escort begins to dwindle till there are only two stubborn lads trotting behind us, each determined to outlast the other.

The sun has risen but gives off no warmth. The wind beats at us across the lake bringing tears to our eyes. In single file, four men and a woman, four pack animals, the horses persistently backing to the wind and having to be sawed around, we wind away from the walled town, the bare fields, and eventually from the panting boys.

My plan is to follow this track till we have skirted the lake to the south, then to strike out northeast across the desert toward the valleys of the ranges where the northern nomads winter. It is a route rarely travelled, since the nomads, when they migrate with their flocks, follow the old dead riverbed in a vast sweep east and south. However, it reduces a journey of six weeks to one or two. I have never travelled it myself.

So for the first three days we plod south and then eastward. To our right stretches a plain of wind-eroded clay terraces merging at its extremes into banks and red dust clouds and then into the yellow hazy sky. To our left is flat marshland, belts of reeds, and the lake on which the central ice sheet has not melted. The wind blowing over the ice freezes our very breath, so that rather than ride we often walk for long spells in the lee of our horses. The girl winds a scarf around and around her and, crouching in the saddle, blindly follows her leader.

Two of the pack horses are loaded with firewood, but this must be conserved for the desert. Once, half buried in driftsand, we come upon a spreading moundlike tamarisk which we hack to pieces for fuel; for the rest we have to be content with bundles of dry reeds. The girl and I sleep side by side in the same tent, huddled in our furs against the cold.

In these early days of the journey we eat well. We have brought salted meat, flour, beans, dried fruit, and there are wildfowl to shoot. But we have to be sparing with water. The marshwater here in the shallow southern fingers is too salty to be drinkable. One of the men has to wade twenty or thirty paces in, as deep as his calves, to fill the skins, or, better, to break off lumps of ice. Yet even the melted ice-water is so bitter and salty that it can only be drunk with strong red tea. Every year the lake grows more brackish as the river eats into its banks and sweeps salt and alum into the lake. Since the lake has no outflow its mineral content keeps rising, particularly in the south, where tracts of water are seasonally isolated by sandbars. After the summer flood the fishermen find carp floating belly-up in the shallows. They say that perch are no more to be seen. What will become of the settlement if the lake grows into a dead sea?

After a day of salty tea all of us except the girl begin to suffer from diarrhoea. I am the worst afflicted. I feel keenly the humiliation of the frequent stops, the undressing and dressing with frozen fingers in the lee of a horse while the others wait. I try to drink as little as possible, to the point even that my mind throws up tantalizing images as I ride: a full cask by the wellside with water splashing from the ladle; clean snow. My occasional hunting and hawking, my desultory womanizing, exercises of manhood, have concealed from me how soft my body has grown. After long marches my bones ache, by nightfall I am so tired that I have no appetite. I trudge on till I cannot put one foot in front of the other; then I clamber into the saddle, fold myself in my cloak, and wave one of the men forward to take over the task of picking out the faint track. The wind never lets up. It howls at us across the ice, blowing from nowhere to nowhere, veiling the sky in a cloud of red dust. From the dust there is no hiding: it penetrates our clothing, cakes our skin, sifts into the baggage. We eat with coated tongues, spitting often, our teeth grating. Dust rather than air becomes the medium in which we live. We swim through dust like fish through water.

The girl does not complain. She eats well, she does not get sick, she sleeps soundly all night clenched in a ball in weather so cold I would hug a dog for comfort. She rides all day without a murmur. Once, glancing up, I see that she is riding asleep, her face as peaceful as a baby's.

On the third day the rim of the marshland begins to curve back toward the north and we know that we have rounded the lake. We pitch camp early and spend the last hours of light collecting every scrap of fuel we can while the horses browse for the last time on the meagre marshgrass. Then at dawn on the fourth day we begin the crossing of the ancient lake bed that stretches another forty miles beyond the marshes.

The terrain is more desolate than anything we have yet seen. Nothing grows on this salty lake floor, which in places buckles and pushes up in jagged crystalline hexagons a foot wide. There are dangers too: crossing an unusually smooth patch the front horse suddenly plunges through the crust and sinks chest-deep in foul green slime, the man who leads it standing a moment dumbstruck on thin air before he too splashes in. We struggle to haul them out, the salt crust splintering under the hooves of the flailing horse, the hole widening, a brackish stench everywhere. We have not left the lake behind, we now realize: it stretches beneath us here, sometimes under a cover many feet deep, sometimes under a mere parchment of brittle salt. How long since the sun last shone on these dead waters? We light a fire on firmer ground to warm the shivering man and dry his clothes. He shakes his head. "I always heard, beware of the green patches, but I never saw this happen before," he says. He is our guide, the one man among us who has travelled east of the lake. After this we push our horses even harder, in a hurry to be off the dead lake, fearful of being lost in a fluid colder than ice, mineral, subterraneous, airless. We bow our heads and drive into the wind, our coats ballooning behind us, picking a way over the jagged salt shards, avoiding the smooth ground. Through the river of dust that courses majestically across the sky the sun glows like an orange but warms nothing. When darkness falls we batter the tent pegs into cracks in the rock-hard salt; we burn our firewood at an extravagant rate and like sailors pray for land.

On the fifth day we leave the lake floor behind and pass through a belt of smooth crystalline salt which soon gives way to sand and stone. Everyone is heartened, even the horses, which during the crossing of the salt have had nothing but a few handfuls of linseed and a bucketful of brackish water. Their condition is visibly deteriorating.

As for the men, they do not grumble. The fresh meat is giving out but there remain the salt meat and dried beans and plenty of flour and tea, the staples of the road. At each halt we brew tea and fry little fatcakes, delicious morsels to the hungry. The men do the cooking: being shy of the girl, unsure of her standing, unsure most of all what we are doing taking her to the barbarians, they barely address her, avoid looking at her, and certainly do not ask for her help with the food. I do not push her forward, hoping that constraint will disappear on the road. I picked these men because they were hardy and honest and willing. They follow me as lightheartedly as they can under these conditions, though by now the brave lacquered armour the two young soldiers wore when we passed through the great gate is strapped in bundles on the pack-horses and their scabbards are full of sand.

The sand flats begin to modulate into duneland. Our progress slows as we toil up and down the sides of the dunes. It is the worst possible terrain for the horses, which plod forward a few inches at a time, their hooves sinking deep in the sand. I look to our guide, but all he can do is shrug. "It goes on for miles, we have to cross it, there is no other way." Standing on a dune top, shielding my eyes, staring ahead, I can see nothing but swirling sand.

That night one of the pack horses refuses its feed. In the morning, even under the severest flogging, it will not rise. We redistribute the loads and cast away some of the firewood. While the others set out I stay behind. I can swear that the beast knows what is to happen. At the sight of the knife its eyes roll. With the blood spurting from its neck it scrambles free of the sand and totters a pace or two downwind before it falls. In extremities, I have heard, the barbarians tap their horses' veins. Will we live to regret this blood spent so lavishly on the sand?

On the seventh day, with the dunes finally behind us, we make out against the dull grey-brown of the empty landscape a strip of darker grey. From nearer we see that it stretches east and west for miles. There are even the stunted black shapes of trees. We are lucky, our guide says: there is bound to be water here.

What we have stumbled on is the bed of an ancient terminal lagoon. Dead reeds, ghostly white and brittle to the touch, line what were its banks. The trees are poplars, also long dead. They have died since the underground water receded too far to be reached by their roots years and years ago.

We unload the animals and begin to dig. At two feet we reach heavy blue clay. Beneath this there is sand again, then another stratum of clay, noticeably clammy. At a depth of seven feet, with my heart pounding and my ears ringing, I have to refuse my turn with the spade. The three men toil on, lifting the loose soil out of the pit in a tent cloth tied at the corners.

At ten feet water begins to gather around their feet. It is sweet, there is no trace of salt, we smile with delight at each other; but it gathers very slowly and the sides of the pit have continually to be dug out as they cave in. It is only by late afternoon that we can empty out the last of our brackish lakewater and refill the waterskins. In near dark we lower the butt into our well and allow the horses to drink.

Meanwhile, now that there is an abundance of

poplarwood the men have dug two little ovens back to back in the clay and built a roaring fire on top of them to bake the clay dry. When the fire abates they can rake the coals back into the ovens and set about baking bread. The girl stands watching all this, leaning on her sticks to which I have fastened discs of wood to help her in the sand. In the free and easy camaraderie of this good day, and with a day of rest promised, talk flows. Joking with her, the men make their first overture of friendship: "Come and sit with us and taste what men's baking is like!" She smiles back at them, lifting her chin in a gesture which perhaps I alone know is an effort to see. Cautiously she sets herself down beside them to bathe in the glow from the ovens.

I myself sit farther away sheltered from the wind in the mouth of my tent with one of the oil lamps flickering beside me, making the day's entry in the logbook but listening too. The banter goes on in the pidgin of the frontier, and she is at no loss for words. I am surprised by her fluency, her quickness, her self-possession. I even catch myself in a flush of pride: she is not just the old man's slut, she is a witty, attractive young woman! Perhaps if from the beginning I had known how to use this slap-happy joking lingo with her we might have warmed more to each other. But like a fool, instead of giving her a good time I oppressed her with gloom. Truly, the world ought to belong to the singers and dancers! Futile bitterness, idle melancholy, empty regrets! I blow out the lamp, sit with my chin on my fist staring toward the fire, listening to my stomach rumble.

GRAHAM GREENE

Famous for such novels as Brighton Rock, The Power and the Glory, The End of the Affair, The Quiet American, *and* The Human Factor, *Graham Greene took his place in the company of Evelyn Waugh, Peter Fleming, and Robert Byron as a distinguished travel writer of the thirties with the 1936 publication of* Journey Without Maps, *a narrative of his ruinous West African trek by foot through two hundred miles of seediness and mosquitoes, during which he contracted malaria. He followed this book three years later with* The Lawless Roads, *an account of his unhappy journey in Mexico, a country where he was unable to experience much, if any, pleasure. He died in April 1991.*

from THE LAWLESS ROADS

THE LONG RIDE

I left my suitcase behind, and because it seemed absurd to think of rain I foolishly abandoned my cape and took only the net, a hammock, and a rucksack.

At a quarter past four I got up and dressed by the light of my electric torch, folded up the huge tentlike mosquito net. Everybody in Salto was asleep but my guide — a dark, dapper young man of some education

who had come from Las Casas by way of Yajalon —
and his father, who had prepared us coffee and biscuits
in his home. It was the cool and quiet beginning of one
of the worst days I have ever spent. Only the first few
hours of that ride were to provide any pleasure — riding
out of Salto in the dark with one sleepy mongrel raising
its muzzle at the clip clop of the mules, the ferry across
the river in the earliest light, the two mules swimming
beside the canoe, with just their muzzles and their eyes
above the water like a pair of alligator heads, and then
the long banana plantations on the other bank, the fruit
plucked as we rode tasting tart and delicious in the open
air at dawn.

The trouble was, the way to Palenque lay across a bare
exposed plateau, broken only occasionally by patches of
forest and shade, and by nine in the morning the sun
was blindingly up. By ten my cheap helmet bought
in Veracruz for a few pesos was just the damp hot
cardboard it had pretended not be be. I had not ridden
a horse for ten years; I had never ridden a mule before.
Its trot, I imagine, is something like a camel's: its whole
back heaves and strains. There is no rhythm you can
catch by rising in the stirrups; you must just surrender
yourself to the merciless uneven bump. The strain on the
spine to the novice is appalling: the neck stiffens with
it, the head aches as if it had been struck by sun. And
all the time the nerves are worn by the stubbornness of
the brute; the trot degenerates into a walk, the walk into
an amble, unless you beat the mule continually. *"Mula.
Mula. Mula. Echa, mula,"* the dreary lament goes on.

And all the time Palenque shifted like a mirage; my

guide had never been there himself: all he could do on the wide plain was to keep a rough direction. Ten hours away the storekeeper had said, and after four hours I thought I could manage that quite easily, but when we stopped at an Indian's hut about eleven in the morning (six hours from Salto) and heard them talk as if it were now not quite halfway, my heart sank. A couple of wattle huts like those of West African natives, chickens and turkeys tumbling across the dusty floor, a pack of mongrels and a few cows listless in the heat under some thorny trees — it was better than nothing on that baked plateau, and I wished later we had stayed the night. They swung a string hammock up and I dismounted with immense difficulty. Six hours had stiffened me. They gave us tortillas — the flat, dry pancake with which you eat all food in the Mexican country — and an egg each in a tin mug, and coffee, delicious coffee. We rested half an hour and then went on. Six hours more, I said, with what I hoped was cheerfulness to my guide, but he scouted the notion. Six hours — oh, no, perhaps eight. Those people didn't know a thing.

I can remember practically nothing of that ride now until its close; I remember being afraid of sunstroke my head ached so — I would raise my hat for coolness, and then lower it from fear; I remember talking to my guide of the cantinas there would be in Palenque and how much beer and tequila we would drink. I remember the guide getting smaller and smaller in the distance and flogging at my mule (*"Mula. Mula. Echa, mula"*) until I overtook him at a trot that wrenched the backbone. I remember that we passed a man with the

255

mails traveling on a pony at a smart canter and he said he'd left Palenque in the night. And then somewhere on that immense rolling plain, in a spot where the grass grew long, the mule suddenly lay down under me. The guide was a long way off; I felt I could never get up on that mule again; I sat on the grass and tried to be sick and wanted to cry. The guide rode back and waited patiently for me to remount, but I didn't think it was possible — my body was too stiff. There was a small coppice of trees, some monkeys moved inquisitively, and the mule got on its feet again and began to eat.

Can't we stay the night somewhere, I said, in some hut, and go on tomorrow? But the guide said there wasn't a single hut between here and Palenque. It was two o'clock in the afternoon; we had been riding for nine hours, with half an hour's break; Palenque was, he said, about five hours away. Couldn't we string our hammocks up to the trees and sleep here? But he had no hammock and besides, there was no food, no drink, and lots of mosquitoes, perhaps a leopard. I think he meant a leopard — they call them tigers in Chiapas — and I remember how Victorian Dr. Fitzpatrick had met one on his ride across these mountains, standing across his path. It is rather terrifying to believe you cannot go on, and yet to have no choice. . . .

I got back into the saddle, thanking God for the big Mexican pommel which you can cling to with both hands when all else fails, and again the ride faded into obscurity — I didn't talk so much now about the cantina, I grumbled to myself in undertones that I *couldn't* make it, and I began to hate the dapperness of my guide, his rather caddish white riding-breeches — it was nothing to him, the ride; he rode just as he would sit in a chair. And then the mule lay down again; it lay down in the end four times before we saw, somewhere about five o'clock when the sun was low, a little smoke drifting over the ridge of the down. "Palenque," my guide said. I didn't believe him, and that was lucky, because it wasn't Palenque, only a prairie fire we had to ride around, the mules uneasy in the smoke. And then we came into a patch of forest and the ways divided; one way, the guide said — on I don't know whose authority, for he had never been here before — led to the German *finca*, the other to Palenque. Which were we to take? I chose Palenque: it was nearer and the lodging more certain, above all the drink. I didn't really believe in the German and his lovely daughter, and when after we'd been going a quarter of an hour we just came out on the same path, I believed less than ever in them. As the sun sank, the flies emerged more numerous than ever; they didn't bother to attack me; great fat droning creatures, they sailed by and sank like dirigibles on to the mule's neck, grappled fast, and sucked until a little stream of blood flowed down. I tried to dislodge them with my stick, but they simply shifted their ground. The smell of blood and mule was sickening. One became at last a kind of automaton, a bundle of flesh and bone without a brain.

And then a little party of riders came out of a belt of forest in the last light and bore news — Palenque was only half an hour distant. The rest of the way was in darkness, the darkness of the forest and then the darkness of night as well. That was how we began and ended. The stars were up when we came out of the forest, and there at the head of a long parklike slope of grass was a poor abandoned cemetery, crosses rotting at an angle and lying in the long grass behind a broken wall, and at the foot of the slope lights moved obscurely up towards a collection of round mud huts thatched with banana leaves as poor as anything I ever saw in West Africa. We rode through the huts and came into a long wide street of bigger huts — square ones these, raised a foot from the ground to avoid ants, some of them roofed with tin — and at the head of the street on a little hill a big plain ruined church.

My guide apparently had learned where we could get food, if not lodging — a woman's hut where the school teacher lived, and while food was prepared we staggered out on legs as stiff as stilts to find the drink we had promised ourselves all the hot day. But Palenque wasn't Salto; the Salto cantina loomed in memory with the luxury of an American bar. In the store near the church they had three bottles of beer only — warm, gassy, unsatisfying stuff. And afterwards we drank a glass each of very new and raw tequila; it hardly touched our thirst. At the other end of the village was the only other store. We made our way there by the light of electric torches, to find they sold no beer at all: all we could get was mineral water coloured pink and flavoured with some sweet chemical. We had a bottle each and I took a bottle away with me to wash down my quinine. Otherwise we had to try and satisfy our thirst with coffee — endlessly; a good drink, but bad for the nerves. The school teacher was a plump complacent young

258

half-caste with a patronising and clerical manner and a soft boneless hand: that was what the village had gained in place of a priest. His assistant was of a different type: alert, interested in his job for its own sake and not for the prestige it gave him, good with children, I feel sure. After we had eaten, he led us up the street to his own room, where we were to sleep. It was a small room in a tin-roofed hut beside the ruined church, which they used now as a school. He insisted that I should take his bed, my guide took my hammock, and our host tied up another for himself from the heavy beams.

I think the hut had once been a stable; now it seemed to be divided by thin partitions into three. In one division we slept, in another small children cried all night, and behind my head, in the third, I could hear the slow movements and the regular coughing of cows. I slept very badly in my clothes — I had cramps in my feet and a little fever from the sun. Somewhere around midnight there was the sound of a horse outside and a fist beat on the big-bolted barn door. Nobody moved until a voice called, "*Con amistad*" (with friendship), and then the stranger was let in. I put on my electric torch and he moved heavily round the little room tying up a hammock; then he took off his revolver holster and lay down, and again I tried to sleep. It seemed to me that a woman's voice was constantly urging me to turn my face to the wall because that way I lay closer to Tabasco, the Atlantic, and home. I felt sick, but I was too tired to go outside and vomit. The hammocks creaked and something fluttered in the roof and a child wailed. There was no ventilation at all.

VISITING THE RUINS

Fate had got me somehow to Palenque, and so I thought I had better see the ruins, but it was stupid, after the long ride and the feverish night, to go next morning. And it was stupid, too, to start as late as seven, for it was nearly half-past nine before we reached them and the tropical sun was already high. It wasn't so much stiffness that bothered me now: it was the feel of fever, an overpowering nausea without the energy to vomit, a desire to lie down and never get up again, a continuous thirst. I had tried to get some mineral water to take with me, but our purchases had cleared the store right out, and all the time, if only I had known it, I was in one of the few places in Mexico where it was safe to drink the water. Springs rose everywhere; as we climbed through the thick hot forest they sparkled between the trees, fell in tiny torrents, spread out, like a Devonshire stream, over the pebbles in a little clearing. But I didn't drink, merely watched with sick envy the mules take their fill, afraid that the streams might be polluted farther up by cattle, as if any cattle could live in this deep forest: we passed the bleached skeleton of something by the path. So one always starts a journey in a strange land — taking too many precautions, until one tires of the exertion and abandons care in the worst spot of all. How I hated my mule, drinking where I wanted to drink myself and, like the American dentist, chewing all the time, pausing every few feet up the mountainside to snatch grasses.

Nobody had properly opened up the way to Palenque; sometimes the guide had to cut the way with his machete, and at the end the path rose at a crazy angle — it couldn't have been less than sixty degrees. I hung on to the pommel and left it all to the mule and anyway didn't care. And then at last, two hours and a half from the village, the ruins appeared.

I haven't been to Chichen Itzá, but judging from photographs of the Yucatán remains they are immeasurably more impressive than those of Palenque, though, I suppose, if you like wild nature, the setting of Palenque is a finer one — on a great circular plateau halfway up the mountainside, with the jungle falling precipitously below into the plain and rising straight up behind; in the clearing itself there is nothing but a few Indian huts, scrub and stone and great mounds of rubble crowned with low one-storey ruins of grey rock, so age-worn they have a lichenous shape and look more vegetable than mineral. And no shade anywhere until you've climbed the steep loose slopes and bent inside the dark cool little rooms like lavatories where a few stalactites have formed and on some of the stones are a few faint scratches which they call hieroglyphics. At first you notice only one of these temples or palaces where it stands in mid-clearing on its mound with no more importance than a ruined stone farm in the Oxford countryside, but then all round you, as you gaze, they open up, emerging obscurely from the jungle — three, four, five, six, I don't know how many gnarled relics. No work is in progress, and you can see them on the point of being swallowed again by the forest; they have looked out for a minute, old wrinkled faces, and will soon withdraw.

Well, I had told people I was here in Chiapas to visit the ruins and I had visited them; but there was no compulsion to see them, and I hadn't the strength to climb more than two of those slopes and peer into more than two of the cold snaky chambers. I thought I was going to faint; I sat down on a stone and looked down — at trees, and nothing but trees, going on and on out of sight. It seemed to me that this wasn't a country to live in at all with the heat and the desolation; it was a country to die in and leave only ruins behind. Last year Mexico City was shaken more than two hundred times by earthquake. . . . One was looking at the future as well as at the past.

I slid somehow down on to the ground and saw my guide set off with the Indian who guards the site towards another palace; I couldn't follow. With what seemed awful labour I moved my legs back toward the Indian huts; a kind of stubbornness surged up through the fever — I wouldn't see the ruins, I wouldn't go back to Palenque, I'd simply lie down here and wait — for a miracle. The Indian hut had no walls; it was simply a twig shelter with a chicken or two scratching in the dust, and a hammock and a packing case. I lay down on my back in the hammock and stared at the roof; outside, according to authorities, were the Templo de las Leyes, the Templo del Sol, the Templo de la Cruz de Palenque. I knew what they could do with their temples. . . . And farther off still England. It had no reality. You get accustomed in a few weeks to the idea of living or dying in the most bizarre surroundings. Man has a dreadful adaptability.

I suppose I dozed, for there were the Indian and the guide looking down at me. I could see the guide was troubled. He had a feeling of responsibility, and no Mexican cares for that. It's like a disused limb they have learned to do without. They said if I'd move into the other hut they would get me coffee. I felt that it was a trap: if they could make me move, they could make me get on that mule again and then would begin the two-and-a-half hour ride back to Palenque. An hour had lost meaning; it was like a cipher for some number too big to comprehend. Very unwillingly, very slowly, I shifted a dozen feet to another open hut and another hammock. A young Indian girl with big silver ear-rings and a happy sensual face began to make corn coffee — thin grey stuff like a temperance drink which does no harm. I said to the guide, without much hope, "Why shouldn't we sleep here?" I knew his answer — mosquitoes; he was a man who liked his comforts. He brought up again that dream of a German with a beautiful daughter; I lay on my back, disbelieving. The *finca*, he said, was only a little way from Palenque. We'd go there tonight in the cool. I went on drinking corn coffee, bowl after bowl of it. I suppose it had some tonic effect, for I have a dim memory of suddenly thinking, "Oh, hell, if I'm going to collapse, I may as well collapse in the village where the damned guide won't worry me. . . ." I got on the mule and when once I was up it was as easy — almost — to sit there as in a hammock; I just held on to the pommel and let the mule do the rest. We slid down slowly over the tree roots toward the plain. I was too exhausted to be frightened.

And when time did somehow come to an end, I fell

off the mule and made straight for the schoolmaster's hammock and lay down. I wanted nothing except just not to move. The plump complacent schoolmaster sat on the steps and had a philosophical talk with a passing peasant — "The sun is the origin of life," a finger pointed upwards. I was too sick to think then of Rivera's school teachers in snowy-white blessing with raised episcopal fingers the little children with knowledge, knowledge like this. "That is true. Without the sun we should cease to exist." I lay and drank cup after cup of coffee; the school teachers had lunch, but I couldn't eat, just went on drinking coffee, and sweating it out again. Liquid had no time to be digested; it came through the pores long before it reached the stomach. I lay wet through with sweat for four hours — it was very nearly like happiness. In the street outside nobody passed: it was too hot for life to go on. Only a vulture or two flopping by, and the whinny of a horse in a field.

ERIC HANSEN

Born in 1948, Eric Hansen is a graduate of the University of California at Berkeley, and has traveled extensively in the Middle East and Asia. In 1982 he spent seven months walking across Borneo and back. What follows is a crucial part of this intrepid expedition when, mistaken for a bali saleng, *or a collector of blood offerings for coastal construction projects, Hansen encounters trouble among village people in the Kayan River valley. His most recent book is* Motoring with Mohammed.

from STRANGER IN THE FOREST

"The people are afraid," Pa Biah warned me. "Don't travel by yourself; it is not safe. The people know you have come to the valley. They may hurt you if they see you alone in the jungle."

The red glow from Pa Biah's cheroot gradually faded, and as he coaxed the fire back to life with his foot, we sipped hot bitter tea from chipped enamel mugs. Ibu Iting, his wife, sat nearby. She was making thread by pulling strands of cotton from the edge of an old piece of fabric. While holding the ends of two strands in her left hand, she twisted them together by rubbing them between her right hand and thigh. She threaded her needle and continued to listen to our conversation as she patched a well-worn pair of trousers.

"Last year," Pa Biah continued, "*bali saleng* was described as a brown-skinned man with long black hair and pointed teeth. He wore a powder blue, short-sleeved, military-type shirt with matching shorts. He had a special set of spring-powered shoes that enabled him to jump four meters in the air and ten meters away in a single bound. He could spring through the air to cover long distances quickly and capture people by surprise. After tying up his victim with strips of rattan, he would take the blood from the wrist or the foot with a small knife and a rubber pump. The corpse would then be hoisted with vines up into the jungle canopy so that searchers could not find it."

Listening attentively, I tried to imagine a police department's composite sketch of such an individual. The image of *bali saleng* was still too farfetched for me to take seriously.

"A *bali saleng* cannot be killed by man," Pa Biah continued. "Bullets bounce off him, spears cannot pierce his body, and when he gets old he will take on a young man without family and train him."

Pa Biah went on to tell me that the year before a pregnant woman was reported to have been killed by a *bali saleng* near the village of Long Ampung. Pregnant women are considered prime targets because they contain the blood of two people.

That night the people of Long Nawang locked themselves into their family quarters and did not open their doors until daybreak.

I listened to Pa Biah's stories with interest, but I failed to recognize my own imminent danger. I was placing too much confidence in my knowledge of the language and too little importance on the power of fear. Instead of accepting the people's beliefs as something real and adjusting my behavior accordingly, I was relying on a false sense of security. With nearly eighteen hundred jungle miles behind me, I had become careless.

The next morning I got up and left at dawn — alone. I didn't get far. Four hours up the valley, as I followed the Kayan River southeast from Long Nawang, I was attacked in the village of Long Uro. The first thing I heard was the frantic pounding of children's feet along hardwood planks of the longhouse porch. There were a few startled cries from the women then the sound of men's voices. It all happened very quickly. It took me a moment to realize that I was the cause of the commotion.

A group of about two dozen men, some armed with spears, came down to the trail where I was standing. After some excited questioning and gesturing (not all of which I understood), I felt their hands on me. I was stripped of my pack and forced to the ground. I didn't resist. I sat in the dirt with my back to a drainage ditch as the men formed a tight semicircle in front of me. For the next two hours they fired accusations at me in Indonesian. I was repeatedly questioned and cross-examined. My mind became alert, and I was careful not to show any fear. They wanted to know why I was by myself, why I didn't have a cooking pot, what I was doing in the Kayan River valley, and how I had come over the mountains from Sarawak. My answers didn't sound very convincing, and I soon realized how vulnerable I was. The experience of facing so many frightened people was intimidating. My belongings were ransacked; shotgun shells, diaries, salt, clothing, and half-finished letters to friends littered the ground. I was repeatedly asked about the contents of my pack. After two men had gone through everything, I realized that they had been looking for spring-powered shoes, the small blood knife, and the rubber pump.

Over and over they repeated two questions: "Why do you walk by yourself?" and "Why aren't you afraid of *bali saleng*?"

The fact is that no one in Borneo walks by himself in the jungle. It is too easy to fall down or to get lost or sick. Every year people disappear in the rain forest without a trace. Solo travel isn't done except by the spirits. It was difficult to explain to these villagers why I had no fear. By now hours had passed, and I felt my energy fading. These frightened, angry people, with their excited sing-song manner of speaking, were exhausting me. Here in a village of practicing animists was a middle-class Westerner arguing about evil spirits in their jungle. By consistently basing my answers on logic and reasoning, I was only making the situation worse. I would have merely increased their suspicions if I had claimed not to believe in spirits. How could I possibly be convincing? I asked myself. It became irrelevant and unimportant to me whether they understood who I really was. By this time I wanted only one thing: to be able to leave the village safely. I realized that I had to accept their fear and deal with it on their terms. It was absurd for me to try to convince them that one of their greatest fears was unfounded. A solution came to me unexpectedly.

The Kenyah, as do all the inland people, have a tradition of amulets, charms, and spell-breakers. The collective term for these items is *jeemat*. A *jeemat* can be made from a wide assortment of materials; the most common are seedpods, bones, wood shavings, crushed insects, beeswax, cowrie shells, and odd-shaped black pebbles known as hook stones. A *jeemat* can be made by man or found, but the most powerful ones (the hook stones) are given by a spirit or ghost. Directions for their use are revealed during a dream. It is very bad luck to lose or give away a charm that has come from the spirits. *Jeemats* are usually worn around the neck or wrist and are an important part of one's personal adornment. They are visible proof of one's faith in the power of the spirit world.

With this in mind, I remembered I was wearing a small, stuffed fabric banana pin that a friend had given me before I started my trip. The pin was about three inches long and had a bright yellow, polka-dot peel. The banana was removable. It could be dangled at the end of a short safety string. Until that moment in Long Uro, I had used the pin only to amuse people.

"This," I said, gesturing to the pin, "is my *jeemat*. It protects me from *bali saleng*." It caught them off guard; it also aroused their interest. One of the men came forward to touch the banana, but I cautioned him not to. He stopped three feet away from me.

"It has very strong *obat*," I said. *Obat* has many

definitions: magic, power, or medicine. "Be careful, this charm was made especially for me by a spirit. That is why I'm not afraid to walk alone in the jungle." The mood of the interrogation changed as interest shifted to my banana pin.

"Where did it come from?" "What is it made of?" "Do you have more?" "How much would one cost?" they wanted to know.

I did not concoct my banana-pin story because I thought my tormentors were simple-minded or childish. Quite the opposite. The Kenyah have a highly developed relationship with the spirit world. I couldn't think of any other story they might believe. From generations of experience, they know how to coexist with both good and bad spirits. Firmly rooted in the twentieth century, I certainly didn't have anything to teach them. I was the outsider, the ignorant one. I had great respect for all the inland people. With their unique forms of architecture, social organization, and sophisticated farming techniques, they have established themselves in an incredibly difficult environment. The decision to present the banana pin as a powerful charm not only helped save me in this situation, but also forced me to reconsider how I was responding to the people. I stopped being the observer and began to accept their supernatural world, and my journey was never the same. In that single moment I grew much closer to my experiences.

The tension eased after I had revealed the power of the banana-pin charm. A few obstinate older men insisted on going over the fine points of my story, but the rest seemed to think I was probably harmless. I was flushed with relief. The blood and adrenaline pounded through my body and made my fingertips and toes ache. I felt light-headed and blessed to have survived this incident unharmed.

I was free to go, but it was too late to continue up the valley to my original destination — Long Sungai Barang. I had to spend the night in Long Uro. Dozens of eyes stared at me through knotholes and cracks in the rough wooden walls as I ate a miserable and lonely dinner. I was served half-rotten fish pounded in a mortar, bones and all. Having finished my meal, I strung my mosquito net in a filthy corner, unrolled my mat, and escaped into an exhausted sleep.

During the night there must have been more discussion because in the morning, just after I left the village, I came upon a young man standing at the side of the pathway. He was barefoot, well muscled, and dressed in blue shorts. He wore white gloves and held a large unsheathed parang at his side. He didn't respond to my greeting as I approached, but as I passed he fell into step a few feet behind me. I continued on for a short while then decided it would be better to confront him. I turned to speak, but he had vanished into the undergrowth. I knew that he could be no more than fifty feet from where I stood, but I couldn't see him. For months this jungle had seemed so benign and giving. How quickly it had become frightening. It was clear to me that at any moment I might be ambushed and killed.

Farther up the valley I passed abandoned farm huts and stopped briefly in the village of Lidung Payau to

271

ask directions to the village of Long Sungai Barang. On the far side of Lidung Payau, I saw what I soon realized was a cage fashioned out of logs six inches in diameter. The structure was raised off the ground and had a slat floor that let excrement out and the flies in. The cage measured six feet by five feet by four feet and had a shingled roof. It was "home" not to an animal, but to a man. There were no doors or windows. I later learned that the inhabitant, barely visible between the gaps in the horizontal logs, had lived in the cage for more than two years. I don't know what his crime was. The cloud of furiously buzzing blackflies must have driven him mad. I looked upon this wretched man as a fellow sufferer, but when I tried to speak with him, he moved to the far side of his cage, and I could sense his fear of my presence.

I no longer had my sense of security and self-confidence. I lost track of time. As my anxiety mounted, a few hundred yards began to seem like miles. My thinking became erratic and unsound. There was no turning back, and for the first time since leaving Long Sungai Anai three days earlier, I began to panic. I sensed that I was being watched. Soaked in perspiration, I paused frequently to look over my shoulder and listen for the sound of human voices or of jungle knives slashing through the undergrowth. I scanned the surrounding walls of impenetrable green and brown foliage, but I could detect nothing. There were only the normal sounds of the jungle: the wind, the flutter of leaves, dripping water, and rubbing branches. I could see black hornbills perched nearby, so I called to them. I wanted to hear something friendly and reassuring, but their calls came back to me sounding like strangled pleas.

I hurried on to Long Sungai Barang, hoping that word of the incident in Long Uro hadn't preceded me. I wanted a fresh start. I now realized the full extent of my naiveté, my incredible stupidity. I was completely alone and vulnerable. I didn't know what else to do except to keep walking and to try to relax. I stopped frequently, considered going back, couldn't decide, then continued on. Whenever I sat down to rest and clear my mind, a new wave of anxiety would engulf me.

I knew that Long Sungai Barang was the last village in the upper Kayan River valley. If the people there weren't friendly, I would be trapped. Four hundred miles of primary rain forest separated me from the most accessible coast.

It was late afternoon by the time I entered the longhouse at Sungai Barang. I was disoriented and confused, and my legs were bleeding freely from the leeches and barbed vines. I was led to the headman's room. While he was being summoned, I was surrounded by about a dozen Kenyah men. I could feel the deep, painful grooves that the straps of the rattan pack had cut into my shoulders. My shirt was pasted to my back from the heat of the day. The men seemed relaxed and curious, but I felt they looked right through me and sensed my uncertainty.

We talked about the approaching rice harvest for perhaps ten minutes; then to my left I heard the familiar creak and slam of a sapling-powered hardwood door. In midsentence I looked up, expecting to see the headman, but there before me stood a young, white-skinned woman with golden hair. She was dressed in a flowered sarong and a blouse. She was barefoot, pretty, and smiling. I was completely unnerved. It just wasn't possible for her to be there. I became incredulous and even more confused. Finally I just smiled back and felt my pent-up fears and anxieties begin to dissolve.

The first thing I noticed as she stood there was the fragrance of her skin. It wasn't the scent of soap or perfume; it was the scent of another culture, another world, a fresh, wonderful smell that made me question my attraction to smoky jungle campfires and eating wild animals. We spoke Indonesian. There was no urgency to our voices. In Kenyah fashion we began with trivial matters in order to mask the real intent of our conversation, and gradually we led up to the important questions. More people came into the room. They sat quietly, watched, and listened. Eventually the temptation to speak our own language was overwhelming. The woman smiled again and in perfect English said, "I'm Cynthia. I live next door. The headman won't be back until late tonight. Would you like to come over to my place for a visit?"

REDMOND O'HANLON

Redmond O'Hanlon was born in Dorset in 1947 and educated at Marlborough and Oxford. His doctoral thesis combined his interests in nature and the English novel, and in 1984 he published Joseph Conrad and Charles Darwin. *In that year he also published his first travel book,* Into the Heart of Borneo. *In his second,* In Trouble Again: A Journey Between the Orinoco and the Amazon, *he can be seen traveling in South America in the same ironical, bug-infested tradition as Evelyn Waugh and the wandering naturalists of the nineteenth century. O'Hanlon is a Fellow of the Royal Geographic Society and lives with his wife and children near Oxford.* African Signs *was published in 1991.*

from IN TROUBLE AGAIN

The Baria is not the easy waterway which Spruce imagined it to be. Four days into its dendritic delta it seemed the most difficult place on earth. The yelping toucans, the big Amazon parrots, the paired flights of macaws, the rattling cry of the ringed kingfisher, the giant herons, the anhingas, the swallow-tailed kites — all the birds of the open river had long since disappeared. Even the big blue morpho butterflies and the bats, the tiny grey bats that fluttered in flocks like blown woodsmoke from one dead branch to another as we approached — even they had gone. The trees in the labyrinth met overhead, knotted together with lianas, their foliage thickened with epiphytic orchids and umbrella-leaved bromeliads. The sun only reached the black-water channels of the Baria when a storm or old age or a collapsing bank had felled a tree and left a gap in the canopy.

Woken at four-thirty in the morning by the one clock still functioning, a cheap Classa alarm which I kept in a plastic bag, I shone my torch across the leaf litter and carefully noted the positions of two scorpions. Small, mean and black, with a serious-looking whip-over sting, there would be a scorpion, I had calculated, under every eleventh leaf. They, too, caught by the rising water, had to camp with us on islands that were never more than ten yards by twenty. We had to share these small outcrops with all the refugees from the jungle floor. I changed fast out of my dry clothes, made a brief tick check by torchlight, pulled on my wet clothes and steeled myself for the first personal trauma of the day. In my own utopia I would elect to shit only in a lead-lined chamber half-a-mile underground, safe from enemy radar. Shitting two yards from Simon and five yards from Chimo was, I found, difficult. I hung on to a sapling with one hand, switched off my torch, took down my trousers and squatted over the black, swirling water.

"Don't look," I said.

"Who's interested?" said Simon, leaning out of his hammock and pointing his torch straight at me.

"Push!" yelled Chimo.

"Bit runny today," said Simon.

*　*　*

Dawn filtered down. Frogs and cicadas began to call. The mosquitoes scrambled. And, as we folded up the wet tarpaulins, there came four loud blasts on a whistle, followed by a noise of sucking, then clickings of disapproval.

"Viudita carablanca," said Chimo, putting his fingers to his cheeks, drawing in his breath, and making sucking and clicking noises in his turn. There was no reply. Somewhere up in the green tangle, a troop of White-faced sakis were watching us.

Chimo, Culimacaré and Pablo cut fresh poles and we set off, punting the heavy canoes slowly forward. It was not easy to find a purchase for the ten-foot-long poles — the channels, although never more than six to fifteen feet wide, were far too deep for us to touch bottom — so we pushed against submerged branches or roots on the soft bank. Most of the time we could not punt at all, but pulled the boats forwards, standing on submerged branches up to our waists or necks, easing the hull over fallen trees, hacking a way through their dense, upstanding, lateral shoots.

At such times, when standing out of the water, the main discomfort was the ants, not the dangerous veinte-cuatro and catanare who seemed to confine themselves to well-marked territories on shore, and not the army ants, but just thousands of ordinary biting ants (I counted fourteen different species) which went for your head and neck and fastened onto your back inside your shirt. "Hormiga! Hormiga!" Culimacaré would shout when he struck a particularly ant-rich bush, but there was not much you could do to avoid them. At other times we would crouch low, easing the dugouts beneath larger trees which had fallen, but which were still supported lengthwise above the ground and the river by their broken branches, forming bridges for leaf-cutter ants. I grew fond of these fundamentally non-homicidal insects, fully engaged in their perpetual harvest: neatly clipped leaf-sections, held upright, jerkily processed above our heads.

One species of wasp and one species of hornet, in small separate colonies, hung their nests from twigs or fixed them to the backs of leaves suspended over the water. As we cleared a passage with our machetes it was impossible to spot their yellow-brown upended cones. One tremor along a branch, one near cut, and they ejected through the entrance at the base, coming for us with extraordinary speed and concentration. A cry of "Avispa!" really galvanized your limbs: wherever you were, you dived for the water and held your hat across your face to protect your eyes. A wasp sting on the back was tolerable, one on the neck was very painful; five wasp stings on the back equalled one hornet sting on the back. Simon, who disliked the cold, black water on principle and tried to keep his clothes dry for as long as possible each day, moved a fraction slower than the rest of us and, as the last available target, was often stung on the back of the head.

At water level, there were a surprising number of hunting spiders, no bigger, in total extent, than the palm of your hand, which jumped across the surface. Tiny tree frogs, a bright, translucent green as if fashioned in glass, some with little red eyes and feet, dislodged from the foliage as we passed, would fall into the boat or the current, and, pausing to collect themselves, hop or swim to shore; and about twenty times a day we would see the cazadora, the hunter, the long, thin green vine snake, its slim head raised above the water, towing its Vs of ripples.

At normal eye level, we edged past the bases of a seemingly endless variety of tree species, their trunks wrapped with lianas and furry with lichens, their bark smooth or ridged or ringed with spines, and supported on the ground with mats of root fibres, or buttresses, or prop roots like wigwam frames or birdcages, or, occasionally, they were themselves dead or imprisoned in the grasp of a buttressed, hollow, parasitic fig tree which grows from a seed wiped from a bird's beak on some high branch, puts down the slow roots like giant fingers, and throttles its host.

About two hundred yards downstream from our camp-site, after an hour and a half of travelling, we met our first serious obstacle: a trunk across the channel which was so large its mass descended some two feet below the water surface and rose about four feet above it. But the tree was big enough, and had fallen recently enough, to open a clearing in the canopy. In the sudden warmth, our clothes began to steam slightly. A screaming piha was calling, unseen, as it did all day, every day.

"And that's another thing," said Simon, lying back on our shared thwart against our packs under the tarpaulin, stretching in the sun and putting his hands over his ears, "just when that moronic bird stops going *hum hum hum up your bum* all night, this bloody idiot starts whistling."

"It's sex," I said, "they're telling the girls they've got their patch."

"Leave it out," said Simon, "you're going soft in the head."

Pablo brought the second dugout up and Culimacaré started clearing the mass of shoots and shrubs from one end of the tree trunk, whilst Chimo and Pablo laboured at the other.

A tiny blue-black hummingbird, perhaps a fork-tailed wood-nymph, suddenly appeared above us; it whirred to and fro like a dandelion seed in a thermal and then hovered purposefully, obviously curious, repeating the manoeuvre, drawing closer.

"Quick, Simon, where's your camera?" I said.

Simon drew the body with the long lens on it out of a plastic bag beneath the tarpaulin, and the bird flew off like a bumblebee.

"Mira!" yelled Chimo, pointing at the leaves in front of him. "Mira! Mira!"

Pablo and Culimacaré stopped cutting. It was a startling picture. It was a full frontal. It was a short, dangerous, angry coral snake, banded bright red and black to warn its predators, a pattern which even at night tells everyone how deadly it is: and it hung down from its twig-coiled tail, its head up, its white mouth open, hissing.

"For Christsake, take that!" I said.

Simon thrust himself right back against the tarpaulin, his camera clutched across his chest for protection.

"I ain't taking no fucking pictures of no fucking snakes," he shouted, *They give me the creeps*."

Valentine ran forward and knocked it into the river with a punt pole.

Culimacaré, Pablo and Chimo took it in turns to axe through the tree. I went ahead with my machete and hacked at the easy vegetation. I felt eaten up inside with little white maggots of rage.

* * *

Two hours later, sitting together down a clearish straight stretch, Simon reached into another plastic bag and drew out his tape recorder diary. He clicked down the record button and put the machine to his mouth: "Dateline May 14th. Place: Baria river. What's new? I ask myself. No rain today, *that's* what's new I tell myself. Hear that" — he held the machine over the side of the boat — "Right? No endless thundering buckets of piss crashing down on my head all day. Well, you can take it from me, Angel-drawers, the whole ghastly business will start again tomorrow. Up-to-the-minute report: only three wasp stings this morning. No more than 10,000 ants. No hornets. Blissikins, you might say. Oh yes — one more thing before I mosey on out to my favourite pub: Fatso's got the right needle with me just because I wouldn't take a picture of some frigging horrible snake. And how do I know Fatso's got the right needle with me? I know Fatso's got the right needle with me cos he hasn't spoken to me for *two whole hours*."

The rage eased. I laughed. I must fight this anger, I thought; such feelings were as dangerous as they would be in a prison cell. It was an effective weapon, that recorder. I rather wished the mould had grown in it as thoroughly as it had colonised his cameras. I only half-treasured the memory of part of last night's entry, for instance, on which I had eavesdropped from my hammock whilst pretending to be asleep: "In all honesty, Angel," I heard him say, *sotto voce*, "to be perfectly frank with you, Redmond is a selfish bastard. He pretends he likes it here. The Indians, of course, poor geezers, don't know any better. And that Juan is just a nasty little dago who treats me like a moron. Good night. I bite your bum. I miss you. Simon."

* * *

The normal dank, rotting smell of the river bank — or rather the endless series of little islands and interflowing creeks — was displaced by the powerful, musky odour of otter scent and droppings and urine. We passed a muddy patch of firm ground, big enough to camp on, which had been entirely cleared of its undergrowth of shoots and of the usual plants with thick pointed-shovel-shaped leaves; it was a piece of giant otter advertisement which we met three or four times a day.

"The pong those guys make," said Simon. "It's about as close as you get to comradeship around here. There's not a lot else on offer, not so as you'd notice."

We rounded a bend and came to a small pool where four little streams met, and there, barring the way, were the otters themselves. Five large, dark-brown, tightly furred heads, flattened on top, stuck out of the water in a line.

"Ha! Ha! Uh! Uh! Oof!" they said.

Chimo imitated their chatter and they grew agitated, looking at each other, at the boats, then diving and surfacing right beside us.

"Jesus," said Simon, "knock it off, will you Chimo? They're huge. There's no room in here. *I don't want my nuts nicked off.*"

They had small, laid-back ears, large brown eyes, blotches of white on their big chests, and efficient-looking teeth. Drops of water slid off their long side-whiskers.

"Go on boys," said Simon, waving his arms at them, "piss off and scrag a fish."

The otters submerged and reappeared in a creek to the left.

"Christ," said Simon, getting his cigarettes out of the plastic bag.

"They grow to six foot long," I said.

"Surprise me," said Simon, inhaling.

"They're just curious," said Juan, laughing, "they've never seen people."

"That's why they thought we were fish," said Simon.

We ate our manioc-and-water on a strip of sandy mud beneath another sudden gap in the canopy, where a legume tree lay across the stream: it must have fallen in the storms of the last few days because its outsize, broad beanlike seed-pods were still fresh. Everyone except Simon gathered handfuls, brushed off the ants and opened the long, green, knobbly cases with a thumb; we sucked the sweet, white, protective fur from each bean, spitting out the bean itself.

"No wonder you've got the shits," said Simon, turning away to pee on the sand.

Several round-winged, yellow butterflies settled on his slightly steaming urine; and almost at once they were joined by a solitary kite swallowtail which jostled its way to the centre of the patch: its triangular wings were a filmy white translucence, edged with black, and striped across their veining with black lines of varying lengths, some fringed with scarlet, some with a light green, some running from the leading edge to the scalloped rear and continuing down the long blades of its two swordlike tails

"Bit like you," said Simon, sitting on a fallen branch, rubbing the scabs on the back of his neck, and watching the butterfly with distaste. "Looks all right to start with — you'd never guess it had such nasty habits. You'd never think it would eat bird-gut soup with froth on top, piss, anything."

The swallowtail pumped up the warm liquid in its proboscis at one end and jetted it out again, in little spurts, from its anus. It was so exposed, so obvious a target for any passing antbird or gnatwren or tanager that I wondered idly if its warning colours were a copy of some poisonous, plant-feeding species; perhaps it was a party to that Darwinian bluff, Batesian mimicry, which Bates had discovered on his travels in the Amazons to the south.

Culimacaré, Pablo and Chimo, working in relays,

took an hour to axe through the legume tree and clear our passage back into the dark tunnel ahead of us. And three trees later, in the early evening, as Chimo looked in vain for an island in the black maze of streams which might be large enough to camp on, we emerged, without warning, into an open river.

"Told you so!" said Chimo, lying through his gums and so pleased with himself that he forgot his ritual greeting. "The Maguarinuma!"

Released into space, sky, clouds, a land with horizons, we were silent, allowing our eyes to roam. A pair of swallow-tailed kites were gliding low over the palms of the left bank and eight black vultures were stacked above us, wheeling overhead, the highest only just visible. We laid our poles down the edge of the tarpaulins; Chimo and Pablo tilted the hitched-up engines back into the water, pulled their strings and opened up the throttles. We rounded a couple of bends — and there, straight in front of us, were the dark, lowering, canyon sides of the mountain, three-quarters wrapped in cloud.

The light began to fade; the bushes and then the trees on the bank darkened. The clouds, hanging like slow eruptions of steam from the great peaks to our right, turned pink along their undersides and spread their reflections across the water. To our left the high cliffs and the gullied slopes beneath them grew purple, seemed to increase in size and, as night fell, moved toward us until their shadow finally engulfed the jungle and the river in a massy blackness.

WILFRED THESIGER

Wilfred Thesiger was born in Addis Ababa in 1910 and educated at Eton and Oxford. During the war he served in Abyssinia, Syria, and the Western Desert. Since then he has traveled endlessly, by foot, animal, and boat in such remote regions of the world as Southern Arabia, Kurdistan, the Marshes of Iraq, the Hindu Kush, and northern Kenya. He is the recipient of many honors and awards and his books include The Marsh Arabs *and* The Life of My Choice. *In the desert-traveling tradition of C. M. Doughty before him and Michael Asher after him,* Arabian Sands *recounts his journeys in Arabia from 1945 to 1950. In late 1946 he set out on his first crossing of the parched Empty Quarter, the unexplored desert-within-a-desert virtually unknown to Europeans. His name among the Arabs here was Umbarak.*

from **ARABIAN SANDS**

To rest the camels we stopped for four hours in the late afternoon on a long gentle slope which stretched down to another salt flat. There was no vegetation on it and no salt bushes bordered the plain below us. Al Auf announced that we would go on again at sunset. While we were feeding I said to him cheerfully, "Anyway, the worst should be over now that we are across the Uruq al Shaiba." He looked at me for a moment and then answered, "If we go well tonight we should reach them tomorrow." I said, "Reach what?" and he replied, "The Uruq al Shaiba," adding, "Did you think what we crossed today was the Uruq al Shaiba? That was only a dune. You will see them tomorrow." For a moment, I thought he was joking, and then I realized that he was serious, that the worst of the journey which I had thought was behind us was still ahead.

It was midnight when at last al Auf said, "Let's stop here. We will get some sleep and give the camels a rest. The Uruq al Shaiba are not far away now." In my dreams that night they towered above us higher than the Himalayas.

Al Auf woke us again while it was still dark. As usual bin Kabina made coffee, and the sharp-tasting drops which he poured out stimulated but did not warm. The morning star had risen above the dunes. Formless things regained their shape in the first dim light of dawn. The grunting camels heaved themselves erect. We lingered for a moment more beside the fire; then al Auf said "Come," and we moved forward. Beneath my feet the gritty sand was cold as frozen snow.

We were faced by a range as high as, perhaps even higher than, the range we had crossed the day before, but here the peaks were steeper and more pronounced, rising in many cases to great pinnacles, down which the flowing ridges swept like draperies. These sands, paler coloured than those we had crossed, were very soft, cascading round our feet as the camels struggled up the slopes. Remembering how little warning of imminent collapse the dying camels had given me twelve years before in the Danakil country, I wondered how much more these camels would stand, for they were trembling violently whenever they halted. When one refused to go on we heaved on her headrope, pushed her from behind, and lifted the loads on either side as we manhandled the roaring animal upward. Sometimes one of them lay down and refused to rise, and then we had to unload her, and carry the water-skins and the saddlebags ourselves. Not that the loads were heavy. We had only a few gallons of water left and some handfuls of flour.

We led the trembling, hesitating animals upward along great sweeping ridges where the knife-edged crests crumbled beneath our feet. Although it was killing work, my companions were always gentle and infinitely patient. The sun was scorching hot and I felt empty, sick, and dizzy. As I struggled up the slope, knee-deep in shifting sand, my heart thumped wildly and my thirst grew worse. I found it difficult to swallow; even my ears felt blocked, and yet I knew that it would be many intolerable hours before I could drink. I would stop to rest, dropping down on the scorching sand, and immediately it seemed I would hear the others shouting, "Umbarak, Umbarak"; their voices sounded strained and hoarse.

It took us three hours to cross this range.

On the summit were no gently undulating downs such as we had met the day before. Instead, three smaller dune-chains rode upon its back, and beyond them the sand fell away to a salt-flat in another great empty trough between the mountains. The range on the far side seemed even higher than the one on which we stood, and behind it were others. I looked round, seeking instinctively for some escape. There was no limit to my vision. Somewhere in the ultimate distance the sands merged into the sky, but in that infinity of space I could see no living thing, not even a withered plant to give me hope. "There is nowhere to go," I thought. "We cannot go back and our camels will never get up another of these awful dunes. We really are finished." The silence flowed over me, drowning the voices of my companions and the fidgeting of their camels.

We went down into the valley, and somehow — and I shall never know how the camels did it — we got up the other side. There, utterly exhausted, we collapsed. Al Auf gave us each a little water, enough to wet our mouths. He said, "We need this if we are to go on." The midday sun had drained the colour from the sands. Scattered banks of cumulus cloud threw shadows across the dunes and salt flats, and added an illusion that we were high among Alpine peaks, with frozen lakes of blue-and-green in the valley, far below. Half asleep, I turned over, but the sand burnt through my shirt and woke me from my dreams.

Two hours later al Auf roused us. As he helped me load my camel, he said, "Cheer up, Umbarak. This time we really are across the Uruq al Shaiba," and when I pointed to the ranges ahead of us, he answered, "I can find a way through those; we need not cross them." We went on till sunset, but we were going with the grain of the country, following the valleys and no longer trying to climb the dunes. We should not have been able to cross another. There was a little fresh *qassis* on the slope where we halted. I hoped that this lucky find would give us an excuse to stop here for the night, but, after we had fed, al Auf went to fetch the camels, saying, "We must go on again while it is cool if we are ever to reach Dhafara."

We stopped long after midnight and started again at dawn, still exhausted from the strain and long hours of yesterday, but al Auf encouraged us by saying that the worst was over. The dunes were certainly lower than they had been, more uniform in height and more rounded, with fewer peaks. Four hours after we had started we came to rolling uplands of gold and silver sand, but still there was nothing for the camels to eat.

A hare jumped out from under a bush, and al Auf knocked it over with his stick. The others shouted "God has given us meat." For days we had talked of food; every conversation seemed to lead back to it. Since we had left Ghanim I had been always conscious of the dull ache of hunger, yet in the evening my throat was dry even after my drink, so that I found it difficult to swallow the dry bread Musallim set before us. All day we thought and talked about that hare, and by three o'clock in the afternoon could no longer resist stopping to cook it. Mabkhaut suggested, "Let's roast it in its skin in the embers of a fire. That will save our water — we haven't got much left." Bin Kabina led the chorus of protest. "No, by God! Don't even suggest such a thing"; and turning to me he said, "We don't want Mabkhaut's charred meat. Soup. We want soup and extra bread. We will feed well today even if we go hungry and thirsty later. By God, I am hungry!" We agreed to make soup. We were across the Uruq al Shaiba and intended to celebrate our achievement with this gift from God. Unless our camels foundered we were safe; even if our water ran out we should live to reach a well.

Musallim made nearly double our usual quantity of bread while bin Kabina cooked the hare. He looked across at me and said, "The smell of this meat makes me faint." When it was ready he divided it into five portions. They were very small, for an Arabian hare is no larger than an English rabbit, and this one was not even fully grown. Al Auf named the lots and Mabkhaut drew them. Each of us took the small pile of meat which had fallen to him. Then bin Kabina said, "God! I have forgotten to divide the liver," and the others said, "Give it to Umbarak." I protested, saying that they should divide it, but they swore by God that they would not eat it and that I was to have it. Eventually I took it, knowing that I ought not, but too greedy for this extra scrap of meat to care.

MICHAEL ASHER

Born in Great Britain in 1953, Michael Asher was a teacher in the Sudan from 1979 to 1982, where his interest in the nomadic tribes of the Sahara was born. His In Search of the Forty Days Road *is based on his journeys there with the nomads. In the following excerpt from his second book,* A Desert Dies, *he is attempting to travel through the desert by camel to visit some Kababish families in Abu Tabara with his guide, Jibrin. A devastating drought has displaced thousands of nomads in the Sudan by December 1984, where it is much hotter than normal and the grazing has vanished. At this point the two men have been riding six days and are suffering from a severe shortage of water.*

from A DESERT DIES

That evening we camped on a rock shelf beyond the ridge. We cooked porridge, but our mouths were too dry to enjoy it. As the next day dawned I saw to the north a long wall of black rock. It looked no more than ten kilometres away, and had two rock chimneys rising above it. I guessed that it was the southern edge of the legendary Jabal Abyad "The White Mountain," where Kababish herds had grazed in past times. There was a high peak marked on the map as Burj al Hatab, but this was nowhere to be seen. The country to the west was hammada with patches of sand rising to naked peaks of basalt here and there. The day was another hot one, without the solace of a cloud to veil the full power of the sun. We had been riding for six days, most of them under summer conditions, and the camels were tired and thirsty. Working in these temperatures they needed to drink every three or four days, and the grain we fed them increased their thirst. As the day grew hotter, I felt my spirits sink. The lining of my stomach felt tight with a sick, acid sensation. I could think of nothing but water. The thirst was an acute pain, like a nagging toothache that all my powers of concentration could not dismiss. We rode through a region where the rocks were weathered into the shapes of nightmare creatures and strange deformed reptiles. It was a dead, dry, moonscape world where men did not belong. By the middle of the morning, on that sixth day, I was almost dropping from my camel with thirst, my body bent and hunched up over the saddle horns. I guessed Jibrin felt the same, for he had assumed the same hunched position. I knew now that the ability to resist thirst was psychological, not physiological. Experiments had proved that an acclimatized European has exactly the same requirements in the desert as a nomad. One had to have the will to endure it.

Jibrin exclaimed, "By God, it is hot!"

"Let's drink," I said. We couched our camels and drew a single mug of water, half each. At once I felt the moisture seeping into my blood and reactivating my cells and muscles, uncloying and lubricating the tight walls of my stomach that had seized up and fused together.

"Let's go," Jibrin said, and on we went, crossing the huge boulder-strewn plain, two tiny black specks in its midst.

Once we came across the tracks of two men and eight camels. Jibrin grew excited. "These are the tracks of my relations!" he said. We followed them a short way, but they veered drunkenly from side to side in great sweeps and soon petered out amongst the rocks. Still, it was cheering to know that we were on the right trajectory, and our spirits rose a little. But by the time the darkness came our optimism had faded.

The night closed in around us. We ate porridge, chewing it mechanically and retching from its dryness. We drank a little water afterwards, but not enough to quench our thirst. I looked at our remaining supply. Both waterskins were empty and there remained about a gallon in the jerrycan. I could hardly believe that we had used so much. That gallon would last us for the next morning; it might last us all day if we did not eat. That meant that it was essential to find Abu Tabara sometime during the next day. We had no leeway. The chances would be firmly against us, even if the weather changed.

In all my travels in the desert by camel, I had never been in a position as serious as this. I had been thirsty before; I had gone for days without drinking, but then the temperature had been relatively low and our navigation assured. I thought longingly of the bulging skins I had seen in Ed Debba. Why had I not persuaded someone to sell me one? I remembered bathing in the shallow inlets on the waterfront at Debba, and thought of the water pots the river people left outside their houses. I could think of nothing else. I said to Jibrin, "If we do not find Abu Tabara tomorrow we are in big trouble!"

"We shall all die when it is time for us to die," the Arab said. "God is generous."

I rolled over on to my stomach and switched on my torch. The way ahead looked grim, and I felt angry with myself. My navigation had failed. My map had failed. Even Jibrin's knowledge had failed. How on earth could we find Abu Tabara? Now all we could do was to resign ourselves to what came, or fight back. Jibrin, true to his culture, had chosen resignation. I, true to mine, wrote in my journal: "As long as there is the will in me, I shall struggle to survive."

Later we curled up in our blankets. After about half an hour I was still awake when I heard the distant growl of a motor vehicle. The sound swelled and died, then swelled again. It sounded like a truck that had got bogged down in the sand. I jumped up and woke Jibrin. He sat up reluctantly. The sound came again, unmistakably. "Don't you hear it?" I asked him. "No," he replied dully. The sound suddenly ceased, and the desert was quiet again. "There is nothing," my companion said. "You imagined it. It is strange what thirst will do. Go back to sleep. You will need your sleep if we are to find Abu Tabara tomorrow." I lay down straining my ears. There was no sound but the humming breath of the camels. Perhaps I had imagined it after all. I reasoned that Jibrin's senses must be more acute than mine. I did not know that he had suffered mumps as a boy, and was deaf in one ear.

Our departure next morning was grim and silent. We moved off, walking as usual through the mystical landscape of moulded rock and drifting sand. My eyes had become accustomed to the washed-out, pastel hues of the desert scenery, so when my gaze swept over the landscape ahead, I picked out a brilliant yellow-and-silver shape amongst the rocks. I was drawn to it like a magnet. A few paces farther on I realized that it was certainly something man-made. Then Jibrin said, "It *is* a trick, by Almighty God! There are two of them!"

As we approached, we saw that there were two silver-grey Fiats parked amongst the boulders. They were loaded with sacks and carried yellow covers. There were six men with the vehicles, who gathered together to stare at us when we approached. We left our camels hobbled at some distance and went to greet them.

The two drivers were fat townsmen with black faces and fuzzy hair. Their faces dropped in amazement when they realized I was a European. I greeted them formally in the manner of the nomads and ignored their expressions. This was enough to prevent too many tedious questions. They were friendly and called for tea. They told us that they had come from El 'Atrun and were taking rock salt for sale in Dongola. They had not been to Abu Tabara, but they thought it was ahead.

"What grazing have you seen on the way?" Jibrin

asked. I was dying to ask for water and could hardly stand the tension, but I thought it better to let my companion talk.

"Well, there was some grass and trees about half an hour from here," said one of the drivers.

"What kind of trees?" Jibrin asked.

"Thorny ones," answered the other.

I saw Jibrin smile almost pityingly. We drank the tea that the lorry-boys brought us and squatted down in the hearth with them. Jibrin behaved formally and with great dignity. He sipped his tea as if it were his fifth cup. I took my cue from him, even though I was desperate. I realized that it would be a disgrace to display thirst before these townsmen. After we had drunk, Jibrin casually mentioned that we needed some water. The driver told one of the boys to half fill one of our skins. The squelching vessel was laid in front of us. I tried to avoid looking at it. Instead I thanked the men and told them our names.

"Why don't you travel by lorry? It's much easier!" said one of the drivers.

"You can't learn anything in a lorry," I told him. "If you are in a lorry you are not in the desert." He looked at me in bewilderment, but Jibrin's eyes glowed in understanding.

The men climbed aboard the great machines and started the engines. The desert was filled with the sound of their buzzing, and with fumes of oil. The drivers waved and wished us good luck, and we thanked them again. We grabbed the headropes of our camels to prevent them bolting as the vehicles lumbered off, billowing smoke, slowly gathering speed until they disappeared into the landscape.

Then Jibrin poured out a mugful of water and held it out to me. I was too thirsty to worry about protocol. I drank it down greedily in steady gulps. It tasted like cream. When it was finished, I exclaimed, "Praise be to God!" and meant it. Then Jibrin drank. As we reloaded the camels, he muttered, "Those people don't even know they are travelling. There are some trees here . . . some grass there . . . 'thorny ones' indeed! They know nothing of the desert!"

"You cannot know the desert if you travel by motor vehicle," I said.

"Yes," he agreed. "There is nothing better than a camel in the desert. The lorry is fast but you cannot enjoy it." I had always hated motor vehicles, yet I knew that this time they had saved my life.

We walked for almost four hours over the carcass of the desert. Soon the rocks gave way to a basin of brown dust with a great edifice of jagged black rock on the horizon. We mounted up as the time passed, not daring to halt, for the half skin of water would soon be used up and we could waste no time. In the middle of the plain was a withered *tundub* and at its base lay the tangled skeleton of a camel, the dry hide twisted around the bones. There were a few leaves on the tree and we let our camels browse. Jibrin joked, "Was this camel a male or a female? It doesn't matter much now does it! Was it brown or red? Who cares anyway!"

We pressed on, but now the camels were faltering. "This one will be dead soon if we do not find water!"

Jibrin declared. At midday we crossed a dune and saw from the top a depression filled with massive slabs of rock, black and silver, weathered and carved into weird figures and half-buried by furrows of sand. The sun was so hot it took our breath away. As we descended the dune slope, Jibrin said, "It must be here."

I knew he was right. This was the lowest land as far as I could see, and the water course must be in a depression. Then we saw a trail of droppings scattered in the sand. They looked very old. We moved on, weaving in and out of the boulders. There were no other signs of humans or herds, and I was beginning to wonder if this was really the place when Jibrin cried, "See the last of the tents! This is it!" Looking down, I saw many pieces of torn *shuggas*, half covered in sand, with broken pots, useless leather buckets, split saddlebags. "This is Abu Tabara," Jibrin said, smiling. We climbed a hump of sand, and he showed me the single well, covered in flat stones. "They have all gone," he said. "They must have left only days ago." It was disappointing to find the place uninhabited, but the survival instinct was stronger: I was overjoyed to find water.

Near the well we spied an immense block of granite that had split in half. The fissure was easily large enough to take us and all our luggage. As we sat down in the shade both of us said, "Praise be to God!" and were silent for a moment. Jibrin exclaimed "By Almighty God! This is where we were, all that time ago! There were Awlad Huwal and Hamdab here then. I wonder what happened to them all!"

I walked down to the well head. There was a basin

of dried clay, and the well was covered with five flat stones. I crouched down and removed them carefully. Then I dropped a pebble into the gaping hole. The "plunk!" and the rippling of water was a holy sound in this appalling dryness. Abu Tabara was a holy shrine devoted to this end. Jibrin brought the well bucket and hoisted up some of the liquid. It was clean and clear and its taste as untainted as the desert wind. It seemed like a miracle. Here, in the middle of the most dangerous desert on earth, there was water. Here there was life.

ERIC NEWBY

Eric Newby was born in London in 1919 and edu-cated at St. Paul's School. In World War II he was captured off the coast of Sicily on a secret mission and was kept a prisoner-of-war from 1942 to 1945. His many books of adventure and travel include The Last Grain Race, Slowly Down the Ganges, Love and War in the Apennines, The Big Red Train Ride, *and* A Traveller's Life. *A* Short Walk in the Hindu Kush *narrates the story of his amateur mountain-climbing experiences in Asia with his friend Hugh Carless. In the following passage they are attempting to scale the summit of Mir Samir in Nuristan, having already taken five hours instead of two just to reach their present position on a ridge, only to find that the summit is still invisible. We are reminded of Wilfred Thesiger's observation: "Who, after all, would dispute that it is more satisfying to climb to the top of a mountain than to go there in a funicular railway?" Mr. Thesiger, of course, was in the desert.*

from A SHORT WALK IN THE HINDU KUSH

First we tackled the castlelike knob to our left, going up the north side. It had all the attributes of an exposed face, together with a truly awe-inspiring drop of three thousand feet to the east glacier, and it was bitterly cold; like everywhere else we had so far been on this aggravating mountain there were no good belays. Up to now in the most difficult circumstances we had managed a few grim little jokes, but now on the face of this abominable castle our capacity for humour finally deserted us.

From the top of the castle there was the choice of the north side which was cold and grim or the south, a labyrinthine chaos of rock, fitted with clefts and chimneys too narrow to admit the human frame without pain. In one of these clefts that split a great boulder twenty feet long, we both became wedged and only extricated ourselves with difficulty. Sometimes exasperated with this lunatic place we would force a way over the ridge through the soft snow only to find ourselves, with no way of going on, forced to return by the way we had come.

But as we advanced, the ridge became more and more narrow and eventually we emerged on to a perfect knife edge. Ahead, but separated from us by two formidable buttresses, was the summit, a simple cone of snow as high as Box Hill.

We dug ourselves a hole in the snow and considered our position. The view was colossal. Below us on every side mountains surged away it seemed for ever; we looked down on glaciers and snow-covered peaks that perhaps no one has ever seen before, except from the air. To the west and north we could see the great axis of the Hindu Kush and its southward curve, from the

Anjuman Pass around the northern marches of Nuristan. Away to the east-northeast was the great snow-covered mountain we had seen from the wall of the east glacier, Tirich Mir, the twenty-five-thousand-foot giant on the Chitral border, and to the southwest the mountains that separated Nuristan from Paryshir.

Our own immediate situation was no less impressive. A stone dropped from one hand would have landed on one of the upper glaciers of the Chamar Valley, while from the other it would have landed on the east glacier. Hugh, having determined the altitude to be 19,100 feet, now gave a practical demonstration of this by dropping the aneroid, which fell with only one bounce into the Chamar Valley.

"Bloody thing," said Hugh gloomily. "I don't think it was much use anyway." Above us choughs circled uttering melancholy croaking noises. "We've got to make a decision about going on," he said. "And we've got to be absolutely certain it's the right one, because our lives are going to depend on it."

Anywhere else such a remark would have sounded over dramatic. Here it seemed no more than an accurate statement of fact.

"How long do you think it will take to get to the top?"

"All of four hours and then only if we don't go any slower."

It was now one-thirty; we had been climbing for nine hours.

"That means five-thirty at the summit. Going down, four hours at least to the Castle, and then twenty minutes to the *col* on the ridge. It'll be nine o'clock. Then there's the ice slope. Do you think we can manage the *col* to the camp in the dark?"

"The only alternative is to sleep on the ridge. We haven't got any sleeping-bags. I'm afraid we wouldn't last out. We can try if you like."

For a moment we were dotty enough to consider going on. It was a terrific temptation: we were only seven hundred feet below the summit. Then we decided to give up. Both of us were nearly in tears. Sadly we ate our nougat and drank our cold coffee.

The descent was terrible. With the stimulus of the summit gone, we suddenly realized how tired we were. But, although our strength and morale were ebbing, we both agreed to take every possible precaution. There was no mountain rescue service on this mountain. If anything happened to one of us, a bad sprain would be enough, it would be the end for both. As we went down I found myself mumbling to myself again and again, "One man's death diminishes mee, one man's death diminishes mee."

Yet, though we were exhausted, we felt an immense sense of companionship. At this difficult moment the sense of dependence on one another, engendered perhaps by the fact we were roped together and had one another's lives in our hands, produced in me a feeling of great affection for Hugh, this tiresome character who had led me to such a spot.

At six we were at the *col* below the Castle, exactly as he had prophesied. The conditions were very bad. All the way down from the Castle a tremendous wind had been blowing and the mountainside was flooded in a ghastly yellow light as the sun went down. As the clouds came up the wind became a blizzard, a howling gale with hail and snow battering us. We had come down from the Castle without crampons. Now to cross the head of the *col* in this wind on the frozen snow, we had to put them on again. Still wearing them, we lowered ourselves one by one over the overhanging crest into a gully on the south face.

The south face was a grey desolation and the gully was the wrong one. It was too wide for an easy descent and was smooth ice the whole way for two hundred feet.

Twice we had to take off and put on our crampons, almost blubbering with fatigue and vexation, as the straps were frozen and adjusting them seemed to take an eternity. Worst of all the wind on the ridge was blowing snow into the gully, half blinding us and sending down big chunks of rock. One of these hit Hugh on the shoulder, hurting him badly, and I thought he was going to faint. The gully was succeeded by a minute chimney full of ice, down which I glissaded on my behind for twenty feet until Hugh pulled me up. Very stupidly I was wearing my crampons attached to a sling round my middle and I sat on them for the full distance, so that they went in to the full length of the spikes, scarring me for life in a most interesting manner.

By now it was quite dark. We had an hour on the rocks, now covered with a fresh sheet of ice, that I shall remember for the rest of my life. Then we were home. "Home" was just the ledge with the two sleeping bags, some food and the stoves, but we had thought of nothing else for hours.

As we stumbled on to it, a great dark shape rose up and struck a match, illuminating an ugly, well-known face with a wart on its forehead. It was Shir Muhammad, most feckless and brutal of drivers, come up to find us.

"I was worried about you," he said simply, "so I came."

It was nine o'clock; we had been climbing for seventeen hours.

By now we were beyond speech. After a long hour the contents of both cooking pots boiled simultaneously, so we drank tea and ate tomato soup at the same time. It was a disagreeable mixture, which we followed with a pot of neat jam and two formidable-looking sleeping-pills that from their size seemed more suitable for horses than human beings.

"I don't approve of drugs," were Hugh's last words before we both sank into a coma, "but I think that under the circumstances we're justified."

We woke at five. My first thought as I came to was that I had been operated on, an illusion heightened by the sight of Hugh's bloody bandaged hands gripping the mouth of his sleeping bag. Mine were now in the same condition as Hugh's had been two days previously; his were worse than ever.

It took us both a long time to dress and Shir Muhammad had to button our trousers, which was a difficult operation for someone who had never had fly buttons of his own. It was the only time I ever saw him laugh. Then he laced our boots.

As soon as I started to move I realized that my feet were beyond boots, so I decided to wear rubber shoes.

By the time we left the platform it was like a hot plate. Shir Muhammad went first, skipping downhill like a goat bearing a great load. Soon he became impatient with our funereal progress and left us far behind.

At the head of the glacier Hugh stopped and took off his pack.

"What's the matter?"

"Rope," he croaked. "Left a rope. Got to go back."

"Don't be an ass."

"Might need it . . . another try."

"Not this year.

It was useless to argue with him. He was already crawling uphill. My return to fetch the karabiner on the other glacier had created an impossible precedent.

The glare of the small snowfield was appalling. My goggles were somewhere in my rucksack, but I had not the will power to stop and look for them. Soon I developed a splitting headache. With my rubber shoes on I fell continuously. I found myself becoming very grumpy.

At the top of the *moraine* Abdul Ghiyas was waiting for us. He had passed Shir Muhammad without seeing him, somewhere in the labyrinth on the lower slopes of this provoking mountain, and was clucking to himself anxiously.

"Where is Carless *Seb*?"

"Up."

"He is dead?"

"No, he is coming."

"You have climbed the mountain?"

"No."

"Why is Carless *Seb* not with you?"

It was only after much pantomime that I was able to convince him that Hugh was not dead, sacrificed to my own ambition, and he consented to follow me down, carrying my load.

But at the camp we waited an hour, two hours for Hugh; there was no sign of him. I began to be worried and reproached myself for not having waited. The three drivers, huddled over the fire preparing a great secret mess in honour of our arrival, were mumbling, "Carless *Seb*, Carless *Seb*, where is Carless *Seb*?" droning on and on.

Finally Hugh appeared. With his beard full of glacial cream and his cracked lips, he looked like what he in fact was, the survivor of a spectacular disaster.

"Where have you been? We've been worried stiff."

"I got the rope," he said, "then I went to sleep under a rock."

PETER MATTHIESSEN

Peter Matthiessen graduated from Yale in 1950 and helped found The Paris Review *the following year. Among his novels are* At Play in the Fields of the Lord, Far Tortuga, *and most recently,* Killing Mr. Watson. *His numerous nonfiction works include* The Cloud Forest, Wildlife in America, *and* Men's Lives. *In 1973 he set out from Pokhara, Nepal, and walked for five weeks across the snowy Himalaya to reach the Crystal Mountain on the Tibetan plateau, where he and his friend and fellow traveler, biologist George Schaller, hoped to glimpse the rarest of great cats, the snow leopard. His account of that journey, including his return through the high passes, is an often stark and sometimes luminous record of an accompanying search for inner peace. It won the National Book Award.*

from THE SNOW LEOPARD

The camp is less than a thousand feet below the Namdo Pass, and so this morning there is biting cold, with no warmth in the frozen sun when it appears over the eastern rim. This canyon plunges eventually into a maelstrom of narrow, dark ravines that must emerge into that eastern arm of Phoksumdo that we saw on October 25, for there is the aura of a void between one spine of summits and the next where the turquoise lake of the great demoness lies hidden.

Despite the cold, Tende and Chiring Lamo sit near naked on a sheepskin by their daybreak fire, the child's head laid amongst the beads and amulets and cold silver on Tende's round brown breasts. But Dawa is sick this morning; through Tukten, he tells me that even before leaving Shey, he suffered from dysentery and internal bleeding. That last is worrisome; it might well lead to worse. Perhaps he should rest, but we cannot stay in this wild place between high passes. And of course it is only luck that he came out with us; had it not been for Gyaltsen's fear of Tukten, Dawa might have remained behind and died there, without ever speaking up, less out of fortitude than in that peasant apathy and fatalism that is so often taken for stupidity.

I give him something for his dysentery; it may kill him. In his weakened state, Dawa longs to be taken care of; it pleases him to be reminded that he must wear a snow mask, so as not to complicate his sickness with snow blindness. He stands before me in knee britches, big head hanging, like a huge disobedient child.

The yak route descends into night shadows, crossing the ice rivers of this canyon and emerging again on sunny mountainside. Here where sun and shadow meet, a flock of Himalayan snow cock sails away down the steep mountain. To the north and west, across the canyons, the thorn-scrub slopes are cut by cliffs, and soon blue sheep come into view, two far pale bands, one of nine, and the other of twenty-six. I search in vain for sign of the snow leopard.

Down in the shelter of a gully, a yak caravan is preparing to set out; two men strap last loads on the balky animals. Before long, there appears another caravan, this one bound north; having discharged its salt and wool, it is headed home with a cargo of grain, lumber, and variegated goods, its yaks rewarded for their toil with big red tassels on their packs and small orange ones decking out their ears. The dark shapes of the nomads glint with beads and earrings, amulets, and silver daggers; here are the Ch'ang Tartars of two thousand years ago. With their harsh cries and piercing whistles, naked beneath filthy skins of animals, these wild men bawling at rough beasts are fit inhabitants of such dark gorges; one can scarcely imagine them anywhere else. The Redfaced Devils are inquisitive, and look me over before speaking out in the converse of the pilgrim.

Where do you come from?

Shey Gompa.

Ah. Where are you going?

To the Bheri.

Ah.

And so the wary dogs skirt past, we nod, grimace, and resume our paths to separate destinies and graves.

* * *

Winding around beneath towers of rock that fall away into abyss after abyss, the path wanders randomly in all directions. In the cold shine of its ice, this waste between high passes is a realm of blind obliterating nature. The labyrinth is beautiful, yet my heart is touched by dread. I hurry on. At last the ledge trail straightens, headed south, and I reach the foot of the last climb to the pass just before noon. On a knoll, there is a prayer wall and a stock corral for those who come too late in the day to start the climb. Plainly, we shall not reach Murwa before nightfall, despite Karma's assurances to the contrary; we shall have to press hard just to cross the pass and descend far enough below the snows to find brushwood to keep warm. Lacking mountain lungs, I am slow in the steep places, and I start the climb at once, without waiting for the others to come up.

Looking back every little while as I ascend, I see that Karma, arriving at the prayer wall, sets out a sheepskin and lies down, while Tende, Dawa, and Tukten perch on rocks. No doubt Karma will build a fire here and delay everyone with a lengthy meal, thus assuring himself and his wife and child the miserable task, at the end of a long day, of setting up camp in cold and dark, for he is as lightheaded as he is lighthearted, and gives the day's end no more thought than anything else. Every piece of information that this smiling man has offered has been wrong: the climb to this pass, it is plain to see, is not only steeper but longer than the last one.

In the cold wind, the track is icy even at midday, yet one cannot wander to the side without plunging through the crust. The regular slow step that works best on steep mountainside is difficult; I slip and clamber. Far above, a train of yaks makes dark curves on the shining ice; soon a second herd overtakes me, the twine-soled herders strolling up the icy incline with hands clasped behind their backs, grunting and whistling at the heaving animals. Then black goats come clicking up the ice glaze, straight, straight up to the noon sky; the goat horns turn silver on the blue as, in the vertigo and brilliance of high sun, the white peak spins. The goatherd, clad from head to boots in blood-red wool, throws balls of snow to keep his beasts in line; crossing the sun, the balls dissolve in a pale fire.

Eventually the track arrives at the snowfields beneath the summit rim; I am exhausted. Across the whiteness sails a lammergeier, trailing its shadow on the snow, and the wing shadow draws me taut and sends me on. For two more hours I trudge and pant and climb and slip and climb and gasp, dull as any brute, while high above, the prayer flags fly on the westering sun, which turns the cold rocks igneous and the hard sky to white light. Flag shadows dance upon the white walls of the drifts as I enter the shadow of the peak, in an ice tunnel, toiling and heaving, eyes fixed stupidly upon the snow. Then I am in the sun once more, on the last of the high passes, removing my woolen cap to let the wind clear my head; I sink to my knees, exhilarated, spent, on a narrow spine between two worlds.

To the south and west, glowing in snow light and late sun, the great white Kanjirobas rise in haze, like mystical peaks that might vanish at each moment. The caravans are gone into the underworld. Far behind me and below, in the wastes where I have come from, my companions are black specks upon the snow. Still breathing hard, I listen to the wind in my own breath, the ringing silence, the snow fire and soaring rocks, the relentless tappeting of prayer flags, worn diaphanous, that cast wind pictures to the northern blue.

I have the universe all to myself. The universe has me all to itself.

Time resumes, there comes a change in mood. Under the pack, my back is sweating, and the hard wind chills me. Before I am rested, the cold drives me off the peak into a tortuous descent down sharp rock tumulus, hidden by greasy corn snow and glare ice, and my weak legs slip between the rocks as the pack's weight pitches me forward. A thousand feet down, this rockfall changes to a steep snow-patched trail along an icy stream. Toward dusk, in the painful going, I am overtaken by Tukten in his scanty clothes and sneakers. Tukten's indifference to cold and hardship is neither callous nor ascetic: what it seems to be is calm acceptance of everything that comes, and this is the source of that inner quiet that makes his nondescript presence so impressive. He agrees that Murwa is out of the question, and goes on down, still quick and light, to find fuel and a level place to camp.

The steep ravine descending from the pass comes out at last on sandy mountainside that drops into the upper canyon of the Murwa River. Dusk has fallen, and I keep my distance from two herders' fires for fear of the big dogs. Farther on, as darkness comes, I call out, "Tukten, *Tuk-ten*," but there is no answer. Then, below, I see him making a fire; the inspired man has found a stone shed by a waterfall.

Dawa turns up an hour later, and lies down in the shed without his supper. Every little while we call to Karma and his family, but another hour passes, the stars shine, and no one comes. This morning a yawning Karma had excused his reluctance to get up by saying we would arrive at Murwa in midafternoon. Doubtless it was this feckless minstrel who told Jang-bu, who told me, that "one hard day, one easy one" would take us from Saldang to Murwa: two hard days and one easy one are now behind us, and still we are not there. In his airy way, Jang-bu concluded that we could cross both passes in a single day, since neither one, so he was told, was as high or as arduous as the Shey Pass, not to speak of the Kang La. Being ignorant, I didn't argue, though I had to wonder why, if this were true, the wool traders, coming from Saldang, had chosen the Shey Pass-Kang La route over the other. Tonight I know. Because the icy north face of Kang La is too steep for yaks, the traveler must break his own trail in the snow; otherwise that route is much less strenuous than the Shey-Murwa route, in which three passes must be crossed. And the descent from the third pass up there, in snow conditions, is as wearing as the climb. I hate to think of Chiring Lamo in the ice and starlight, swaying along near-precipices on Tende's small and tired shoulders; these ledge trails should not be traveled in the night, without a moon.

However, I am too tired to act, or even think. I am already in my sleeping bag when this innocent family appears out of the darkness; hearing Tukten's voice, I end these notes and go to sleep.

JOHN MILLS

Born in England in 1930, John Mills came to Montreal as an odd-jobber in the mid 1950s, worked on the DEW Line in the North, and ended up an English professor at Simon Fraser University in Vancouver. He has published three novels, The Land of Is, The October Men, *and* Skevington's Daughter, *and a collection memoirs and reviews,* Lizard in the Grass. *He was nineteen when he had the following journey in Scandinavia.*

THE NIGHT OF LUCIA

Östersund, Sweden — about the middle of December, 1949. Our first day out was bleak but relatively mild. The landscape lay under a frigid, grey mist through which the outlines of the thin pines showed blurred and dark grey. The sky was dark, for thick clouds had grown slowly during the night and fused with the mist on the low hills. I never knew whether the road itself was paved or not. Perhaps by now it has become a concrete superhighway — Sundsval to Trondheim with exits for Hammerstrand, Brecke, Östersund and Åre — but then it was covered with a layer of snow and gravel which had frozen together to produce a dense substance, the surface of which seemed hard as diamond. I could feel

316

every ice-embedded pebble in it through the thin soles of my rubber boots — Wellington boots: the kind a man wears in England for a quiet day's weeding in the garden. The warmer weather rendered the ice slippery — a boot would skate on the heavier gravel and I'd totter wildly, trying to regain balance, plunging the other boot around for a foothold, but it would slip, in its turn, and I'd land with a bone-shaking crash on the steel-hard road. So from time to time, I'd give up and walk on the heaps of packed, brownish snow on the road's shoulder, but this had become almost as treacherous, to my useless boots, as the gravel itself and it was like slithering over glass-coated screes. Beyond the shoulder was a drainage ditch filled with light, powdery snow under a brittle crust — a boot whacked into the ditch would sink straight down with a crunching sound and fill itself with this finer snow which would melt, then gel into thick, transparent icicles in the tops of my socks. My rucksack was too heavy and too cumbersome, for strapped to the top of it, was a small valise. The arrangement did its best to pull me out of the vertical and would swing heavily to complete the job of throwing me to the ground whenever I started to topple off balance. I improved its stability when we stopped to eat by jettisoning some of the rucksack's contents and stuffing the valise inside.

We had seen no building of any sort, so at noon we stumbled through the unstained, shallow snow of a disused loop road — a resting place for maintenance vehicles. We found some logs and, placing them side by side, built a twig fire in the space between and started the long job of melting snow for coffee. Sam poked at

317

the fire singing under his breath a song popular in those dark, post-war days. "Evening shadows make me blue," he muttered, but without much conviction. He'd not had too bad a time of it, for his boots were of the solid, Vibram-soled type and, what's more, they fitted him. He'd fallen a couple of times but he was by no means the bruised, numbed, and useless object he was trying to encourage. Apart from this, however, he had the invaluable knack of accurate focus. For example I was a man trying to get to Norway against time and under the pressure of future hunger; he, on the other hand, was a man walking along the road, who had stopped for lunch, and who, dressed in warm clothing, was also solving the problem of keeping on his feet. I wished to act in such a way that my movements were planned, meaningful and patterned. . . . Sam knew, without even thinking about it, that coherence lies only in the present moment, and that he would do, in the future, whatever needed to be done. I wanted something to come of whatever I did; Sam did things for their own sake and could not have cared less about the result. He was even, I think, beginning to enjoy himself at that stage.

The two cups of coffee took over an hour to make. We thawed out the sardines, whose oil had become thick and opaque, and I bared my feet, wrapped a towel around them, picked icicles from my socks, then dried the latter near the fire.

It was dark when we started off again.

We had seen no traffic at all, once or twice, we walked past a farm. These had been invisible in daylight, for they were well off the road, but now we could see their lights, a long way off the road, flickering through the trees. We should look, I said, for paths leading toward this river on our left and find a barn to flop in for the night. Let's push it a bit, Sam answered, and see what turns up. This was the last we said to each other for several miles.

Just after dark it began to snow. It was light, small-flaked stuff that seemed, in the darkness, to spurt gently against the skin like drops of ether. It fell into my hair, melted, and began to drip down my face in long uncontrollable and infuriating streaks which disappeared into the neck of my shirt. But two hours after dark the snow stopped, the sky cleared and suddenly it grew intensely cold. We could see the moon through huge, expanding gaps in the clouds. The strands of my hair began to freeze together and I shoved on a balaclava helmet preferring the constant dripping of water down my face to a frostbitten ear. Except for the echoing crunching of our boots on the fresh snow there was a deep silence into which each sound seemed swallowed, like water in quicklime. We could see the pines as black, feathery silhouettes against the blue-black sky punctured with stars. I became almost hypnotized by the silvery patches of light thrown by the soles of my boots against the snow as I trudged along and it was too cold, now, for my boots to skid easily.

It must have been just before nine o'clock when we heard the car coming.

It began as a tiny, vaguely sensed disturbance in the matrix of silence around us, growing, slowly, until we heard and recognized it, quite suddenly, as a car's engine. I turned, and a mile or so back on the chord across the valley where the road curved, I saw a horizontal cone of white light, dipping and swinging round toward us.

Quick I said, stand in the road.

Stand in the road be buggered, Sam replied, he'll run us down.

The driver swerved slightly to avoid us and swept past, the air eddies in front of the car whipping up thin gauzes of snow and drawing them across the road like the hems of bridal veils. The headlights silvered the telephone wires around the curve ahead.

Bastard, Sam said.

Wait a minute. . . .

The sound of the engine, almost faded into the distance, stopped.

He's stopped for us, I shouted, let's run.

We hobbled forward as fast as we could. My rucksack began to sway heavily until one of the straps broke and it lurched into the snow. Sam shuffled ahead while I hoisted the rucksack on one shoulder and clenched the broken strap against the other. But Sam had stopped on the brow of the hill. The road, after the curve, climbed, then dropped into a valley. There was a house on the left, then another, then two more. Round another bend and we were in a small village, walking along a main street lined with Christmas trees gay with coloured lights. One or two well-fed fur-hatted Swedes passed us on the sidewalk and looked us up and down. The car had not pulled up for us, of course, but at some house in the village. We never even discovered the name of the place. We walked straight through it — no place for the penniless — as though we knew where we were going, struck off along a side path a mile beyond, and found a barn.

* * *

After our night in the barn we woke cold, cramped, and ravenously hungry. I spliced my rucksack strap with a piece of rope while Sam crept out of the barn, sneaked toward the road and stole a can of cream that stood amid milk churns on a platform by the entrance to the farm. We stirred the mixture of ice and thick cream until it was drinkable and counted our supplies — two cans of sardines, one of beans, half a loaf of bread and a tin of Nescafé — we had no money at all. We gobbled the sardines this time without bothering to warm up the congealed oil. There was no time — we had to be on the road to catch the early morning traffic.

There wasn't any. Two cars went by, then a milk truck whose driver merely shook his head at us. To keep warm we began to walk.

As the sky grew lighter I had the curious sensation that we were back twenty miles or so, starting afresh from Östersund. There was the same wide valley cut between low hills, the same mist and dark sky, the same interminable, featureless, gently curving highway. It was colder and easier on the feet, for the fresh powdery snow provided a little friction, but, within an hour I had become hungry again and with hunger there grew in me, for the first time, a willingness to discuss alternatives. We can go on like this, I thought, until we drop from starvation, exhaustion, exposure. We were in a part of the country apparently inhabited by suspicious xenophobes who would like as not turn us in to the police as vagrants if we appealed to them for help. And the police would hand us over to our respective consuls who'd confiscate our passports, label us, and send us home D.B.S. — Distressed British Subjects. So much, then, for my dreams of self-sufficiency. It would be the end of the Norway scheme and probably of my relationship with Joan, its other begetter. What love could survive such humiliation? So Sam and I would have to stay on the road and, if we persevered, we'd undoubtedly stumble into Trondheim, miles ahead, a big town with jobs, money, and shelter to offer.

But something else occurred to me. If we hit the frontier without money, bearded, hungry, and ragged, we stood a very good chance of being thrown back. And it was no use trying to enter Norway illegally if I wished to work there and make it my home. The alternative would be to find some place between here and the frontier to find work for a few days, and enter by train and in comparative style. Jumping freight trains was out — there was a railroad along the valley, but again, we had to stay this side of the law.

I thought again about the Swedes — they had been hospitable enough so far — perhaps I was being a little paranoid about them. Surely no one would turn us into the cops purely for begging at his doorstep. On the other hand, northern Sweden in those days was unused to beggars and suspicious of foreigners, particularly those without visible means of support. But it looked as though we'd have to risk it.

We discussed all this at our midday halt. The safest thing, I said, might be to walk back to that village, phone Robert in the Lutheran Mission at Östersund and get him to wire us some of his girlfriend's money. Sam shook his head. Never go back, he said. Something'll turn up.

Take a look at that sky, he said later. We're gunna have snow up the arse by nightfall. . . .

The grey-misty sky had grown black and sullen toward the South and East and heavy nimbus clouds spread slowly toward us like a dark stain. The valley toward Östersund had disappeared, completely . . . swallowed in the cloud.

We packed up hastily and buried the can. Its contents had by no means satisfied our hunger . . . merely whetted it. My eyes felt gummy from the night's uneasy sleep and I could not stop myself from yawning. I knew that my body was covered in bruises from the tumbles of the day before. My kneejoints creaked as I got up to go, hoisting my leaden rucksack with difficulty over my shoulders. Sam was in slightly better shape but as an Australian was more used, than I was, to large meals. He began to bitch as we walked slowly down the road, about his empty stomach and his increasing physical weakness . . . My gut's shrunk right up, he complained. When did we eat last? . . . Properly, I mean . . . I don't count that bloody porridge at the mission . . . two days ago . . . that's when it was . . . we can't go on much longer, boy, we're gunna drop in our tracks . . . to think I could be back in Stockholm alonga those French bastards . . . they'll be sitting in the warm, laughin' at

323

us . . . stealin' our women . . . keep yer eyes skinned for a house.

But no sooner had we ratified this decision to risk the cops by begging, then the opportunity, such as it had been, to do so, vanished. We had begun, very slowly, to leave the wide valley with its scattered farms and frozen river behind us. The road twisted slightly and rose higher above the valley floor to work its way into denser forest. Ahead of us, in the dusk, the road seemed to be driving toward the flank of a long, high ridge. It looked as though we were going to cross a watershed into the system of glens and lakes that wound their way toward the Norwegian border. There was unlikely to be a farm for many miles. Behind us the sky was black and within ten minutes it had swallowed the grey twilight and we felt the first, hesitant lash of windborne snow. As we got into the trees the wind dropped but the snow began to pelt down — huge, dry flakes of it which built up on our shoulders and packs and found every gap and join in our clothing. The snow rapidly became ankle deep and then high enough to spill into our boots. The visibility sank to zero. At one point I left the road altogether in the darkness and plunged up to my waist in the ditch. Sam pulled me out and I lay panting and exhausted on the road with the snow building up mercilessly around me. With great difficulty I got to my feet, took two or three steps, then sank into the ditch again. The makeshift strap on my rucksack broke and with a savage oath I released the other strap and threw the whole bloody thing aside. I rested my arms on the edge of the drift, and gasped for breath. I could see only the snow falling rapidly in front of my face and of the road itself and the trees I could see no sign. I could hear Sam shouting in the darkness. I yelled back and he lit his cigarette lighter while I called directions to him. I could see the flame drop suddenly as he stumbled into a soft drift and the light vanished to reappear again a minute or so later. I heaved myself out of the hole I'd dug and lay on the snow. I no longer knew which was road and which was ditch. Sam found me and shook the snow from his clothes and hair and helped me to my feet. The snow began to settle on us as we stood gingerly in one spot, rolling and lighting a couple of sodden cigarettes.

We're off the road, he said. We must've missed the son-of-a-bitch in the dark and gone up one of those bloody farm tracks by mistake . . . and now we've even lost *that*.

As far as we could tell we'd ended up in a tiny clearing surrounded by an almost impenetrable forest of low pines. The tracks we'd made were now completely obscured and even the holes we'd made in the snow drifts were beginning to fill. With Sam's help I found my rucksack and ripped a dozen pages out of a copy of Gibbon I'd been carrying for sustenance and which, of course, I'd not opened until now. We pulled a dead branch off a neighboring pine, shook the snow off it, and broke its twigs. We snapped the branch into three pieces, laid them together on the snow, and stood over the twigs until, with the aid of Gibbon's noble prose, they began to burn. Snow hissed into the fire as we left it to round up more fuel. The fire flickered badly and its light danced back from the wall of timber which surrounded us. Our hunger had died down and left an increasing feebleness which made each step we took an almost impossible effort.

At one point I found myself gaping and dozing numbly in a foxhole my body had inadvertently prepared for me in a snow bank by the trees. I watched myself gazing vacantly at the hissing flames, and at Sam's dancing, gigantic shadow. I heard the damp, smoking crackle of the logs. Then with a snapping sound, and couple of red sparks, the light went out as though it had been flicked off with a switch. Sam had dozily allowed the three branches to burn through and dunk the flame they bore into the snow. I dragged myself upright and forced my way through the waist-high snow to where he stood tearing up my Gibbon and thumbing his lighter.

It's useless, I said. It'll take all we've got to keep the damn thing going. Let's find that path again and make for the farm.

Both of us knew just how mere a gesture this would be. In such deserted country the farm could be miles off along what would now be an almost impenetrable path. But the highway, if we ever found it, would be just as useless . . . there was nothing back the way we'd come and very little chance of there being a village ahead of us. The fire had shown up that the clearing was shaped like a pear and we knew, roughly, where the narrow end of it was. We pushed our way towards it and almost immediately became entrapped by trees. But the snow did not fall so rapidly here and the going proved a little easier. I felt my feet graze rock and once or twice I tripped on a buried deadfall and slid over the other side of it up to my waist. It seemed as though we were fighting our way round the trunks of trees, penetrating deeper and deeper into the forest. Half an hour of it and we gave up. We were far too exhausted to either go farther or to return the way we came.

I shucked my rucksack onto the snow. Let's hole up, I said. Sam nodded and said nothing. We burrowed under the spreading branches of a tree and, with our last remaining energy, dug out a snow cave.

If it quits snowing, Sam said, we stand a chance . . . but if it goes on for a couple of days, we'll've had it.

It was my turn to nod.

I no longer felt cold, nor hungry. I had begun to doze and my body seemed to be floating, upwards on soft eiderdown. I could hear my own blood pulsing slowly around my body and as a faint background whisper through which I heard, every now and again, the creaking of a branch under its load of snow, the snapping of a twig as Sam shifted his position. This, I remember thinking, is not a bad way to die. There's none of the choking terror of drowning, or the agony of death by fire. Here one's life begins to ebb out of the body slowly and painlessly, flowing gently into the cold, dead forest. We'd disappear, that was the only trouble with it . . . it might be years before we were found in this thick, untravelled bushland. We would vanish like dry ice in warm air . . . there would be enquiries from England . . . a perfunctory search . . . but no one would find us here. The cold and my exhaustion had drained me of any regrets . . . at nineteen I was perhaps too young to die like this but at least I'd be spared the horrors of cancer, or the sudden whiplash of angina . . . life's no joke, I thought, when all's said and done . . . a finite series of hot dinners, as a friend of mine once put it . . . it was nothing, and neither was death.

I began to doze.

Sam Harstein was shaking my shoulder. A light! he was saying, there's a light ahead. I staggered to my feet. Outside our miniature cave it had stopped snowing. Had we continued for a few more minutes, fighting through the bush, we'd've come out of the trees onto a huge field. I could see it now, plainly — a lovely expanse of bare snow sparkling in the moonlight. At the far side of it was a house with lighted windows. With a final effort we ploughed our way toward it and bashed on the door.

*   *   *

The man who answered our frenzied knocking did not, as the poet sings, gaze about him with a wild surmize. He was clearly a man of action. He rushed us upstairs into hot showers and warm bathrobes then suggested that when we were ready for it we should join the company in the dining room. We'd struck it rich. In the kitchen were the remains of a lavish smörgåsbord — we made short work of it and inroads upon a bottle of aquavit. Only then, with the numbness beginning to leave our feet, did we feel relaxed enough to join the group of people gathered together in a comfortable, bourgeois room which, in itself, was satisfactory contrast to the life we had been living for many weeks.

They are from England, our host said, introducing us, and ignoring Sam's pained expression. And I think perhaps they have walked the whole way.

We sank into deep, luxurious chairs while an old lady in a multicoloured gown explained what had happened to us. Had we not left the road, she said, we would've found that it bends northwards and passes through a village, the first of a chain of them, for we were now in that part of Sweden called Jämptland, a winter sports area on the Norwegian border and which, compared to what we'd come through, could be described as "populated." We'd stumbled on a cart track in the dark — a path which cuts straight across the bend, over a low hill, and into a village. Now it's stopped snowing, she told us in good, though accented English, you'll see the village lights from our windows. Lucky you'd kept to the left, she said, or you'd've landed in dense forest and you'd've had a hard time finding your way out again.

We forced a chuckle.

As it is, she said, you can certainly stay with us tonight and in the morning apply for work at one of the hotels. . . .

We nodded. We'd had enough of the road.

Then we told her about our journey on foot from Östersund and about the hut in the forest where we had tried to become loggers.

These two are luckier than their friends, the host said. Because tonight they're going to see something genuinely Swedish. Have you ever heard of the Night of Lucia?

We shook our heads and Sam raised an eyebrow in enquiry but, just at that moment, a bowl of tiny, icing-star decorated cakes was placed on the table by one of the women, while another carried around a trayful of what looked like small teapots but which contained hot, spiced wine.

It's called glög, our host said. Every year at this time we celebrate the anniversary of Saint Lucia — the Queen of the Light. We eat these little cakes you see here. . . .

And drink the glög? Sam said.

You will see.

My escape from an anonymous death in the woods was still rather too uppermost in my mind for me to enter fully into this festivity, whatever it was. The warmth of the room, the good food, and the civilized company had done much to soothe me but I had begun, irrationally, to worry about the future. How would I get to Norway? Clearly I would have to take whatever job I could find locally but how much of a delay would be involved? I thought anxiously about Joan locked into her ghastly family and into a nursing job she could not stand. To change one's life in England, in those days, needed more than an act of the will — it needed a remarkable stroke of luck; the operation, if you like, of Grace.

It occurred to me that the Norway scheme would amount to very little. Already this journey had taken too long; there was little work to be had and what there was did not last. It was not probable that things would be any better in Trondheim. I grappled with the idea of failure — failure followed by ignominious return and that unfinished business with the British Army.

I got up and walked over to the window. The farmhouse was set on a little hill so that I could see across the whole village. Each house glowed with lighted windows and small Christmas trees starred with coloured lights which reflected back from the snow in soft patterns. The December sky was black — cold and hard as polished leather. I stood for awhile, restless and uneasy, but thinking of nothing. There was a small commotion in the room. I turned from the blackness of the window. A door opened and a girl came in. She was young and lithe but solemn in manner: "did seem too solemne sad." There were tiny lighted candles arranged in a crown upon her head and she wore a white dress that looked like a bridal gown. There was complete silence.

Softly, with incredible sweetness, she began to sing.

ANNE MICHAELS

Anne Michaels, born in Toronto in 1958, is the author of two books of poems, The Weight of Oranges *and* Miner's Pond. *She has composed music for the theatre and taught writing at the University of Toronto. "Pillar of Fire" is based on the log entries of Captain Watson of the HMS* Charles Bal *during the huge eruption of Krakatoa in 1883. This interest in historical travel is part of Michaels' persistent interest in memory and exile, loss and the irrecoverableness of narrative truth. Michaels lives in Toronto and has recently completed a novel.*

PILLAR OF FIRE

At Katimbang, dead birds rained out of the sky.
Statues walked.

Whole forests — strewn like driftwood.
Tides so fast, fish were stranded,
then picked from the ground like a crop.

Father, I remember when we first
sailed through together —
how simple fear was, then.
Docked at Merak you told the story
of Sunda ghost, a sailor

who paid for the sins of this life
in the next, by having to gather
all the islands in the Strait.
The lights of port behind you;
breeze snapping the ropes:
"at night you'll hear him howling,
his hands full and his work half done."
My hair jumped when I first heard the sound.
You kept me scared. Then told me
about orang-utans, who'll howl like babies
when the weather's shifting.
Now I can tell you,
Sunda Strait is surely haunted.

Our destination was Hong Kong,
carrying cargo from Belfast.
As usual, the first day we pull from shore,
each man was busy with his own thoughts.
And as usual, Willy — John's son — was below,
sleeping off his leave;
he never came aboard on his own legs.

At first it sounded like cannon fire, a distress;
but not a ship in sight.
The threat of damnation isn't always
something you can see.
Then a line of weather covered half the sky.
I shortened sail, turned south-west to face the wind.

Like meteors, like white comets chained with flame,
the pumice fell — stones bigger than a man's head,

the size of pumpkins —
then smaller ones, almost worse
because they came so fast; in seconds
we were deep in ash.

The sea was a swaying field of pumice,
frozen foam.
And then — a jungle floated towards us,
palms standing straight up;
as if we sailed through dry land.

Midnight, suffocating
on a sea that looked like dirty ice.
Choked with sulphur,
eyes burning into our heads.
Cinders everywhere; the air itself was on fire.
The sea boiled.
Father, at thirty fathoms,
the lead came up hot!
Mastheads and yardarms — lined with spark.

By morning, the strait was clear.
We even laughed when Willy,
who'd slept through it all,
came up for watch and wouldn't believe a word.

But then we saw the lighthouse at Fourth Point
snap like a stem.
And day was night
land was sea,
the earth fell out of the sky.

Noon, and we were in a darkness you could feel.
Burning mud, glowing green and blue,
slapped the deck —
the sound that hits a coffin.
We shouted constantly, because we couldn't see;
and dug, for fear of sinking under the weight.
I called for the sidelights
and sent the two James's forward.
The mate and second in either quarter,
and someone to keep mud off the binnacle glass —
though we were blind as the dead.

Lightning lit our faces,
ugly with work.
The air — smeared solid.

When it stopped
we fell where we stood, as if we'd had only
the exact amount of strength.

The dark was full of stories,
of names of wives and children;
stories that, when light returned,
would never be spoken again.

It lightened enough to see the horizon.
Our first sight of land was West Island.

A mist of sand began to fall.
Krakatoa roared, ear-aching loud,
though we were a full seventy-five miles away.

The *Charles Bal* — from truck to waterline,
spars, sails, and ropes —
hard with mud;
as if she'd been raised from the bottom.

A miracle, not a man hurt.
But — in Anjer, Merak,
all the villages of the Java Coast!

Father, the places you stopped so often
for water and wood, meat and fruit
have vanished.

They say that when the blast came,
in the streets of Katimbang
mud galloped fast as horses;
that burning ash pushed through floors
like pillows bursting their stuffing.
They say that when people ran through the streets
they left red footprints of fire.
That their bare arms looked like torn sleeves.

We knew them.

They say that even now, even far as Ceylon,
when you cut open fish
you find jewellery that belonged to the dead.

The town of Tjiringin is now ocean.

ACKNOWLEDGEMENTS

The editor wishes to express deep appreciation for the generosity shown by all of the following authors, publishers and copyright holders who have allowed their work to be used freely in this anthology, in order to benefit Canada India Village Aid.

PART ONE
Lucking Out With a Bad Patch of Road

NORMAN LEWIS from *Golden Earth* Copyright © 1952 by Norman Lewis. First published by Jonathan Cape Limited. Reprinted by Eland Books 1983. Used by permission of Eland Books and the author.

PATRICK MARNHAM from *Road to Katmandu* Copyright © 1971 by Patrick Marnham. Used by permission of The Putnam Publishing Group and International Creative Management, Inc.

STEPHEN BROOK from *Honkytonk Gelato* Copyright © 1985 by Stephen Brook. Used by permission of Hamish Hamilton Ltd.; Pan Macmillan Ltd.; and the author.

MARK ABLEY from *Beyond Forget* Copyright © 1986 by Mark Abley. Used by permission of Douglas & McIntyre Ltd.; Sierra Club Books; and the author.

338

TED CONOVER from *Rolling Nowhere* Copyright © 1981, 1984 by Ted Conover. Used by permission of Viking Penguin, a division of Penguin Books USA, Inc.; Sterling Lord Literistic, Inc.; and the author.

PART TWO
Writers and the Effects of War

IRVING LAYTON "Postcard" from *The Pole-Vaulter* Copyright © 1974 by Irving Layton. Used by permission of the Canadian Publishers, McClelland and Stewart, Toronto, and the author.

DIRK BOGARDE from *Backcloth* Copyright © 1986 by Dirk Bogarde. Published by Viking Penguin, a division of Penguin Books USA, Inc. Used by permission of A. D. Peters & Co. Ltd.

JAMES FENTON from *All the Wrong Places* Copyright © 1988 by James Fenton. Used by permission of the Atlantic Monthly Press and A. D. Peters & Co. Ltd.

P. J. O'ROURKE "The Piece of Ireland that Passeth all Understanding" from *Holidays in Hell* Copyright © 1988 by P. J. O'Rourke.

GAVIN YOUNG "The Murder of Hué" from *Worlds Apart* Copyright © 1987 by The *Observer*. First published by Hutchinson in 1987. Used by permission of Century Hutchinson Ltd.; Aitken & Stone Ltd.; and the author.

PART THREE
Classic Questers in Extremis

J. M. COETZEE from *Waiting for the Barbarians* Copyright © 1980 by J. M. Coetzee. Used by permission of Viking Penguin, a division of Penguin Books USA, Inc.; Martin Secker & Warburg; and the author.

GRAHAM GREENE from *The Lawless Roads* Copyright © 1939 by Graham Greene. Published by William Heinemann, Ltd. and The Bodley Head, Ltd. Reprinted by Penguin Books. Published in USA as *Another Mexico*. Used by permission of Viking Penguin, a division of Penguin Books USA, Inc.; Laurence Pollinger Ltd.; and the author.

ERIC HANSEN from *Stranger in the Forest* Copyright © 1988 by Eric Hansen. First published by Houghton Mifflin, Inc. Reprinted by permission.

REDMOND O'HANLON from *In Trouble Again* Copyright © 1988 by Redmond O'Hanlon. Published by Hamish Hamilton and Viking Penguin. Used by permission of A. D. Peters & Co. Ltd.; Hamish Hamilton Ltd.; and the author.

WILFRED THESIGER from *Arabian Sands* Copyright © 1959, 1984 by Wilfred Thesiger. Used by permission of Curtis Brown Group Ltd. and the author.

MICHAEL ASHER from *A Desert Dies* Copyright © 1986 by Michael Asher. Used by permission of St. Martin's Press, Inc., and David Higham Associates.

LARGE PRINT

ISIS publish a wide range of books in large print, from fiction to biography. A full list of titles is available free of charge from the address below. Alternatively, contact your local library for details of their collection of ISIS books.

Details of ISIS unabridged audio books are also available.

Any suggestions for books you would like to see in large print or audio are always welcome.

**ISIS
7 Centremead
Osney Mead
Oxford OX2 0ES
(0865) 250333**

TRAVEL, ADVENTURE AND EXPLORATION

Jacques Cousteau	**The Silent World**
Peter Davies	**The Farms of Home**
Patrick Leigh Fermor	**Three Letters From the Andes**
Keath Fraser	**Worst Journeys**
John Hillaby	**Journey to the Gods**
Dervla Murphy	**The Ukimwi Road**
Freya Stark	**The Southern Gates of Arabia**
Tom Vernon	**Fat Man in Argentina**
A Wainwright	**Wainwright in the Limestone Dales**
Dylan Winter	**A Hack in the Borders**

(A) Large Print books also available in Audio

WORLD WAR II

Paul Brickhill	**The Dam Busters**
Reinhold Eggers	**Escape From Colditz**
Fey von Hassell	**A Mother's War**
Dorothy Brewer Kerr	**The Girls Behind the Guns**
Vera Lynn	**We'll Meet Again** (A)
Vera Lynn	**Unsung Heroines**
Tom Quinn	**Sea War**
Frank and Joan Shaw	**We Remember the Battle of Britain**
Frank and Joan Shaw	**We Remember the Blitz**
Frank and Joan Shaw	**We Remember D-Day**
William Sparks	**The Last of the Cockleshell Heroes**
Anne Valery	**Talking About the War**

POETRY

**Long Remembered:
Narrative Poems**

INSPIRATIONAL

Thora Hird	**Thora Hird's Praise Be! Notebook**

REFERENCE AND DICTIONARIES

The Longman English Dictionary
The Longman Medical Dictionary

01 fee

GENERAL NON-FICTION

Eric Delderfield	Eric Delderfield's Bumper Book of True Animal Stories
Caroline Elliot	The BBC Book of Royal Memories 1947-1990
Joan Grant	The Cuckoo on the Kettle
Joan Grant	The Owl on the Teapot
Helene Hanff	Letters From New York
Martin Lloyd-Elliott	City Ablaze
Elizabeth Longford	Royal Throne
Joanna Lumley	Forces Sweethearts
Vera Lynn	We'll Meet Again
Desmond Morris	The Animal Contract
Anne Scott-James and Osbert Lancaster	
	The Pleasure Garden
Les Stocker	The Hedgehog and Friends
Elisabeth Svendsen	Down Among the Donkeys
Gloria Wood and Paul Thompson	The Nineties
The Lady Wardington	Superhints for Gardeners
Nicholas Witchell	The Loch Ness Story